W9-AAS-629

© 2007 by SCALA Group, S.p.A., Firenze, su licenza E-ducation.it, Firenze

This 2007 edition published by Barnes & Noble, Inc. by arrangement with SCALA Group, S.p.A.

Texts: Alice Cartocci, Gloria Rosati
Project director: Cinzia Caiazzo
Editor-in-chief: Filippo Melli
Design: Gruppo Bandello Comunicazione
Graphics: Puntoeacapo srl
Translation: Shanti Evans

ISBN-13: 978-0-7607-8883-7
ISBN-10: 0-7607-8883-9

Printed and bound in China

1 3 5 7 9 10 8 6 4 2

EGYPTIAN ART

Alice Cartocci

Gloria Rosati

BARNES & NOBLE

NEW YORK

TABLE **OF CONTENTS**

TABLE OF CONTENTS

TABLE OF CONTENTS

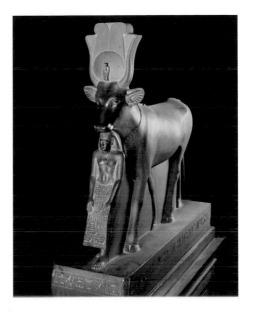

1. Prehistory: The Birth of Egyptian Art

limatic conditions in the Nile Valley at the end of the 4th millennium permitted a rapid and flourishing development of society and technology. The different stages of the transition from prehistory, which is given the name of the Predynastic period, to protohistoric times and then to the complex and highly-structured society of the Old Kingdom are revealed through archeological finds. However, the boundaries between one period and another are not always clear. The society evolved rapidly, passing from a structure of small isolated villages to a unified state with a central government. The centralized state gave a decisive impetus to the organization of resources and the development of art, which from the outset displayed technical features and iconographic themes that were to remain typical of Egyptian art, while other motifs disappeared over time.

1. Facing page:
Ceremonial palette
with dogs and giraffes,
Predynastic period. Paris,
Musée du Louvre.

2. Vase in the form of a
bird, Predynastic period.
Berlin, Ägyptisches
Museum.

3. Statuette of a woman,
about 5th millennium BC.
London, British Museum.

BEFORE THE PHARAOHS EXISTED: THE PREDYNASTIC PERIOD

In the predynastic period the repertoire of symbols available to the artist was far smaller than later on, and the subjects are all clearly inspired by nature. A few images from the prehistoric era survived to become part of the heritage of the dynastic period, although in the majority of cases the iconography was at least partly modified. The natural environment conditioned artistic production not only in the choice of subjects, but also through the raw materials that it supplied in abundance. This period launched enduring techniques for working with clay and stone. Astonishing levels of quality were attained.

Clay was used to make pots and votive figurines, essentially to be placed in graves. But many objects had everyday uses as well, especially the shiny red pots with a black mouth whose production is typical of the Naqadah phase.

Many examples of this type of pottery have been found, some in an excellent state of preservation, showing that the model was widespread. The forms are extremely varied, but all the pieces are characterized by the luminosity of the polished and shiny red surface, which contrasts with the black rim of the mouth, creating a remarkable chromatic effect.

The oldest ceramic production of the Predynastic period also includes pots of red clay with white geometric decorations. A fine example of this is a bowl with four applications in relief in the shape

4

4. Red and black pots, from Abydos, Predynastic period. Cairo, Egyptian Museum.

64910

**5. Jar with painted
decoration, about
3500-3100 BC. Cairo,
Egyptian Museum.**

of crocodiles, now in the Cairo Museum, where geometric decorations are combined with naturalistic images.

Typical of the subsequent phase of the predynastic era are the pots made of pale clay and painted with dark red motifs. It is still difficult to interpret their decorative themes; one of the most common is the stylized representation of long boats with many oars that anticipate the typical form of the vessels which would be used for navigation on the Nile in the dynastic period.

Alongside these boats, the decorations include geometric patterns like spirals, triangles, wavy lines and plant elements with stylized traits. The most frequent form of this pottery is ovoid with an everted lip and very small tubular and perforated handles. Despite the difference in material and technique, the same form was also used for many vases carved out of stone. Other articles made of clay include statuettes of human beings for votive use, like the famous Merimda head or the figurine of a woman with raised arms from Mamariya, perhaps representing a dancer.

As is often true of prehistoric works, the abstraction of the forms and the evocative and communicative power of the subjects are on a par with, and sometimes even surpass, those of the products of modern currents of art.

The meaning of these statuettes remains obscure: the most likely interpretation of the Merimda head is that it is a representation of protective forces intended to drive negative spirits away.

The figurines of women, on the other hand, may have been representations of the archetype of femininity or images created for votive purposes and for use as grave goods. In any case, we can exclude the possibility that their creators had any intention of portraying a specific individual.

7

8

6. Facing page: Head, from Merimda, end of 4th millennium BC. Cairo, Egyptian Museum.

7. Bowl decorated with crocodiles and geometric patterns, from Gebelein, about 4000-3500 BC. Cairo, Egyptian Museum.

8. Statuette of a woman with raised arms, from Mamariya, Predynastic period. New York, Brooklyn Museum of Art.

A superficial look at the art of ancient Egypt might leave the observer with the impression that the artistic production of that civilization remained unchanged over three thousand years of history, since there were very few significant innovations and changes. The continuity of styles and themes is in reality the consequence of a culture dominated by a natural landscape shaped by regular rhythms, and by strong and contrasting situations. Universal order, established at the dawn of time, had to be maintained and guaranteed. So art too followed the rules of creation and adhered to them with extreme rigor. The uniformity of style was deliberate, and almost obstinately pursued, for three millennia. There were times when, as a result of political upheavals or at the behest of central authority, the artistic tradition modified the parameters of iconography and style, but every moment of rupture with the past was always followed by a return to the origins. Art, in ancient Egypt, had a very different role and significance from the ones to which we are accustomed today. In the Egyptian conception of the world reality was pervaded by divine powers; religion was everything and everything was religion. In a world in which every human activity and every natural phenomenon were seen through the prism of faith, art in particular was a

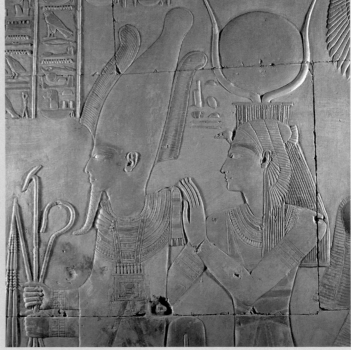

I

II

I. The goddess Hathor and King Seti I, from the tomb of Seti I at Thebes, about 1280 BC. Paris, Musée du Louvre.

II. The god Osiris and the goddess Isis. Abydos, Shrine of Horus, Temple of Seti I.

vehicle for values linked to religion: it never arose out of aesthetic needs but always had a practical function, that of veneration of divine forces or protection from negative influences. The magical aspect is strongly present in the work of art, and often provides the main key to interpreting its meaning. Thus nature, creation of the gods and a living expression of them, was the matrix of artistic forms. It determined and conditioned the subjects, even if the Egyptian artist was capable of abstracting and isolating forms and concepts as icons of natural reality. The markedly cubic conception of space, for example, was naturally suggested by the elements of the landscape: the Nile flowing from south to north and intersecting with the daily journey of the sun provided the geometric system of reference. The landscape is also characterized by strong contrasts, without transitional stages: fertile land gives way abruptly to the harshest desert; the narrow Nile Valley suddenly opens out into the plains of the Delta. From this stemmed a distinctly dualistic conception of the world, always reflected in the work of art. The implacable natural cycles dictated by the flooding of the river, the country's sole source of life, may also have helped to determine the sense of mathematical rigor that conditioned artistic creation. Little room was left for individual

creativity: the artist was not much more than a skilled craftsman. He sought with all the mastery and the accuracy of which he was capable to reproduce forms laid down by a strict canon: any deviation was seen as a departure from the preestablished order, and thus as something negative. The rules governing proportions, established very early on, in the Predynastic period, were preserved until the 26th dynasty, over two thousand years later. Pure geometric forms were the clearly identifiable skeleton of artistic and architectural compositions, and even the relations between forms were dictated by principles of proportionality. Yet we must be careful not to make an error of interpretation: the work

III. Hunting scene in a papyrus grove, about 1550-1295 BC. Thebes, Tomb of Nakht.

IV. The goddess Hathor and the god Osiris, 664-525 BC. Bahariya Oasis, Tomb of Bannantiu.

of art was neither a copy nor an imitation of reality, and verisimilitude was not the artist's sole motivation. The making of an artistic object amounted to a new "creation": a statue of a dead man was not his effigy; it was the dead man himself, on whose behalf it performed several functions. In the same way painted or carved scenes served a concrete purpose on the walls of the tombs or temples that they decorated, ensuring the deceased's safe passage through the dangers of the afterlife or facilitating sacred ceremonies in the temple. Art was the creation of a living and potent reality, capable of acting in the perceptible world as well as in the invisible world of the divine powers by virtue of its magic. The artist sought verisimilitude in order to make his creation coincide as far as possible with its purpose, but at the same time he drew on a vast stock of symbols. Symbolism, omnipresent in Egyptian art, is in fact the logical consequence of all this: the symbol condenses the essential elements of an object, and is thus able to evoke its essence and have its same efficacy.

V

VI

V. The dwarf Seneb and his family, about 2500 BC. Cairo, Egyptian Museum.

VI. Statue of Rameses II as a child with the god Haurun, about 1270 BC. Cairo, Egyptian Museum.

THE ART OF STONE

In the Predynastic period, the carving of vases and votive tablets out of stone developed in parallel with ceramics. Some of the elements, forms and subjects were the same as those used in the medium of clay, and the technique of working stone reached very high levels of quality. Theriomorphic (animal-shaped) vases are typical of predynastic art. The body of the animal is extremely stylized, turning into an almost abstract geometrical form, and constitutes the actual container, while the legs and head, also highly stylized, are external appendages that function as supports or handles, as well as playing the role of decorative elements.

The modeling of the forms is astonishing, always perfectly smooth even when carved from the hardest stone, while the inside of the vessel is hollowed out completely to produce very thin walls. The cosmetic palettes carved from green slate belong to the same artistic tradition, and the earliest of them have the highly stylized forms of animals: fish, turtles, birds, antelopes. Palettes of this kind originally served to grind the malachite-based pigment that was used as makeup to protect the eyes from infections, and were very soon given the shape of animals, in all probability for symbolic reasons. On some of them it is still possible to see green stains and the marks of wear. At a later stage the palettes were decorated with highly detailed and realistic carvings, in apparent

9

9. Vase in the form of an antelope, 4th millennium BC. Cairo, Egyptian Museum.

contrast with the linear and abstract style of the earlier period. In reality this was a consequence of the fact that the palettes dating from the late Predynastic period had lost their practical function and taken on an exclusively symbolic and votive meaning, although they often still had a space at the center that recalled their original purpose, the grinding of cosmetics. They are the earliest examples of objects created to give thanks to the god who had assured a military victory, and therefore to celebrate an event whose memory it was considered important to preserve. Hence the scenes comprise details that identify the episode, such as symbols of cities or regions conquered by the king, or representing the amount of spoils that were brought back from the war. Also very frequent are images of symbolic animals, like the lion, associated with strength and royal power. A large number of the themes typical of the art of the dynastic period appear in these palettes in a sudden, it could almost be said abrupt manner. In fact, although it is possible to find elements of continuity with earlier predynastic artifacts, their style and iconography are already in keeping with the canons of the dynastic age. All at once the reliefs fill up with details, the first pictographic signs of the hieroglyphic script appear and the decoration is already organized in an orderly and logical manner into several superimposed rows. Even the repertoire of symbols is much larger than before, with themes that will become typical of the Egyptian art of the following period. Among them, the bull, an emblem of the virility and power of the sovereign, and the cow's head as an image of the goddess of the sky, who would later come to be known by the name of Hathor. The stylistic features used for human and animal figures are already the

10

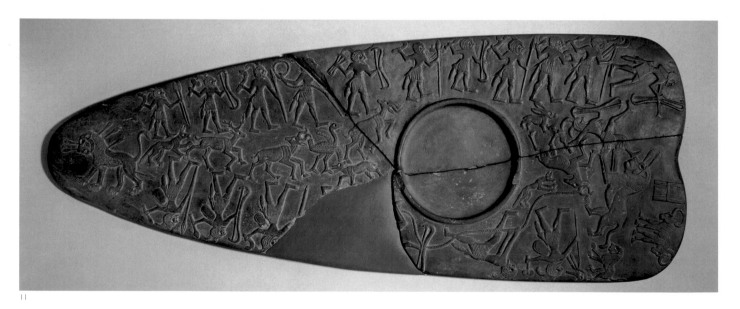

11

10. Palette with two heads of birds, from Amra, about 3100 BC. London, British Museum.

11. The "Hunter's Palette," Predynastic period. London, British Museum.

classical ones, as is the iconography used for the foreign enemies and bound prisoners. Surprisingly, then, Egyptian art emerged at the end of the Predynastic period with codes and an iconography that were to evolve in the protodynastic era (the period of the first two dynasties), assuming all the characteristics that would already be found in a mature form in the Old Kingdom. The techniques and experiments of the prehistoric age were the foundations on which the artistic production of the following millennia would be built.

12

**12. Palette with animals
and plants, about 3000 BC.
Cairo, Egyptian Museum.**

KING NARMER AND THE ORIGINS OF EGYPTIAN ART

The beginning of the pharaonic period is dated, conventionally, to shortly before 3000 BC. The process of evolution of what was perhaps the first unitary state in history had commenced in the previous millennium, and had led to an organization of the territory and its resources, irrigation and farming, and to an economy controlled by an absolute monarch with the authority of a god-king. The archeological evidence, especially for the later periods, suggests that a number of centers were historically important: among them Buto in the Delta and Hierakonpolis in Upper Egypt, which preserved a sacred aura throughout Egyptian history and played a major part in its mythology. It is no coincidence that the monument considered to be almost the "foundation" of Egyptian art, the one where "everything started," comes from Hierakonpolis. This is a

siltstone tablet that reproduces, on a larger scale (it is some 25 in or 64 cm high), the palettes used to pulverize the minerals (by pounding them with a pestle) from which cosmetics for the eyes were made. Thus an object of practical use was assigned a symbolic function. On the palette we find all the conventions of two-dimensional representation and the themes that were to characterize celebration of the ruler and his functions as guarantor of the state in subsequent periods. One side, in fact, is dominated by the king called Horus Narmer in the act of killing an enemy he has seized by the hair, an image that will be repeated dozens of times in the historical era. In this scene the king wears the crown emblematic of Upper Egypt, while on the other side of the palette, the one with the cavity for the cosmetic, he appears in the upper row inspecting the corpses of his defeated enemies and wearing the crown of Lower Egypt. This document has been regarded as the celebration of a fundamental event, which could be the unification of the state. Yet by

14

15

13. Facing page: Tablet with the sovereign represented as a bull trampling the enemy, about 3100 BC. Paris, Musée du Louvre.

14. Narmer Palette, back, from Hierakonpolis, about 3000 BC. Cairo, Egyptian Museum.

15. Narmer Palette, front, from Hierakonpolis, about 3000 BC. Cairo, Egyptian Museum.

Narmer's time the unitary Egyptian state may have been a reality, and art, which had already defined its means of expression and its motifs, was here employed to celebrate not an event, unification, but a fact, royal power as such. According to tradition it was the first king of Egypt, the mythical Menes, who founded the capital Memphis at the northern end of the Nile Valley, just before it broadens into the Delta. In its vicinity (southwest of modern Cairo) still stand the vast necropolises of Saqqarah and Giza, which provide the principal documentation of the architecture and royal and private sculpture of the following period, the Old Kingdom (3rd-6th dynasty). However, recent archeological research in the Memphis area has begun to yield evidence confirming the presence of a city of considerable size in the early dynastic era, perhaps already the administrative center of the state. The rulers of Egypt of the 1st and 2nd dynasty came originally from the city of Thinis, which has not yet been identified by archeologists but was certainly near the extremely important religious center of Abydos, about 200 miles or 500 kilometers south of Cairo. This is where the oldest royal tombs have been found: underground chambers reached by "shafts" lined with stone or brick

and covered by a mound of sand, where the stelae with the name of the sovereign were located. While apparently modest, these monuments were associated with funeral enclosures resembling fortresses, built a mile or almost 2 kilometers further north, which took their inspiration from the royal palace and the structures connected with it.

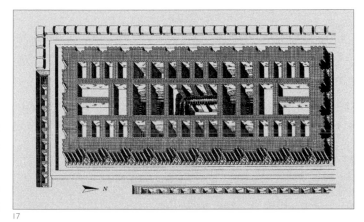

17

18

EGYPTIAN ART

16. Facing page: Narmer Palette, detail of the back, from Hierakonpolis, about 3000 BC. Cairo, Egyptian Museum.

17. Reconstructed plan of a tomb at Saqqarah, about 3000 BC (from R. Schulz, M. Seidel, *Egypt*, Cologne 1998, p. 33, fig. 47).

18. Funeral complex of King Qa'a, about 2890 BC. Abydos.

THE PROTODYNASTIC PERIOD, BRIDGING PREHISTORY AND HISTORY

The first two dynasties of rulers of ancient Egypt cover a span of time that Egyptologists define by convention as the Protodynastic period: a bridge between prehistory and history proper. In fact the birth of a unified state marked a fundamental turning point for the society, and one which had repercussions on art as well: the new needs of administration and those of the pharaoh and his court gave fresh impetus to artists and craftsmen, who had to tackle unprecedented themes and subjects and develop new techniques or improve familiar ones. In addition, the resources of the country, now managed by the central structure of government, could be channeled into the production of art, giving it a great boost: in this way a class of artists and craftsmen in the service of the court was formed. From this period dates the first evidence of writing, on objects found in royal tombs or in the necropolises of Abydos and Saqqarah. The hieroglyphic script had slowly developed over the preceding period and was now the means of communication adopted in the administration of the state. Typical of the Protodynastic period are the bone plates that were tied to the necks of vases with string and which identified their contents; the more elaborate of them specified not only the product but also the quantity, the place of origin or the destination of the vase and the year of the reign or the name of the ruler. The elements of the hieroglyphic script are already clearly delineated and the convention of inscribing the ruler's name inside the serekh established. This is a complicated sign in the shape of a palace and surmounted by a falcon, a symbol (indicating the Horus name of the pharaoh) that would be abandoned in the dynastic period and replaced by the cartouche. Many objects used for other purposes were also enriched with hieroglyphic inscriptions, inaugurating the custom, typical of Egyptian art, of utilizing writing as a means of decoration. They included votive objects, funerary stelae, vases and

19

20

19. Ivory tablet with written signs, about 2920-2770 BC.

20. Comb of King Djet, from Abydos, about 2950 BC. Cairo, Egyptian Museum.

statues, which according to religious tradition acquired greater efficacy by virtue of the inscription that accompanied them and specified their function. The unification of the country also led to the establishment of regular trade links with Palestine and Mesopotamia. In this period, in fact, it is possible to discern a Mesopotamian influence in the decorations and themes of some Egyptian artifacts: examples of this are the interlaced spiral called a guilloche and the iconography of the bearded man with rounded headgear. These elements are found, for instance, on the ivory handles of some ritual knives made of flint, whose blades also provide an example of the degree of sophistication achieved in the working of stone in the prehistoric era. Unfortunately the large constructions of the temples and the royal palaces have been lost as they were built out of unfired brick, matting and wood. To understand the structure of these buildings it is necessary to look at constructions in stone (a material chosen because it was considered eternal) of the 3rd dynasty, which imitate the forms of older temples.

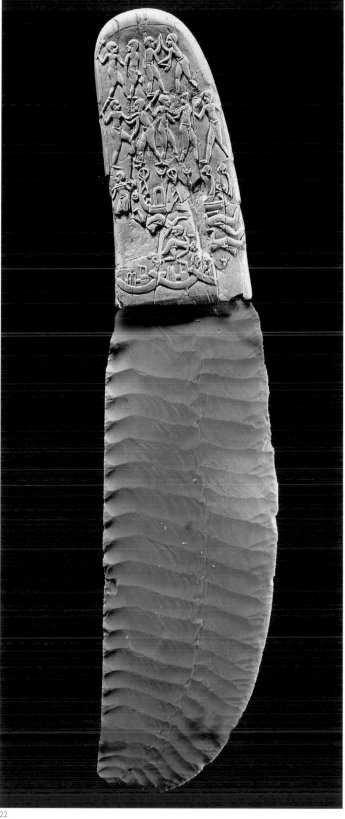

21

22

21. Narmer in the form of a baboon, about 3000 BC. Berlin, Staatliche Museen.

22. Dagger, from Gebel el-Arak, Protodynastic period. Paris, Musée du Louvre.

FUNERARY STELE OF DJET

about 2950 BC
Paris, Musée du Louvre

SUBJECT

The stele, from Abydos, was found in the vicinity of the tomb of Djet, fourth king of the 1st dynasty. The composition is very simple and shows the "Horus name" of the ruler inside the representation of a palace façade called the serekh. Above the serekh, as if to protect the king's name and palace, is the falcon symbolizing Horus. It is an expression of his power on earth..

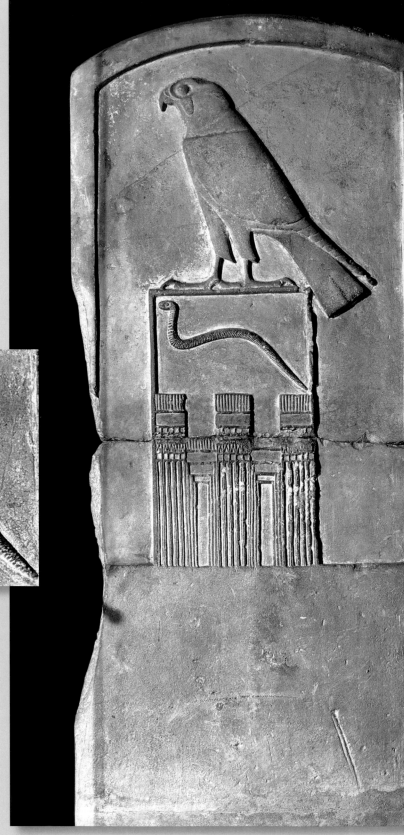

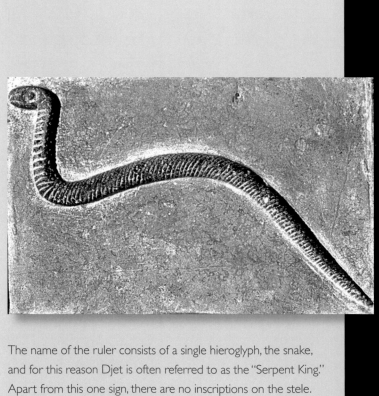

The name of the ruler consists of a single hieroglyph, the snake, and for this reason Djet is often referred to as the "Serpent King." Apart from this one sign, there are no inscriptions on the stele.

COMPOSITION

The excellent state of preservation allows us to appreciate the quality of the precise and clear carving, and the essentiality of the image. The slightly projecting relief creates remarkable effects of light and shade on the white limestone, bringing out the design, which would otherwise blend into the background. This effect is enhanced by the deeper incision of some details, like the falcon's eye.

The grooves in the front of the palace, finally, create an impression of depth. As is frequently the case in Egyptian art, the symbols are used to summarize fairly complicated concepts, simplifying the composition of the work. The palace is depicted "in the Egyptian manner," with its two basic elements represented from different perspectives: the perimeter of the walls and the façade. The former is depicted in a "bird's-eye view," from above, and is presented as a rectangle; the façade on the other hand is viewed from the front and consists of three towers punctuated by regular grooves. Inside the palace, the place of power, the sovereign is "represented" by his name, the hieroglyph of the snake.

THE ARCHAIC STATUETTES OF THE THIRD DYNASTY

Canonical rules for the execution of works of art were already well established at the beginning of Egyptian history; rules that were certainly the fruit of centuries of formulation for which evidence is unfortunately scarce. This results in the strange impression that Egyptian art sprang suddenly into existence, already clearly delineated, out of practically nowhere. Over the course of the 3rd dynasty, however, votive statuettes were carved whose proportions do not conform to the codified ones. It is hard to tell whether these were the products of a provincial workshop or the result of experimentation carried out by the priests who guided the craftsmen, in a search for perfect mathematical and divine proportions.

In any case the production of these statuettes was limited to a very brief span of time and was abandoned for good by the following generation of artists. For the most part they are figures portrayed seated on a chair, sometimes holding a scepter or a mace. The only exception to this rule is the statuette of Hetepdief in the Cairo Museum: the personage is represented squatting on his heels with his hands resting on his knees. What all these statuettes have in common are the compactness and rotundity of their features, as well as the materials chosen, perfectly polished granite or schist. They are never carved from the excellent limestone that was used for the contemporary production of other statues. The first thing that strikes you about these images is that they do not portray the figure in a naturalistic way. Instead, they are characterized by a summary treatment of the limbs and the muscles, which look rough-hewn, while other elements by contrast, such as the braids of the wig, are very well defined.

Moreover, the figure is not at all slender but almost squat, as if it had been squashed, with the neck practically absent and the members short and heavy. The faces, which have high and pointed cheekbones, are unnaturally broad and chubby, with childish features. The eyes, nose and lips are clearly delineated and stand out against the soft surfaces of the rest of the face.

21

25

33

23. Facing page: Statue of Hetepdief, from Memphis, about 2630 BC. Cairo, Egyptian Museum.

24. Granite statue of Ankhwa, master of the adz, about 2680-2610 BC. London, British Museum.

25. Diorite statue of Ankh, priest of Horus. Paris, Musée du Louvre.

Writing was invented at almost the same time by the Egyptians and Sumerians, in the 4th millennium BC. The hieroglyphic script developed in the Nile Valley is of the ideographic type: each sign represents a concept, an object or part of it, and can serve as a true ideogram, signifying what it represents, or be used for its phonetic value. In the latter case the objects represented are irrelevant, in that the signs are linked together to form a phonetic sequence, on the same principle as a rebus. Writing was created as a tool of administration, but very soon began to be employed in art too. In the hieroglyphic script the word had the power of making what was written come true: so from the Old Kingdom onward stelae, statues, tombs and temples were covered with texts that took on a magical value, and then a decorative and artistic one as well; writing was so indissolubly linked to the work of art that they became complementary. The signs of the script

I. Commemorative relief of King Snefru, from Sinai, about 2600 BC. Cairo, Egyptian Museum.

II. Funerary stele of Amenemhet, from Thebes, about 2000 BC. Cairo, Egyptian Museum.

III

III. Stele with Rameses
II represented as a child,
1279-1213 BC. Paris,
Musée du Louvre.

did not undergo a process of stylization but always remained strictly representative of the object; they therefore showed a tendency to become miniatures within the larger works of art, which explains the astonishing degree of accuracy with which even the tiniest details were reproduced. Depending on the context, the signs of the script might be engraved, painted or carved in bas-relief, but in works of great importance, like the tombs in the Valley of the Kings, the signs could be engraved and then retouched with paint, in an effort to create an effect of extreme refinement and accuracy. The inscriptions that cover the walls of the tombs are written in the same style as the ones in the main scenes, where the hieroglyphs have the function of accompanying and describing the contents with magical formulas that will be of use to the occupant in the next life.

At the same time, however, these hieroglyphs constitute a complementary decoration and enrich the images of the deceased or the gods: as these images are not set against a background, they would otherwise appear to be suspended in the void. The most refined examples of painted hieroglyphs are found in the royal tombs of the

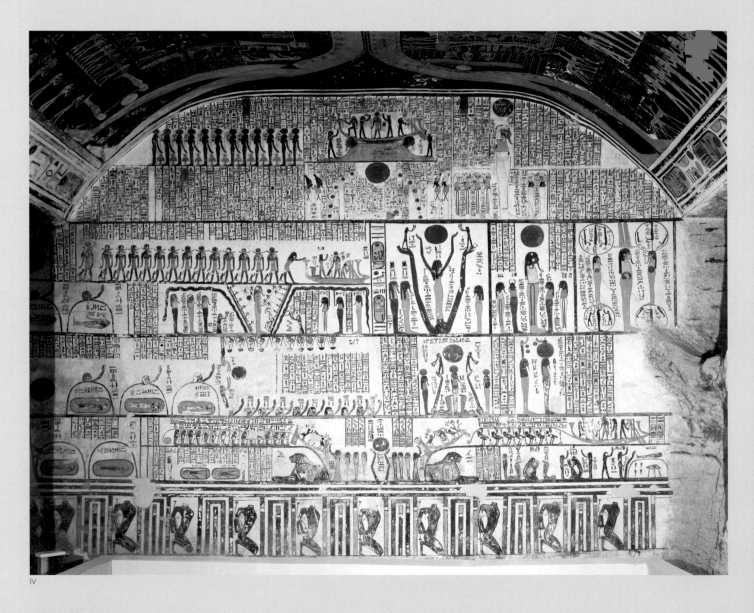

IV

IV. Tomb of Rameses VI, Sarcophagus Room, about 1140 BC. Thebes, Valley of the Kings.

Valley of the Kings, where even the plumage of the wings of the birds and the hair of the human beings are represented with indescribable precision. An exception is the tomb of Thutmosis III, in which the hieroglyphs are more stylized: in all probability this was a deliberate effect, an attempt to imitate writing on a papyrus scroll. As time passed the Egyptian scribes found it necessary to adapt the hieroglyphic signs, designed to be engraved on stone, to writing on papyrus by making them simpler. In some specimens of the Book of the Dead it is evident that the script, while retaining its magic power, has also assumed an artistic value, stemming from the regularity of the line that turns it into an ornament.

In monuments, on the other hand, the hieroglyphs were carved into rock, reserving the techniques of engraving (sometimes with very deep incisions), for the outer walls of the temples, where interesting effects were created by the shadows cast into the incisions. Direct sunlight would have rendered the bas-reliefs inside almost invisible. Instead they were made to stand out, in the semidarkness, by the light that entered at an angle through the gaps in the ceilings.

V

**V. Shrine of Thutmosis III,
about 1430 BC. Luxor.**

2. The Old Kingdom: the Age of the Pyramids

Among the ancient civilizations of the Mediterranean and the Near East, that of pharaonic Egypt was perhaps the one most strongly influenced by the geographical setting in which it developed: a sort of long oasis, watered by the Nile River and hemmed in by the Arabian Desert (to the east) and the Libyan Desert (to the west). Water, sun, sand: strong contrasts conditioned not just the life but also the thought of the Egyptians, who conceived existence as a balance of opposites, perfect yet always under threat. The beneficial repetition of the inundation of the Nile year after year and the daily course of the sun gave them a sense of the cyclicity of time and of eternal recurrence. Surrounded by manifestations of natural phenomena, they recognized the fundamental importance of preserving a preestablished higher order. Guaranteeing its maintenance became the principal duty of every ruler. Thus Egyptian art, destined for eternity and the divine, was an expression of profound convictions; the artist, who almost always remained anonymous, was actually more of a "craftsman," called on to use his skills to give form to ideological messages.

2

3

1. Facing page: Polychrome relief depicting Nefer, the proprietor of the tomb, about 2450 BC. Saqqarah, Mastaba of Nefer and Kahay.

2. Statuette of a slave girl grinding grain, about 2400 BC. Florence, Museo Archeologico.

3. Head of Userkaf, from Abusir, about 2490 BC. Cairo, Egyptian Museum.

THE CANON OF PROPORTIONS

People have always been struck by the constancy with which the figures in the art of ancient Egypt have conformed, over the course of the centuries, to a single style, always remaining perfectly recognizable. The uniformity of the compositions is so great that when we look at the works of periods in which the usual points of reference were no longer followed even the inexpert eye can discern a disturbance in the classical structure of the figure. The backbone of this stylistic continuity was a rigorous canon of proportions that was developed in the Old Kingdom and remained the same until the 26th dynasty.

This rule of mathematical proportions appeared almost out of the blue in the Old Kingdom, although it was in fact the product of a process of elaboration that is still obscure since it is so scantily documented. Even where the origins of the canon, as well as the origins of Egyptian art itself, are concerned, the evidence predating the Old Kingdom is not of much help in clearly defining the break, which there certainly must have been, with the prehistoric era. The mathematical rule that governs the composition of the figures is based on the proportions that were used for the construction of the pyramids in the same period, especially the ratio of 11 to 14, very common in Egyptian art and architecture.

The canon of proportions was a rule of strictly mathematical relations within which the human figure had to be comprised: although it was applied only to the human body, this in turn performed the function of "measure of all things," in that the rest of the composition was adapted to it and developed from it. In any case it was the image of man that had to correspond perfectly to the rules of divine proportions; while

4

4. Pyramid of Khafre, about 2550 BC. Giza.

5. Facing page: Statue of Thutmosis III, from Karnak, about 1430 BC. Luxor, Museum of Ancient Egyptian Art.

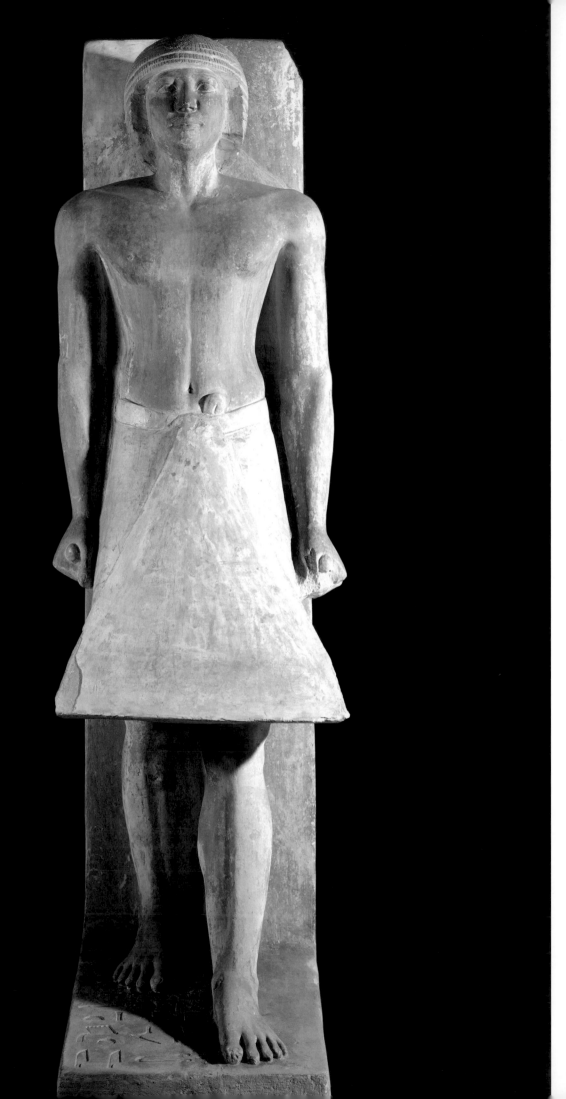

7

representations of animals or plants were also governed by strict stylistic rules, the artist was given a certain amount of license.

The formulation of a rigid canon at the time of the Old Kingdom
stemmed from the need to fix the representation of reality in an
unambiguous and absolute way so that it would conform perfectly to
divine creation. Once an exact correspondence of forms with cosmic
harmony, *maat*, had been achieved, it was impossible for anyone to
represent human and divine beings in an arbitrary manner, as this
would invalidate the magical power of the image.

The human figure was included within a grid of squares: in the case of
the standing figure the grid was 18 squares high, with the 11th representing the waistline, while the width could vary from 9 to 11 squares.
The height was reduced to 14 squares if the figure was seated on the
throne. Some points of the human body were anchored within this
grid: the height of the knee, the position of the feet and in particular

the line of the waist and the height of the eyes. Curiously, the upper-
most square did not correspond to the maximum height of the figure,
but coincided with the hairline: in fact it was not possible to determine
the height of either gods or kings exactly because of the crowns and
various kinds of headdress that these figures often wore.

Drawings found on pieces of sandstone used as rough copies and
on walls of unfinished tombs show that craftsman, before executing
figures on the surface to be decorated, used to trace the basic grid on
the plaster in order to define the proportion of the image.

The figures and hieroglyphs were sketched on this grid in red paint
with a brush. Finally they were retouched by the supervisor of the
work who marked in black ink the corrections that needed to be
made for a harmonious composition. At this point the stonecutters
or painters could start on the actual decoration of the wall, following
the outlines.

**6. Facing page: Statue of
Ti, from Saqqarah, about
2450 BC. Cairo, Egyptian
Museum.**

**7. Relief depicting farming
and craft activities, from
the Mastaba of Kaemrehu,
circa 2350 BC. Cairo,
Egyptian Museum.**

THE TOMBS OF THE RULERS OF THE OLD KINGDOM: THE PYRAMIDS

At Saqqarah, during the reign of Djoser (3rd dynasty, about 2650 BC), a radical change took place: the architect Imhotep designed for the pharaoh a complex built entirely of stone, an everlasting material by definition, in which the structures that had hitherto been constructed out of perishable materials were fixed forever. A high boundary wall of white limestone surrounds a rectangular area of 37 acres or 15 hectares, with a north-south orientation, whose central part is dominated by the tomb of the king. This stands above the burial chambers, located underground, and was conceived as a flight of steps rising into the sky, where it was the pharaoh's divine destiny to reside. It was the first pyramid, or rather a stepped mastaba, i.e. a series of superimposed parallelepipeds that reached a height of nearly 200 ft or 60 m, immediately evoking the idea of ascent. The elaborate group of buildings to the east is even more astounding: here stone was used to reproduce places of worship and pavilions, and therefore what had originally consisted of wooden stakes, rolled-up mats and tree trunks supporting a roof of reeds was carved out of stone, becoming indestructible. The set of structures recreated for the dead king were the ones used for his Sed festival, or jubilee, a ritual intended to renew

8

9

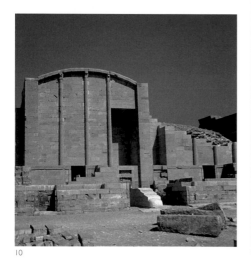

10

8-9. Step Pyramid, funeral complex of Djoser, about 2650 BC. Saqqarah.

10. Shrine of the courtyard of the Sed festival, funeral complex of Djoser, about 2650 BC. Saqqarah.

the ruler's vitality. This ensured the perpetual regeneration of his sovereignty. The following 4th dynasty saw a new evolution, a symptom of a change in religious ideas. Three pyramids are attributed to King Snefru, immense monuments whose construction would have been inconceivable without a perfect organization of labor and broad and unquestioned popular support. One at Maydum and two at Dahshur (the so-called "Bent" or Rhomboidal Pyramid, with a double slope, and the "Red" or Obtuse Pyramid, with a reduced slope), they testify to the phases of development that would lead to the "perfection" of the pyramid built by his son Khufu and, in the same necropolis at Giza, the complexes of Khafre and Menkaure.

The monument at Maydum, which now stands like a tower in the desert, was designed as a stepped mastaba and was only turned into a regular pyramid in the last part of Snefru's reign, a sign that the "message" conveyed by the old architecture was no longer relevant or acceptable. It may seem truly inconceivable, from our rational point of view, that a single ruler could have set in motion a mechanism so perfectly planned and sustained that he was able to complete three such immense projects.

One of them may even have risked turning out a failure (if that "rationality" of ours does not mislead us): the "Bent" Pyramid of Dahshur, the southernmost of the two constructed here by Snefru, was sup-

11

12

13

11. Walls, funeral complex of Djoser, about 2650 BC. Saqqarah.

12. Colonnade, funeral complex of Djoser, about 2650 BC. Saqqarah.

13. Pavilion, funeral complex of Djoser, about 2650 BC. Saqqarah.

14

15

14. Pyramid of King Snefru, about 2600 BC. Maydum.

15. View of the necropolises of South Saqqarah and Dahshur: in the foreground, on the left, the sarcophagus-shaped tomb of King Shepseskaf (about 2500 BC), on the right, the Pyramid of King Pepi II (about 2200 BC). In the background, the two pyramids of King Snefru at Dahshur (about 2590 BC).

posed to have been the first true pyramid, with smooth walls and a height of 451 ft or 137.5 m. But the base soon had to be widened because of internal damage and finally, when it was already 161 ft or 49 m high, the slope was reduced from the initial 54° to about 43°, giving the sides the peculiar bent angle that we can still see today, so that it only reached a height of 341 ft or 104 m. Yet this is the pyramid whose facing is best preserved and whose internal spaces are divided into two groups, linked together at a later date: thus it has two separate entrances and two burial chambers, on different levels, with spectacular corbeled vaults over 56 ft or 17 m high. Snefru's final resting place was probably in the third and last pyramid, a little further north, for which the slope of the upper part of the southern one (43°) was prudently adopted. For a few years now it has been possible to go inside it again: the long corridor from the north seems

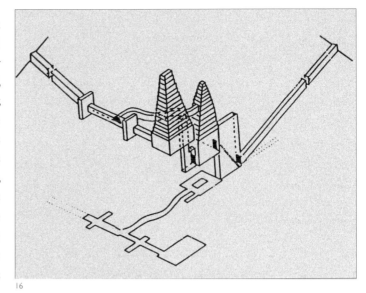

16

17

16. Reconstruction of the system of burial chambers in the "Bent" Pyramid of Snefru at Dahshur, about 2590 BC (from R. Schulz,

M. Seidel, *Egypt*, Cologne 1998, p. 59, fig. 25).

17. The Pyramids of Giza, about 2580-2500 BC.

18

**18. The "Bent" Pyramid
of Snefru, about 2590 BC.
Dahshur.**

to descend all the way to ground level, leading to two antechambers and then, from the top of the second and changing direction (running from east to west), to the burial chamber with its staggering corbeled vault almost 50 ft or 15 m high. The change in the external form may have been due to the spread of sun worship: a pure geometric form that was a sort of crystallization of the primordial hill on which, according to the theologians, the Sun had risen at the first moment of life of the universe to begin the creation. Thus the ruler would have been integrated into a cosmic cycle of rebirth, similar to the daily one of the sun. It is harder to explain the reasons for the construction of complicated internal structures, especially when located in the body of the pyramid itself (the ones built by Djoser, while intricate, were completely underground, and his pyramid or stepped mastaba has no internal chambers), as in the case of the Pyramid of Khufu.

19

20

EGYPTIAN ART

19. *Pyramidion* of the "Red" Pyramid of Snefru, about 2590 BC. Dahshur.

20. Northern or "Red" Pyramid of Snefru, about 2590 BC. Dahshur.

THE GREAT PYRAMID OF KHUFU

The Pyramid of Khufu is the monument that to our eyes (and those of whoever drew up the list of the Seven Wonders of the World) appears the most harmonious in the inclination of its faces and its grandeur, the most complex in its internal structure and the most rigorous in its orientation; in a word, "perfect." It is not yet clear whether changes were made to the design, leading gradually to the final location of the chamber of the sarcophagus, or if the internal arrangement we see today was planned right from the start. Certainly, changing the original design during the construction of such a monument seems an unlikely thing to do. In fact there are three chambers inside the Pyramid of Khufu: an unfinished underground one; another in line with the central axis and roofed by a "pitched" ceiling (improperly called the "Queen's Chamber"); and the final, spectacular chamber of red

granite, which you change direction to enter (it is oriented east-west, like that of Snefru in the Northern Pyramid at Dahshur) after passing through the marvel of the Grand Gallery, over 26 ft or 8 m high and roofed with corbeled slabs of granite. Two small openings set opposite one another on the long sides of the chamber belong to the so-called "air shafts." There are shafts in the middle chamber too, but they are blocked somewhere inside the pyramid, while the outlets of those of the upper chamber, chosen in the end to house the sarcophagus, have been found. The sarcophagus, made of granite and missing its lid today, is the first to have been found inside a pyramid. There will be no end to interpretations of the whole: it seems more likely that the project was carried out without alterations, but it is difficult to find an explanation for all the rooms, in the total absence of clues. The one known as the "Queen's Chamber" may have been the seat of the deceased's "spirit" (*ka*), while the "air shafts" leading to the outside may have symbolized

21

**21-23. Pyramid of Khufu,
about 2570 BC. Giza.**

routes for free movement left open to the immortal soul, fated to survive the body preserved in the sarcophagus. Attention has recently been drawn to the need to study the internal chambers of a pyramid in parallel with the layout of the places of worship located outside it but directly connected with it: since they were intended to fulfill the same purposes, a comparison could show whether they complement each other and help us to understand them.

For the moment one observation awaits evaluation: it appears that pyramids with larger internal spaces have less imposing external temples. The complex of buildings linked with the pyramid was oriented east-west, like the course of the sun, and included a temple located further down, near the end of a canal leading to the Nile, and a causeway 886 yd or 810 m long (in the case of the complex of Khufu; they usually extended for about 550 yd or 500 m) leading to a mortuary temple in front of the pyramid. While history presents an image of Snefru as

22

23

22. **Isonometric projection of the Pyramid of Khufu (from R. Schulz, M. Seidel, *Egypt*, Cologne 1998, p. 63, fig. 33).**

a benevolent ruler, Khufu has been branded as a despot and tyrant, a reputation that seemed to be born out by the scarcity of other monuments to him, in an apparent condemnation by posterity. In recent years, however, there has been growing support for the hypothesis that the most famous sculpture of antiquity, and certainly the largest, the Great Sphinx, was part of his funerary complex and not Khafre's. If this is true the symbol of Egypt itself, and of its fascination, was created for Khufu, with a head reproducing his features set on the body of a lion, the emblem of sovereignty and its power. In all likelihood the Sphinx is connected with the remains of a temple that, now definitely dated to the 4th dynasty, is one of the oldest to have been preserved, at least in part. It was characterized by a large central courtyard that was once surrounded by statues like the nearby valley temple of Khafre; the presence of the Sphinx may have determined its location as well as the oblique angle of the ramp leading to the pyramid.

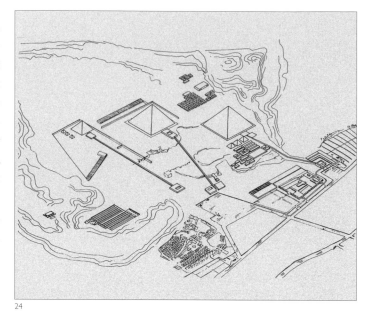

24

25

24. Plan of the complexes of the Pyramids of Giza, about 2580-2500 BC (from R. Schulz, M. Seidel, *Egypt,* **Cologne 1998, p. 63, fig. 36).**

25. Pyramid of Khafre, about 2550 BC. Giza.

26

27

26-27. The Sphinx of Giza,
about 2570-2540 BC.

THE GIZA PLATEAU

To build their imposing pyramids, the pharaohs of the 4th dynasty chose the plateau of Giza, situated a few miles to the north of the city of Memphis.

In fact the difficulties encountered during the erection of the pyramids at Dahshur had persuaded the constructors to look for a site where more solid foundations could be laid than was possible in sand. And the Giza Plateau, consisting of an enormous bed of rock, provided the stability required to support the weight of these immense constructions, and at the same time could be exploited as a source of raw materials. The level attained by the techniques of construction in the Giza complex is distinctly superior to that of all the earlier pyramids: the pyramidal shape was made perfect since the casing, smooth and gleaming under the rays of the sun, concealed the tiers of stone beneath.

On the eastern side of each pyramid stood the mortuary temple used for the worship of the dead king, linked by a raised passageway to a second temple, called the "valley temple," where the boats used for ceremonies were moored during the flood season.

54

I. View of the pyramids,
2580-2500 BC. Giza.

THE GREAT PYRAMID

The Pyramid of Khufu, also known as the Great Pyramid as it is larger than the others, was originally clad with limestone that had been polished to reflect the rays of the sun. The temples of the complex of Khufu and the corridors that linked them to the pyramid have vanished, but the trenches intended for burial of the sacred boats have been discovered, and it has even been possible to reconstruct one of them, found dismantled but perfectly preserved. Despite having magical functions and being intended for the deceased king's voyage in the other world, the boat is on a real scale and had probably been used. On the eastern side a small satellite pyramid had been built, along with three minor pyramids as tombs of the queens; a necropolis made up of the mastabas of court dignitaries and nobles who wished to be buried near their sovereign was laid out on the eastern and western sides.

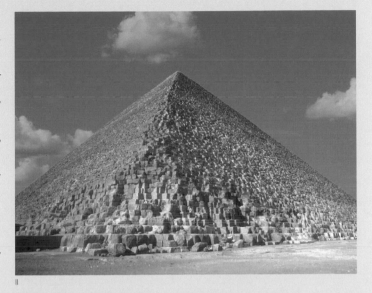

II

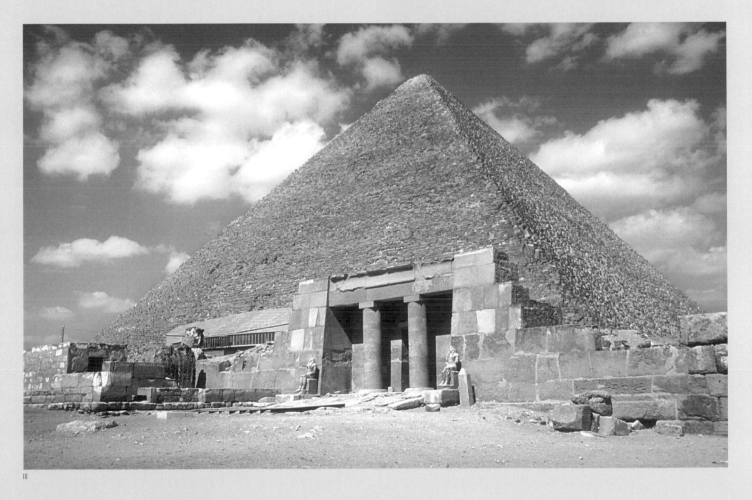

III

II. Pyramid of Khufu, about 2570 BC. Giza.

III. Pyramid of Khufu with the tomb of the dignitary Sheshemnefer in the foreground, about 2570 BC. Giza.

THE PYRAMID OF KHAFRE

Khufu's son built a second pyramid on the Giza site. Not much smaller than his father's, it too was faced with limestone, traces of which can still be seen on the summit. The impressive valley temple and part of the alabaster causeway that connected it with the mortuary temple have also survived. The huge, perfectly laid monolithic blocks of the valley temple, originally faced with red granite, bear witness to the construction skills of the Old Kingdom. The austere architecture was embellished with statues of the seated pharaoh, including the famous one now on display in the Cairo Museum. There was also an effort to create chromatic effects through the use of diorite, whose green color stood out against the red of the granite. In the part adjacent to the valley temple, used as a quarry for the blocks of stone for the pyramid, an enormous statue was carved out of the rock: the Sphinx. It was the largest statue ever created in the Old Kingdom and is the symbol of the Giza complex.

IV

V

**IV. The Sphinx of Giza,
about 2570-2540 BC.**

**V. Pyramid of Khafre,
about 2550 BC. Giza.**

THE PYRAMID OF MENKAURE

Menkaure, sometimes called Mycerinus, was the last ruler to build his tomb on the Giza Plateau. The dimensions of his pyramid are considerably smaller than those of his predecessor, but the complex once stood out for the richness and variety of the materials utilized. The original design must have called for the pyramid to be clad entirely with red granite, and the temples to be lavishly decorated with polychrome materials, but Menkaure's premature death prevented completion of the complex. Alongside the pharaoh's tomb were built three pyramids for his queens, two of which, left unfinished, have a stepped form. Unfortunately the decorated sarcophagus found in the burial chamber was lost when the ship taking it to England sank off the Spanish coast.

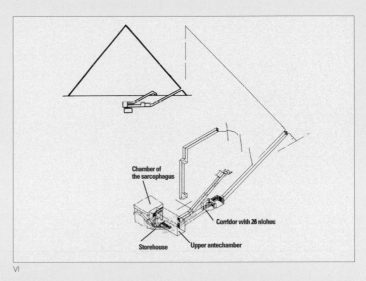

Chamber of the sarcophagus

Corridor with 26 niches

Storehouse

Upper antechamber

VI

VII

VI. Isonometric projection and section of the Pyramid of Menkaure (from R. Schulz, M. Seidel, *Egypt*, Cologne 1998, p. 68, fig. 45).

VII. Pyramid of Menkaure, about 2510 BC. Giza.

THE TRIAD OF MENKAURE

about 2500 BC
Cairo, Egyptian Museum

In 1908 the archeologist George Reisner found a number of schist statues in the valley temple of the complex of Menkaure at Giza, at least four of which were exceptionally intact.

The statues form a triad in which the pharaoh is flanked by the goddess Hathor and the personification of one of the nomes, or provinces, of Egypt, identified by the standard set above her head. There was probably a triad for each nome, and the statues were intended to represent the sovereign's authority over the whole of the country.

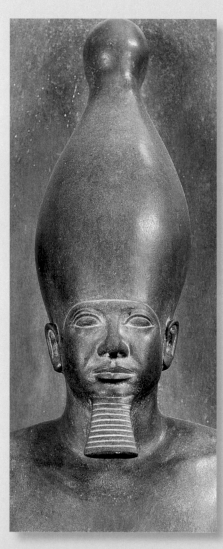

The three figures are not free standing but emerge from the gray surface of the background that frames them and gives the composition a strong sense of unity. Menkaure is wearing the crown of Upper Egypt but the name inscribed at his feet identifies him as "king of Lower and Upper Egypt," evidence that the unification of the country had been consolidated.

The ruler is set slightly forward of the two figures that accompany him and so is located on a different spatial plane.

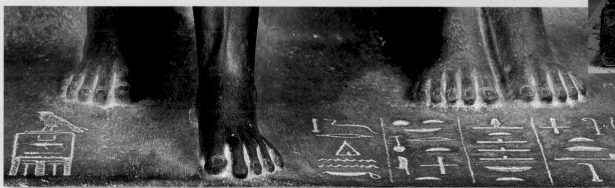

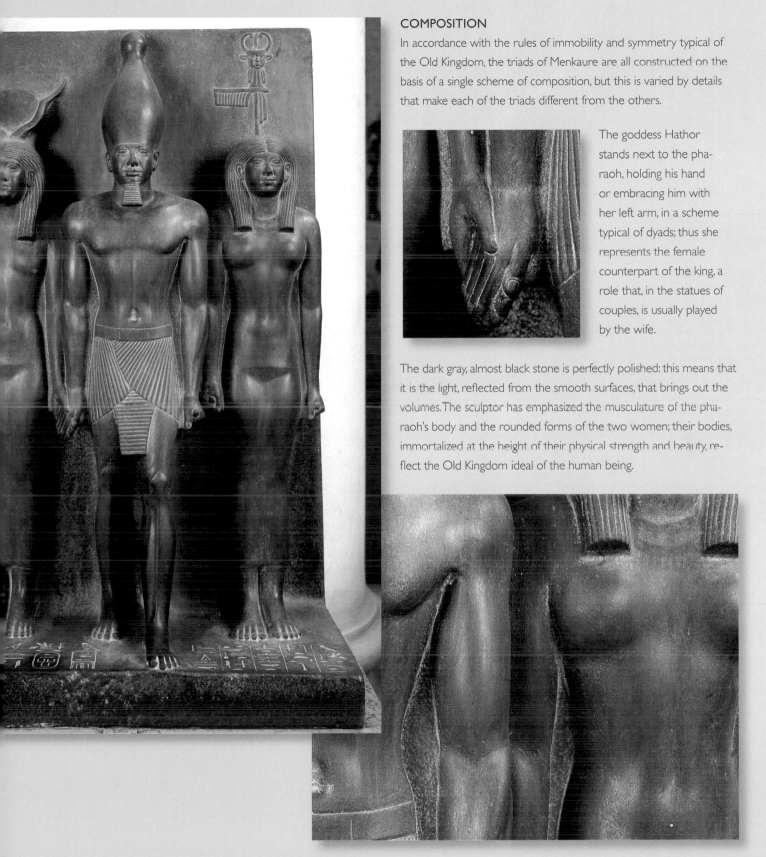

COMPOSITION

In accordance with the rules of immobility and symmetry typical of the Old Kingdom, the triads of Menkaure are all constructed on the basis of a single scheme of composition, but this is varied by details that make each of the triads different from the others.

The goddess Hathor stands next to the pharaoh, holding his hand or embracing him with her left arm, in a scheme typical of dyads; thus she represents the female counterpart of the king, a role that, in the statues of couples, is usually played by the wife.

The dark gray, almost black stone is perfectly polished: this means that it is the light, reflected from the smooth surfaces, that brings out the volumes. The sculptor has emphasized the musculature of the pharaoh's body and the rounded forms of the two women; their bodies, immortalized at the height of their physical strength and beauty, reflect the Old Kingdom ideal of the human being.

THE PYRAMIDS OF THE FIFTH AND SIXTH DYNASTY

Over the course of the following dynasties the structure of the royal funeral complexes showed a tendency to standardize: pyramids of smaller size, but an enlargement of the attached places of worship; similar internal spaces, generally made up of four elements (passageway, antechamber, *serdab*, chamber of the sarcophagus) and always with a change of direction. During the 5th dynasty a monument devoted to worship of the sun seems to have been linked with the royal funeral complex, although separate from it, as in those of Userkaf and Neuserre at Abu Gurab, the only ones studied so far. These were large open courtyards, surrounded by a wall, with a sort of tower in the form of an obelisk with a pyramidal tip standing on a base at the center. The obelisk, to which we shall return, was undoubtedly a solar monument, given that the texts connect it with a sacred stone, perhaps a meteorite, of a presumably conical shape (the *benben* stone) that was kept at the religious center of Heliopolis ("Sun City") and was linked with the solar mythology devised by the local priesthood.

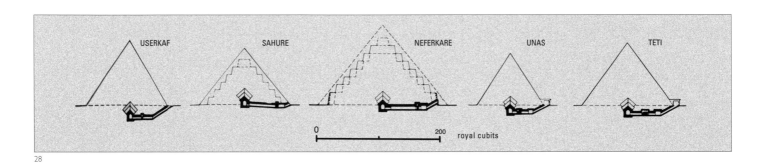

28

29

28. Reconstructive drawings of the pyramids of the pharaohs Userkaf, at Saqqarah, Sahure and Neferkare, at Abusir, and Unas and Teti, at Saqqarah, about 2490-2330 BC (from *Il tempo delle piramidi*, Milan 1979, p. 311, figs. 391-5).

29. Ruins of the sun temple of Neuserre, about 2430 BC. Abu Gurab.

Only fragments of the beautiful reliefs that decorated the areas of worship, with naturalistic themes intended to exalt the life-giving role of the deity, have come down to us. Among them, personifications of the three seasons into which the Egyptian year was divided, each lasting four months: Inundation, with which the year began toward the end of our July, when the Nile flooded; the Emergence, i.e. the resurfacing of land after the flooding and the sprouting of the crops, in the period of our winter, and the Low Water, the season between spring and summer in which the fields were prepared to receive the benefits of the flood.

30

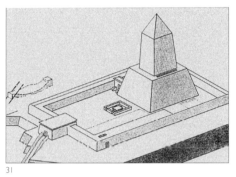

31

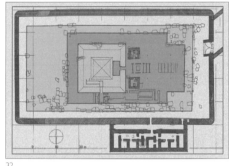

32

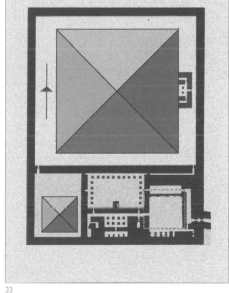

33

30. Relief with birds from the mortuary temple of the Pyramid of Userkaf at Saqqarah, about 2490 BC. Cairo, Egyptian Museum.

31. Reconstructive drawing of the sun temple of Neuserre at Abu Gurab, about 2430 BC (from R. Schulz, M. Seidel, *Egypt*, Cologne 1998, p. 71, fig. 52).

32. Plan of the sun temple of Userkaf at Abusir, about 2490 BC (from D. Arnold, *The Encyclopaedia of Ancient Egyptian Architecture*, London 2003, p. 251).

33. Plan of the pyramid and mortuary temple of Userkaf at Saqqarah, about 2490 BC (from *Il tempo delle piramidi*, Milan 1979, p. 310, fig. 385).

Re, Aton, Harakhte: in Egyptian culture the sun, heavenly body *par excellence* whose intensity conditioned Egypt's very existence, was not a clearly defined entity, as it comprised too many values. Thus for each aspect and each function of the sun there was a separate deity or image. In the dualistic vision of Egyptian culture it was the sun's light that opposed darkness and brought life to the fertile regions, but also death to the desert.

So the sun, whose iconographic emblem was a simple yellow or red disk, had a multiplicity of functions, partly on the basis of the different meanings it assumed in religious symbology. Its daily cycle of death and rebirth gave rise to many funerary traditions, which described its nocturnal journey and the struggle to defeat its enemies, before returning to triumph over the darkness in the morning. This myth magically assured the living that the order of the world was guarded by the deity of light, which inexorably fled the dangers of the dark. In the same way, by analogy, it guaranteed the deceased that they would be able to confront and defeat the dangers of death and live their life in the next world to the full. In addition, the cycle of the sun, which was swallowed every evening by Nut, the goddess of the night sky, and then born again in the morning, was represented on the ceilings of the tombs of the New Kingdom. In these images Nut is shown arched above the earth, her hands and feet resting on the ground, her body covered with stars; one solar disk is set in front of Nut's lips and the other near her hips. In the images linked to the cult of the god, on the

1. Paintings depicting, on the right, Osiris in the guise of the sun god Re, about 1270 BC. Thebes, Tomb of Nefertari.

other hand, the sun is represented in the most varied and unexpected forms: the obelisk, for example, is a potent solar symbol as it is a physical translation of the rays of the sun, as if they had turned to stone at the moment they descended to earth. The pyramid is also a representation of the rays that descend from the sky, although it has a more extensive symbology in which we can recognize many different concepts that have merged with it as time passed.

In divine iconography the solar aspect is always indicated by a disk surmounting the head as an attribute or standard. In the Egyptian pantheon the sun god *par excellence* is Re (sometimes pronounced and written Ra), represented as a man with the head of a falcon or ram and with the solar disk; but many other deities, like the god

Horus and the goddess Sekhmet, also have strong solar aspects. In fact both the falcon and the lion, the totemic animals of these two deities, have a symbolic link with the sun. The solar religion took on new connotations in the New Kingdom, when the pharaoh Amenhotep IV-Akhenaton introduced the worship of a single deity: the god Aton. This god was identified with the solar disk, representing only its physical side: the disk gave off rays of light that descended to the earth, and they too were rendered visible and material. Aton was an extremely benevolent guardian deity and particular emphasis was given to his function as bearer and guarantor of life: the rays that fell to earth, in fact, ended in the form of a hand offering the pharaoh the *ankh*, symbol of life.

II. Head of falcon, about 2200 BC. Cairo, Egyptian Museum.

III. Akhenaton and his family making offerings to Aton, about 1340 BC. Cairo, Egyptian Museum.

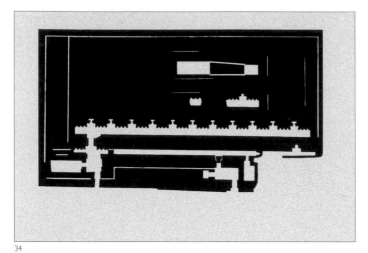

TOMBS OF DIGNITARIES: THE MASTABAS

The eternal abodes of the king's officials and dependants were placed around the great funeral complexes in a topographical arrangement similar to that of a real urban district. The possession of a tomb was considered indispensable to insuring survival after death, protecting the body and guaranteeing the maintenance of its vital energy.

The typical private tomb of the Old Kingdom was the mastaba. With a variable number of rooms located in the structure above ground, the true burial chamber lay underneath, entered through a "shaft" that was closed off after the body had been placed in the

34. Plan of the Mastaba of Hesire at Saqqarah, about 2650 BC (from *Il tempo delle piramidi*, Milan 1979, p. 312, fig. 398).

35. Mastaba of Mereruka, statue of the proprietor in a niche with a table for offerings at his feet, about 2330 BC. Saqqarah.

tomb. The rooms above, sometimes large and numerous, remained accessible for worship and one of the characteristic elements of the superstructure was the so-called false door, located on the eastern side: jambs and lintels reproduced the shape of a door, symbolizing the point of contact between the world of the living and that of the dead. In front of the false door, on a mat or a stone table, were deposited the provisions necessary for the sustenance of the deceased.

Over the course of time the rooms in the superstructure grew increasingly complicated, and the walls were decorated with polychrome images in relief: sometimes very animated, they were intended to represent life.

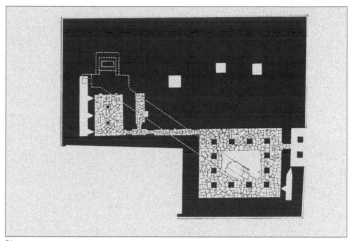

36

37

38

36. Plan of the Mastaba of Ti at Saqqarah, about 2450 BC (from *Il tempo delle piramidi*, Milan 1979, p. 313, fig. 404).

37. False door with polychrome reliefs, about 2450 BC. Saqqarah, Mastaba of Nefer and Kahay.

38. False door of Nikaure, from Saqqarah, about 2460 BC. Cairo, Egyptian Museum.

BAS-RELIEFS IN PRIVATE TOMBS: SCENES OF LIFE

From the 5th dynasty onward the mural decorations in the mastabas of members of the nobility underwent a flowering. This was the consequence of an improvement in their standard of living, as they were given grants of land and other rewards by the pharaoh for their work in the administration of the state. The greater resources at the disposal of the aristocracy made it possible for private individuals to decorate their own tombs for the first time with techniques that had previously been exclusive to the sovereign and utilized for the great temple complexes.

Among other things, the sun temples of the 5th dynasty were decorated with scenes of the labors of the three seasons of the Egyptian year, and these provided models for private decorations. In fact the nobility could not use the same themes as the pharaohs for their tombs, but decorated them instead with images linked to the life of the deceased, or to everyday activities in general: work in the fields, the harvest, fishing and crafts were the most frequent subjects.

The inspiration for these scenes has always to be sought in religious beliefs. Death was seen neither as an annihilation nor as a privation, but as a continuation of life in every sense. In the other world the deceased would go on carrying out the activities he had pursued when alive, and his souls, the *ba* and the *ka*, would have the same need to eat, to dress and to sleep as they had had in life.

To ensure a life without hardships in the next world, everything the deceased would require was placed in the tomb, from clothing to food, from furniture to work tools. But the grave goods were not sufficient, and so to make sure that every need could be satisfied the

39

39. Polychrome relief representing the papyrus harvest, pasturage and hunting, about 2450 BC. Saqqarah, Mastaba of Nefer and Kahay.

40. Facing page: Relief depicting craft activities, about 2450 BC. Saqqarah, Mastaba of Niankhkhnum and Khnumhotep.

walls of the tombs, which were the eternal abodes of the *ka*, were decorated with scenes of daily life: in fact it was believed that images, like writing, had magical powers. Representing work in the fields and the harvest of grain, for example, was a way of ensuring that the *ka* of the deceased would always have the food required for his survival, even when, with the passing of the years, material offerings of bread and beer were no longer made. In general, representing life signified guaranteeing it after death as well.

Magic made the scenes depicted real: so artists strove to execute the decorations in the most complete way possible to make sure the deceased would lack nothing.

Looking at these scenes it is easier for us to understand how in Egyptian culture death was seen as just a stage in the journey of the individual. The decorations also offer us an insight into the daily life of ancient Egypt. The principle that inspired artists was verisimilitude, a quality they sought in order to make the representation more effective. Much care was taken over the details, which took on very great importance. But what were represented with an almost staggering accuracy and realism were the specimens from the world of animals: each species is identifiable thanks to the care with which it was depicted, something which also bears witness to a profound knowledge of the animal kingdom on the part of artists. Stonecutter and painter

41

41. Polychrome relief depicting market and craft activities, about 2450 BC. Saqqarah, Mastaba of Ti.

collaborated, working as a unit in which one made no sense without the other. The bas-relief was developed to be painted in such a way that form and color create an indissoluble unity.

It is almost impossible to distinguish the hand of the individual artist: the decorations are the work of teams of stonecutters and painters, who portrayed the deceased and reproduced his life in the established style. No provision was made for the initiative or creative impulse of the artist since the style was the one defined by the canons adopted for the sovereign: in fact artists got their training on the construction sites of the great works raised by the pharaohs and reproduced the same styles in the decorations of private tombs. The artist is always anonymous: no names of famous sculptors or painters have come down to us. The only concessions made to innovation or change were those related to secondary details of minor importance: in fact deviating from the fixed forms would have meant rendering the magic less effective, and thus nullifying the significance of the images.

Naturally the fundamental scene was the one in which the proprietor of the tomb was depicted "taking possession" of the victuals laid out on a table, as this guaranteed the existence of the necessary food and its legal ownership by the deceased, by concession of the king: a concession on which the possession of the tomb and its decorations also depended.

42

42. Relief showing the preparation and baking of bread, about 2450 BC. Saqqarah, Mastaba of Niankhkhnum and Khnumhotep.

THE GEESE OF MAYDUM
2575-2550 BC
Cairo, Egyptian Museum

SUBJECT

The geese of Maydum are one of the masterpieces of Old Kingdom painting. Originally the painting was part of the mural decoration of the tomb of Nefermaat, a nobleman of the 4th dynasty. His mastaba was found during the excavations carried out at Maydum by Auguste Mariette in 1871, and the frieze with six geese was detached from the wall of the corridor on which it was located and taken to the Egyptian Museum in Cairo, where it can still be seen today.

The frieze represents six geese divided into two symmetrical groups of three, arranged on a thin dark line that acts as a base. The figures, which are also dark, stand out from the light-blue background, unlike the bushes and plants which are painted in pale colors. It was the artist's intention for the picture to represent an indefinite number of birds, as in hieroglyphic script the sign for three was used to indicate the plural in general.

COMPOSITION

The scene conveys a strong sense of symmetry due to the disposition of the two groups, but it is a symmetry that is deliberately broken by a number of details that enliven the composition.

The most significant break can be seen in the middle: the tails of the two birds with their backs to each other are not positioned at the same height, and the two central pairs also differ in their plumage, indicating that they belong to two different species.

The depiction of the plumage is very precise and meticulous, right down to the smallest detail.

The two geese at the ends, with their long necks bent down to the ground, close the composition elegantly and are larger in size, probably so as not to leave empty spaces in the upper part.

In the upper right-hand corner the artist has still felt the need to fill the empty space with a bush that has been left suspended in the air.

EGYPTIAN PERSPECTIVE

In these bas-reliefs it is possible for us to appreciate the construction of the singular system of representation that makes Egyptian art so unique and easy to recognize.

In fact perspective was unknown and, faced with the need to represent three-dimensional reality in just two dimensions, artists devised a system of their own.

The pictures on the walls are laid out in two horizontal bands, with the compositions arranged in such a way that they almost seem to follow the criteria of a "narrative," in which different places and times are identified in succession. There is also an evident search for symmetry in the volumes and gestures. The conventions that were adopted for two-dimensional representation are truly peculiar: the visually essential characteristics of an object or a person were emphasized by projecting them onto a flat surface, without depth.

The basic view was from the front and in profile, along the perpendicular, and when artists wanted to depict an element laid out horizontally, like the top of a table or a stool, they flipped it over so it was seen from above.

Standing or seated, the human figure is presented as a composite of various elements that are intended to show the typical appearance of individual parts of the body: the head is represented in profile, but the eye and eyebrow from the front; the shoulders are also

43

43. Relief representing a sports competition aboard boats, from Saqqarah, about 2494-2345 BC. Cairo, Egyptian Museum.

viewed from the front but the bust is at three quarters and the legs in profile.

This is why the human figure assumes its typical and evocative appearance, as a result of the combination of two different planes of representation in a single figure. In no way does this create difficulties for the artist, who on the contrary is able to make this disjointed image look quite natural.

The figures adhere to the canon of proportions even in group scenes and in movement. Naturally in the groups where the figures are shown carrying out activities we find a greater freedom in the representation, and the arms, legs or pelvis are twisted to give a visual impression of movement.

44

44. Polychrome relief with
scenes of pastoral farming
and fishing, about 2450 BC.
Saqqarah, Mastaba
of Nefer and Kahay.

THE STATUE, LIVING IMAGE

Even before the beginning of the Old Kingdom we have evidence for the carving of wood and ivory to create images of a small size, sometimes conditioned by the original shape of the material used. The tradition of using these more easily worked materials was maintained later on, but it was above all in meeting the "challenge" of stone that Egyptians artists revealed a mastery that has perhaps never been surpassed. The desert around the valley supplied a vast range of high-quality stone: limestone quarries existed in Middle Egypt, but the most sought-after for its firmness and whiteness was mined at Tura, not far south of Cairo; in Upper Egypt there were beds of golden sandstone, as well as pink granite at Aswan; basalt was quarried in the eastern desert and red quartzite near Cairo.

No difficulty seemed to put off the sculptors, who tackled the hardest materials with hammers made of stone (dolerite or gneiss), blades of flint and chisels and saws of copper or bronze, used in combination with powdered quartz.

To bring the figure "out" of the block of stone as if it had been drawn on a cartoon, the sculptor used the same grid of proportions as in reliefs carved on the wall, and projected, to scale, the front, side and rear views onto the four sides of a block, linking them together. It is likely that in Egypt the tradition of carving statues developed out of the cult of the dead ruler: the appearance of the statues was connected with funerary conceptions, and in particular they provided the support for supernatural elements, i.e. they allowed an abstract and invisible entity to be turned into a visible image. Survival after death depended on the preservation of the body, seat of a vital element, the *ka*, that could also reside in statues of the deceased so long as his name was carved on them. The writing authenticated (almost as if it were a "document") the relationship between subject and object, to the point where it was possible to appropriate statues or monuments dedicated to someone else by chiseling out the original names and titles carved on them: the new names that took their place were the "valid" ones. The aim of Egyptian artistic expression was not so much the representation of a reality as its creation. Thus the function of a statue was to create a surrogate, not to reproduce a model, and responded to the need for the effigy to last for an unlimited period of time, independently of whether anyone could see it or not: reality transferred and ideally eternal, destined to prolong the existence of the subject represented in time, in a concrete and living image.

Statues of the pharaohs were located in their mortuary temples, those of private individuals in the closed room called the *serdab*, so they were not seen but could "see," participating in rites and benefiting from offerings. We note, in the structuring of the figure, a tendency to use solid volumes, to avoid a lack of balance between

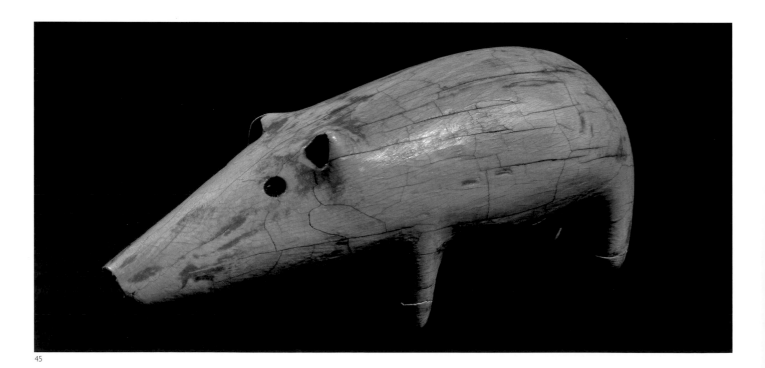

45

45. Ivory statuette of a wild boar, 4th millennium BC. France, private collection.

the various parts; indeed there was a propensity for cubic forms. The person is represented in full maturity, and the body conveys a sense of harmony, prosperity and vital force. The attitude is static, even when, for example, some scribes are shown engaged in reading or writing: in these cases the aim is not to represent a function, but a specific position in society. The immobility may be accentuated by the presence of a base, a dorsal pillar, a seat or other supporting elements with which the statue forms an inseparable unit.

We find these concepts already fully present in the earliest large statue of a king to have come down to us, that of Djoser: this was in fact located inside a sort of enclosed sentry box, inclined at the same angle as the pyramid and set on the north side, next to the mortuary temple at Saqqarah; two small round openings at the level of the eyes allowed the pharaoh to look straight toward the everlasting stars that awaited him. He is represented rigid, fused with his throne and wrapped in the jubilee cloak that also covers the right arm raised to his breast, so that all the attention is focused on the face. This may have an even more solemn appearance today, owing to the shadow that obscures the eyes, which must have once been inlaid and certainly vivid. The heavy wig, only partly covered by the *nemes* headdress, and the long false beard characterize his role, rendered more human only by the touch of the thin mustaches, a fashion that was not to last for long.

46

47

46. Ivory label with the name of Horus-Aha, about 3100 BC. Cairo, Egyptian Museum.

47. Statuette of King Khasekhem, from Hierakonpolis, about 2690 BC. Cairo, Egyptian Museum.

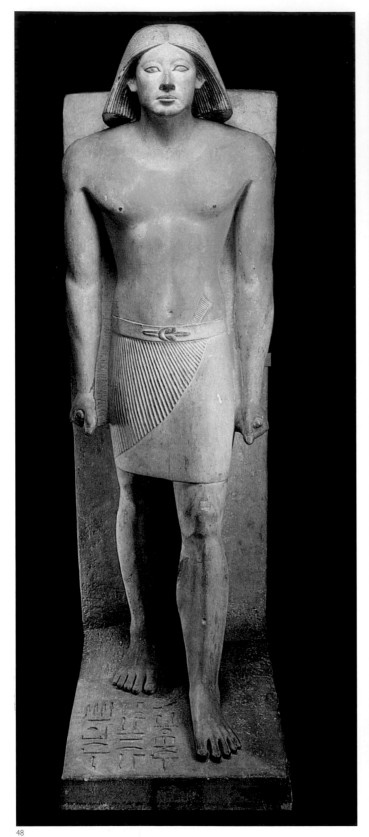

48

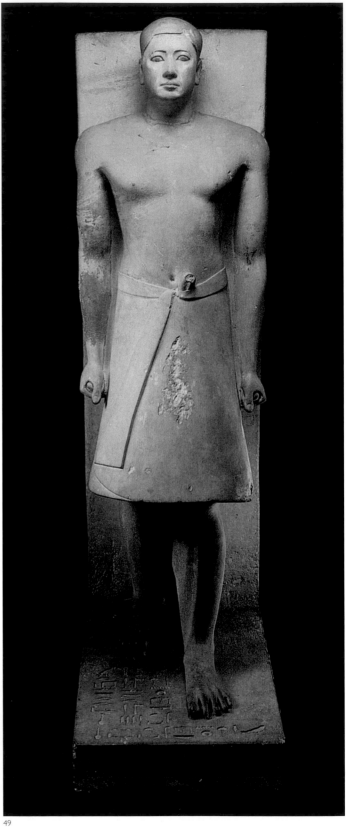

49

48-49. Two statues of Ranefer, with different clothing and hairstyles, from Saqqarah, about 2470 BC. Cairo, Egyptian Museum.

50. Facing page: Double statue of Nimaatsed, from Saqqarah, about 2400 BC. Cairo, Egyptian Museum.

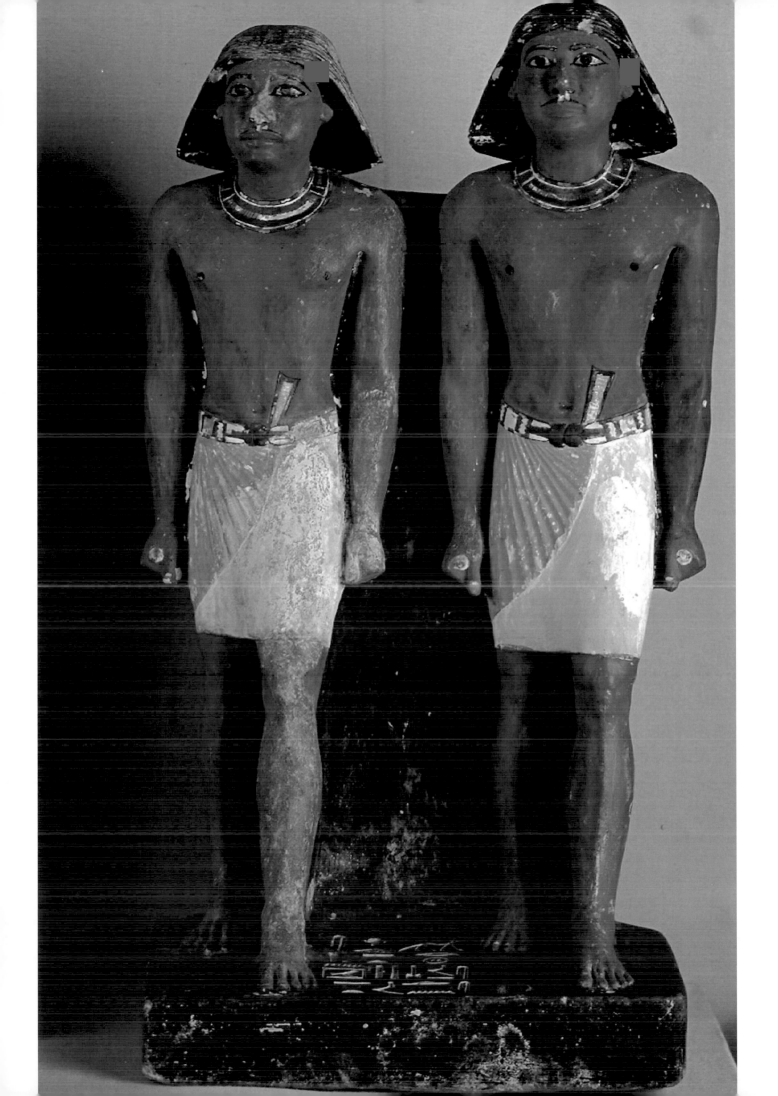

51

**51. Statue of a scribe, from
Saqqarah, 2600-2350 BC.
Paris, Musée du Louvre.**

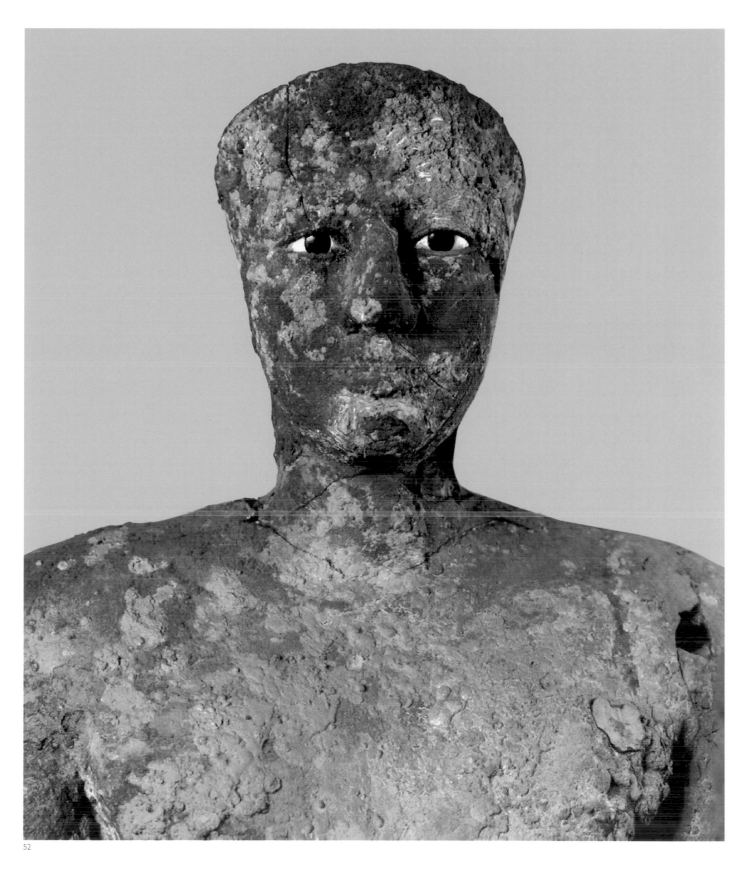

52. Copper statue of King
Pepi I, from Hierakonpolis,
about 2300 BC. Cairo,
Egyptian Museum.

53-54. Statue of Djoser
and detail of the bust,
from Saqqarah, about
2650 BC. Cairo, Egyptian
Museum.

STATUE OF KHAFRE
about 2540 BC
Cairo, Egyptian Museum

SUBJECT

The statue was found in 1860, in a pit in the valley temple of the Pyramid of Khafre at Giza, along with the fragments of eight more. Four of these are of the same material, very dark green gneiss with white veining, one of the most difficult types of stone to work. Despite this, the statue shows a sureness of touch and a refinement in the handling of the translucent surfaces, and is considered the highest expression of regal majesty.

The king is represented seated on the throne, with his arms resting on his legs, the left hand relaxed, the right holding a folded piece of cloth, of symbolic significance, whose ends hang down at the sides.

He is wearing the *nemes*, a cloth headdress with two wide bands that fall onto his breast and, on his forehead, a diadem with a flattened image of the cobra or uraeus, typical attribute of kings.

The pleated kilt or apron called the *shendyt* is composed of two strips of cloth, one wrapped around the hips and one hanging in front.

COMPOSITION

Rather than reproducing particular features, the modeling of the face sets out to create an impression of calm and detachment: the features are regular and harmonious and the chin blends into the royal false beard.

The broad shoulders and the modeling of the bust are a carefully calculated representation of an ideal physique.

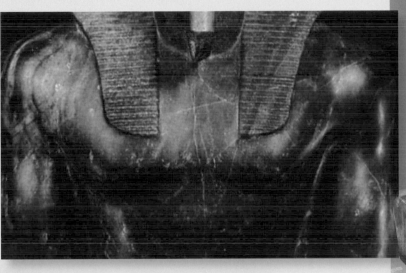

The throne, on whose base is carved the name of Khafre, is a chair with a high back, its sides and legs carved in the form of lions, animals symbolic of royalty.

The sides are decorated in relief with the motif of the "Union of the Two Lands," in which the heraldic plants of Upper and Lower Egypt (the lotus and the papyrus respectively) are knotted around the hieroglyph for "union."

Viewed from the side, we find another element emblematic of the god-king: invisible from the front, the god Horus in his hawk aspect is perched on top of the back, covering the nape of the king's neck with his wings, as if to protect and inspire him, for the pharaohs are his representatives on earth.

55

PRIVATE STATUARY

Among the statues of private persons there are undoubtedly some very fine examples that, while respecting the rules, seem to want to break free of the shackles of tradition and "characterize" their subjects. One of these is the well-known "Village Headman" (*Sheikh el-Beled*), the name given to the painted wooden statue of the priest Kaaper, now in the Cairo Museum, datable to the beginning of the 5th dynasty. The temptation to see in them a tendency to the portrait is strong, especially with regard to images that in our eyes display a marked realism: this is the case, for instance, with

56

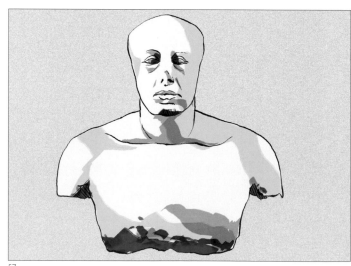

57

55-56. Statue of the priest Kaaper called the *Sheikh el-Beled* and detail of the face, from Saqqarah, about 2450 BC. Cairo, Egyptian Museum.

57. Drawing of the bust of Ankhhaf in the Museum of Fine Arts, Boston, about 2550 BC.

works of the 4th dynasty like the statue of Khufu's architect Hemiunu, in Hildesheim, or the bust of Khufu's son-in-law Ankhhaf, in Boston. This last is a rare type of statue, which should be pictured as "emerging" from the false door of the mastaba to communicate with the living. The realism of the features is undeniable, but they are just one more connotation, no more valid than the name. Another production typical of the 4th dynasty, with which the bust of Ankhhaf may be connected, is that of what are jokingly called "spare heads." Instead of a full-length statue, just a head was deposited in some tombs of that period: cut-off at the neck and sharing common characteristics, all are carved from limestone and not painted, and so white; the hair is treated as a closely-fitting skullcap and the ears are missing, either because they were not provided for or were deliberately chipped away; an incision on top of the head may also be intentional. The sculptor is interested only in the face, whose features are individualized, but certainly idealized and not faithful to reality. They have been interpreted as sculptures that condense the function of a statue, subjected to rituals of which they bear the signs. More recent interpretations prefer to see them, without denying their role as "substitute" statues, as serving a more practical purpose, that of "forms" for funerary masks; the scratches on the head may have been caused by removal of the masks.

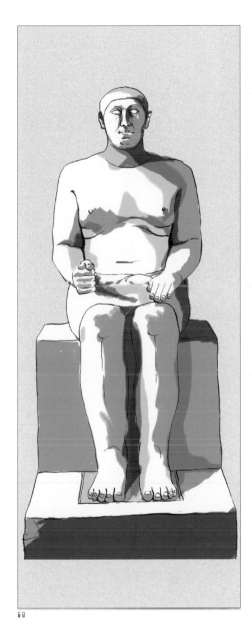

58. Drawing of the statue of the architect Hemiunu in the Roemer und Pelizaeus Museum, Hildesheim, about 2560 BC.

59. "Spare head," about 2550-2500 BC. Cairo, Egyptian Museum.

STATUES OF RAHOTEP AND NOFRET
about 2570 BC
Cairo, Egyptian Museum

SUBJECT

This perfectly preserved pair of statues was found in 1871 in a mastaba at Maydum, where one of Snefru's three pyramids stands. They represent the dignitary Rahotep, thought by many to be the son of Snefru and brother of Khufu, and his wife Nofret.

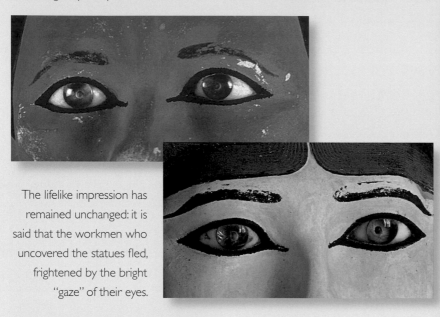

The lifelike impression has remained unchanged: it is said that the workmen who uncovered the statues fled, frightened by the bright "gaze" of their eyes.

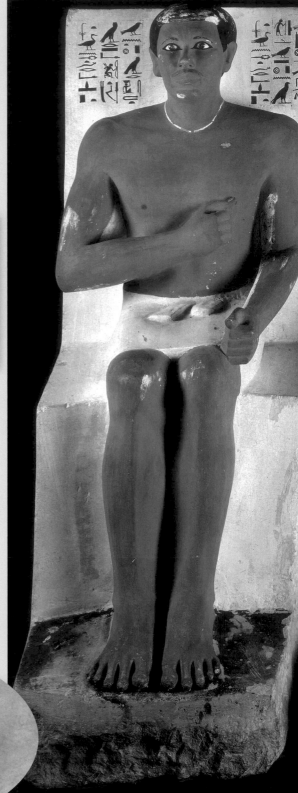

The very high back of the chairs surrounds the figures like a frame and makes them stand out, as if they were emerging from the block of stone. The beautiful hieroglyphs painted on them in black identify the personages and record the important titles of Rahotep.

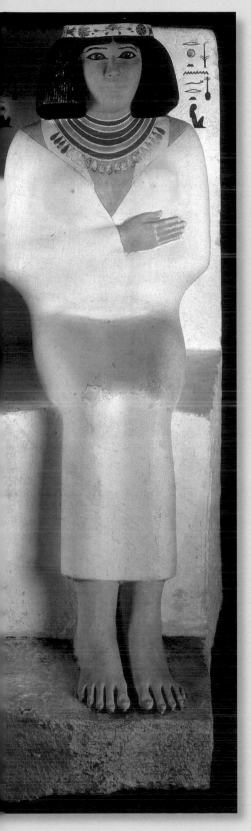

COMPOSITION

Prince Rahotep, "High Priest of Heliopolis" and "Director of Expeditions," is seated with his right hand on his breast and his left on his knee. He is wearing nothing but a short, white kilt. Particular care has been taken over the representation of the bust, athletic and vigorous, with the skin painted a reddish-brown color as convention required.

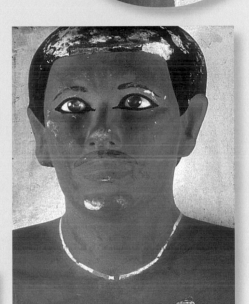

The feet and ankles are handled in a cruder fashion.

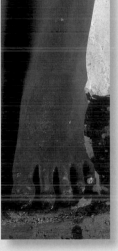

The black hair is set like a skullcap on the face, dominated by the heavily made-up eyes, inlaid in quartz and rock crystal. A crease between the eyebrows augments the impression of energy. Note the thin mustache and, around the neck, a cord from which hangs an amulet.

The strapping appearance of the man is matched by the soft forms of his wife, Nofret, exalted by the mantle in which she is wrapped, from which only her right hand emerges. Against the almost totally white figure stand out the pale yellow ocher of the skin and the colors of her ornaments: the full black wig (her natural hair is seen on the forehead) is ringed by a diadem with floral motifs, intended to represent set stones. A collar of concentric bands hangs over the straps of her tunic.

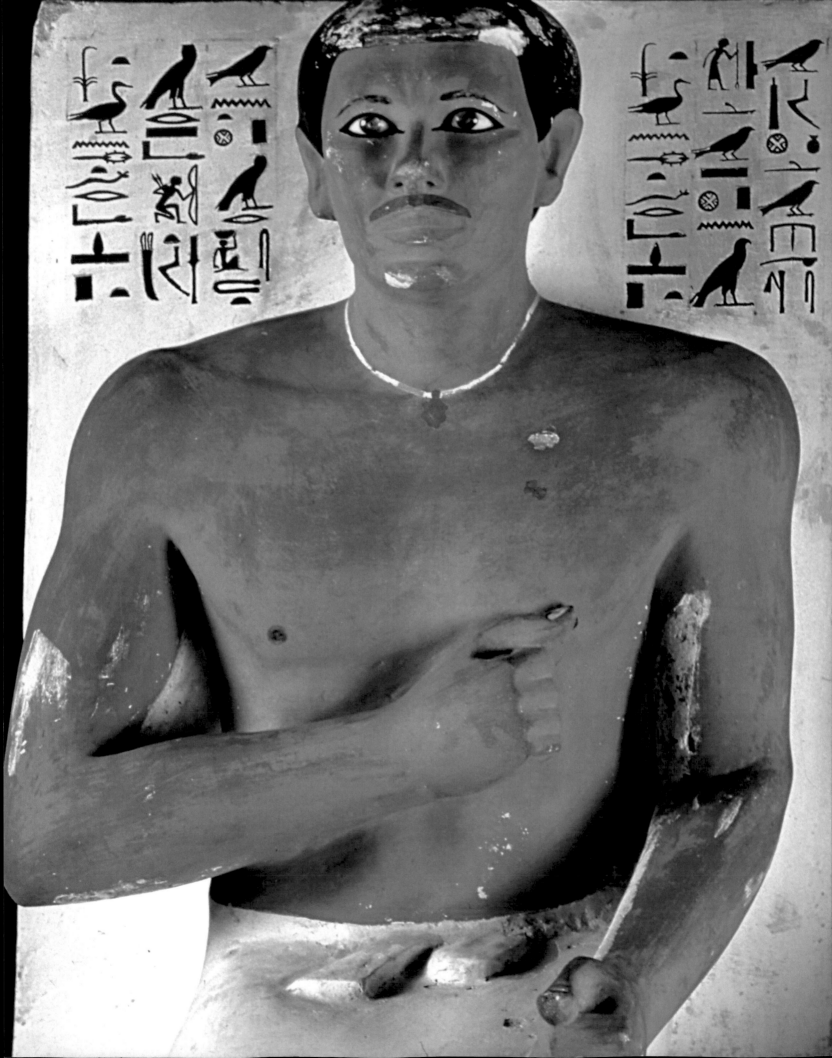

STATUE OF A SCRIBE
about 2470 BC
Cairo, Egyptian Museum

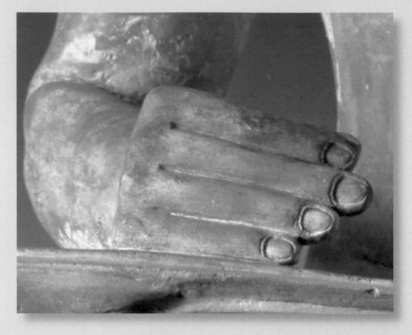

SUBJECT
The excavations conducted by the Antiquities Service at Saqqarah in 1893 brought to light this painted sandstone statue of a scribe of the 5th dynasty. The statue represents the scribe carrying out his functions, seated with his legs crossed and keeping a papyrus scroll open with his left hand while the right used to hold a quill, now vanished.

The eyes, inlaid with rock crystal and semiprecious stones and ringed with copper, are very large and expressive. As in other statues of the Old Kingdom, they are striking in their brilliance, making the statue look alive and present.

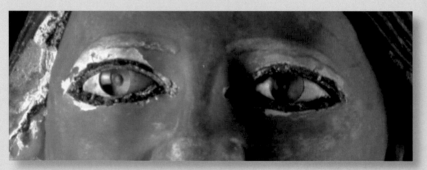

The state of preservation is excellent, not just for the integrity of the stone, which is only lightly scratched, but also and above all for the vividness of the color.

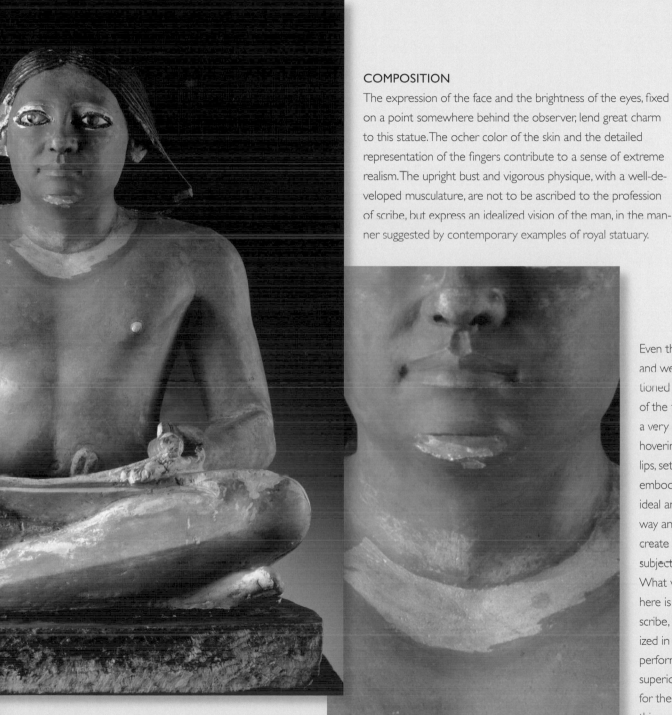

COMPOSITION

The expression of the face and the brightness of the eyes, fixed on a point somewhere behind the observer, lend great charm to this statue. The ocher color of the skin and the detailed representation of the fingers contribute to a sense of extreme realism. The upright bust and vigorous physique, with a well-developed musculature, are not to be ascribed to the profession of scribe, but express an idealized vision of the man, in the manner suggested by contemporary examples of royal statuary.

Even the serene and well-proportioned lineaments of the face, with a very slight smile hovering on the lips, set out to embody a human ideal and are in no way an attempt to create a lifelike and subjective portrait. What we have here is the ideal scribe, immortalized in the act of performing his superior function, for the exercise of this profession was considered a privilege for a few, providing them with access to wisdom. So it appears logical that the men who were invested with this important role should choose to be represented, in their funerary statues, with the distinctive traits of their office.

SARCOPHAGI AND PRECIOUS STONES

Sculpture in stone includes some magnificent examples of monolithic sarcophagi, sometimes without any decoration in order to suggest the idea of protection and an eternal "home" with the pure form in limestone, calcite and granite. During the Old Kingdom these imposing monuments were sometimes decorated in imitation of the architecture of palaces.

They reproduced their façades, with boundary walls punctuated with niches and doors, and even the gratings of windows. In the underground galleries of the Pyramid of Djoser, used in part for the tombs of the pharaoh and the members of his family, but also to house the grave goods, were found large numbers of splendid stone vases dating from earlier dynasties. They bear witness to the mastery achieved by sculptors in the working of even the hardest stone, which they were able to

60

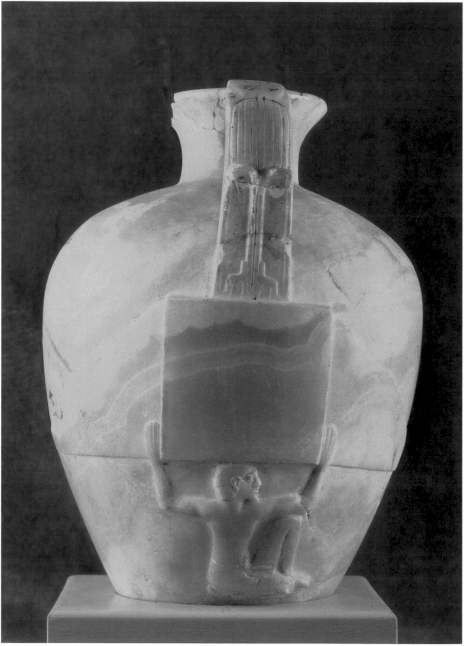

61

98

60-61. Calcite vase with decorative motifs in relief connected with the Sed festival, or jubilee, from Saqqarah, about 2700 BC. Cairo, Egyptian Museum.

handle with skill and even, at times, virtuosity. The production of objects that were in part intended for use soon began to reflect a quest not just for functionality, but for effect, for elegance or fantasy: in pottery, for instance, refined products had been made since prehistoric times. As civilization advanced, the production of the necessary went hand in hand with a growing interest in the "superfluous," and not just the ornamental, with all the connotations that derived from it (display of status through the intrinsic value of precious materials, along with the symbolic values of protection or magical powers attributed to them). Since the first dynasties of the historical period expeditions had been sent in search of gold; in the Sinai they looked for copper, but also for gleaming turquoise. Artists quickly learned to combine precious metal and stones in vivid colors, which could be obtained in Egypt (jasper, cornelian), or by sending expeditions (for example to the Wadi el-Hudi for amethyst).

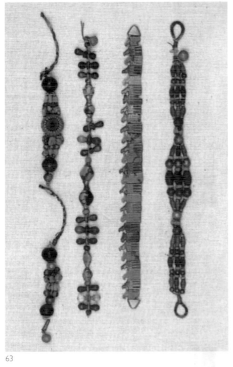
63

64

99

62. Sarcophagus decorated with architectural motifs, from Giza, about 2550 BC. Cairo, Egyptian Museum.

63. Bracelets made of gold and precious stones, from the tomb of the pharaoh Djer at Abydos, about 3000 BC. Cairo, Egyptian Museum.

64. Vases found in the Step Pyramid of Djoser at Saqqarah, about 3000-2700 BC. Cairo, Egyptian Museum.

THE QUEEN'S TREASURE AND THE PHARAOH'S BOAT

The discovery of the contents of the tomb of Khufu's mother in 1925 would have been an even more sensational event if the exploration of Tutankhamun's tomb had not been underway at the same time. And yet the richness and exceptional nature of the finds and a touch of mystery made it a unique case. The contents of the tomb of the king's mother, Hetepheres, wife of Snefru, were found in an intact funerary shaft, excavated to the east of the Pyramid of Khufu. They include Canopic jars, showing that that the queen had been mummified even if the alabaster sarcophagus was empty. In any case it was certainly not the tomb intended for her: perhaps it had been necessary to transfer everything possible into that depository, but without her, and we may never know why. Now, however, we can admire pieces of furniture of astonishing elegance and refinement, which it

has been possible to reconstruct thanks to their decorations or facings of gold or ivory and in spite of the fact that every part made of wood, except the ebony, has turned to dust. Hetepheres' husband had had a canopy of gilded wood made for her, along with the box to transport her drapery. Her son had completed the furnishings with a bed and a litter with ebony finishings and palm-shaped gold knobs on the ends of its poles. The toilet vessels and the razors in their container were also made of gold, and the jewelry casket was gilded; it contained silver bracelets studded with semiprecious stones forming patterns of rosettes and butterflies. But the masterpiece of joinery, if we can call it that, of the period is undoubtedly Khufu's ceremonial boat: to the north and south of the mortuary temple lay two large trenches whose shape immediately suggested the form of a boat. The boat itself was found at the bottom of a pit on the south side, partially dismantled, just as it had been deposited by the executor of

65

67

66

100

65. Chair of Queen Hetepheres, from Giza, about 2580 BC. Cairo, Egyptian Museum.

66. Litter of Queen Hetepheres, from Giza, about 2580 BC. Cairo, Egyptian Museum.

67. Gold vessels of Queen Hetepheres, from Giza, about 2580 BC. Cairo, Egyptian Museum.

Khufu's funeral, his son and successor Djedefra. After restoration it proved to be 141 ft (43 m) long and 20 ft (6 m) wide, with a slender hull terminating in a palm-shaped column at the bow and stern; the planks of cedar and sycamore wood were held in place by ropes, as if "stitched" together, without nails. On the deck, lined with long oars, the elegant cabin with pillars in the shape of papyrus stalks extended to form a veranda. It is possible that the boat was actually used for the funeral ceremonies, but it is likely that its main function was to provide the means of transport for the dead king as he set out to follow the sun in its course.

68. Large trench for a boat in front of the Pyramid of Khufu, 2570 BC about. Giza.

3. The Middle Kingdom: the Classical Age

Toward the end of the 3rd millennium the Memphite monarchy disintegrated under the pressure of economic and social change: over the space of little more than a century, in a historical phase defined as the First Intermediate Period, two cities aspired to hegemony, Heracleopolis, at the entrance to the depression of El-Faiyum, and Thebes, in Upper Egypt. It was an age of disorder and war, but also one that saw the emergence of new social classes, along with different forms of expression from those developed by the palace workshops. While sometimes clumsy, these were spontaneous and brought a breath of fresh air. The renewal would soon be apparent in every sphere: the Theban royal house managed to gain the upper hand and reunify the country, permitting a magnificent flowering of the arts and literature. The pharaohs of the 12th dynasty moved the capital from Thebes to El-Lisht, near the oasis of El-Faiyum, where reclamation work designed to increase the area of cultivable land was concentrated. But it was also an "ideological" return to a location close to the historic city of Memphis, capital of the Old Kingdom, and to its traditions.

2

3

103

1. Statue of Sesostris I, detail of the bust, 1956-1911 BC. Cairo, Egyptian Museum.

2. Relief with the god Horus presenting the symbol of life to the pharaoh, detail, about 1925 BC. Karnak, White Chapel of Sesostris I.

3. Statue of Nofret, wife of Sesostris II, from Tanis, 1877-1870 BC. Cairo, Egyptian Museum.

THE FIRST INTERMEDIATE PERIOD

After the very long reign of Pepi II, at the end of the Old Kingdom the state government found itself in a weakened position with respect to the provincial centers, which had acquired considerable independence. In fact administrative posts, originally assigned by the ruler, had slowly become hereditary, resulting in the formation of fiefdoms within the unified state and leading to a situation in which the unity of that state no longer really existed. With the loss of unity, the stylistic uniformity that had pervaded all works of art in the Old Kingdom also vanished. At first the feudal lords attracted artists trained in the school of Memphis to the provincial centers, but local schools quickly emerged with their own styles to meet the needs of those who wanted to decorate their tombs. The greater part of the production that has come down to us from the First Intermediate Period consists of statues and examples of the decorative arts created for votive purposes: they are the funerary works of the provincial necropolises and not much has survived. In general we see a marked deterioration in formal quality, with a mechanical repetition of themes and subjects typical of the latter part of the Old Kingdom that could not match the excellence of their execution. The roughness of the forms and the stiffness of the features were not due solely to a lack of skill, which the patronage of the pharaoh and his court had certainly stimulated in artists by always coming up with new requirements and proposing new themes, but were a reflection of the social upheaval that was sweeping the country. The literature of the time is also permeated by a deep sense

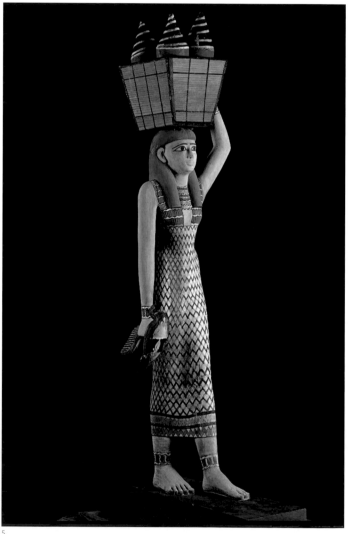

4

5

4. Stele of Inheretnakht, probably from Naga ed-Deir, about 2160-2055 BC. London, British Museum.

5. Statue of woman carrying offerings, from the tomb of Meketra at Thebes, about 2000 BC. Cairo, Egyptian Museum.

6

of pessimism and despair. The order established by the gods, as well as the pharaoh's ability to guarantee *maat* (harmony), had suddenly broken down; in other words, all the certainties on which the culture of the Old Kingdom had been based had vanished and people found themselves living in a difficult and violent world, demoralized and deprived of the points of reference that had hitherto seemed unshakable. This loss of values found expression in art too: the figures no longer had any of the harmony, regularity and perfection typical of the Old Kingdom. Innovations were reduced to flashes of vivacity that brought tired and repetitive themes to life: groups of animals led to pasture are not separated into different breeds but mixed up in a single flock or herd; elsewhere an unwary fisherman ends up in the mouth of a crocodile, and even the scenes of dancing are more lively in comparison with the rigidity of the earlier designs. The figure lost its refinement, but gained a little in animation and movement. Small models and three-dimensional representations of servants, or of farming activities, took the place of the magical paraphernalia of

the tombs, previously made up of images carved and painted on the walls but now left much barer. Several typical scenes, like those of baking bread, were replaced by models of women grinding grain and the number of statuettes of servants increased exponentially. In the First Intermediate Period the human figure, especially in the statuary, had distinctive traits that create an impression of brutal force, power and belligerence. Despite the fact that the artists imitated the subjects of the Old Kingdom, the planes are greatly simplified, the features are crude and extremely harsh, the expressions often convey a certain aggressiveness: on the faces of the statues that have survived we can read the strain of living in a world that had grown difficult and full of violence. The statues were made almost exclusively out of wood: few could afford sculptures in noble materials like stone, although the examples that have come down to us are similar in quality to those of the previous period as far as the technique used to work the material is concerned. It was in this moment of rupture and confusion that the foundations were laid for the art of the Middle Kingdom. The funerary

**6. Fresco depicting a scene
of the transport of grain,
from the tomb of Iti at
Gebelein, about 2100 BC.
Turin, Egyptian Museum.**

7

7. Painted wooden model
of a farmer plowing a
field, about 2160-2055 BC.
Paris, Musée du Louvre.

statues of the first ruler who succeeded in bringing the country back under a single command, Mentuhotep II, still have all the force and intensity typical of the spirit of the First Intermediate Period, whose style was to influence the art of the first part of the Middle Kingdom. Although the evidence is scanty, the decorative arts do not seem to have attained the level of quality they had in the Old Kingdom, but were fairly rough and simplified, while maintaining the elements of vivacity introduced in this period. Royal statuary preserved the sense of force and power typical of this time of confusion, which was to last up until the kings of the 12th dynasty. The expression on the face of these rulers conveys both concern and the firmness needed to govern the state. The composed calm and sense of absolute superiority displayed by the sovereigns of the Old Kingdom seem to have vanished. Only in the second half of the Middle Kingdom would the faces of the pharaohs recover their serenity, at times becoming almost idealized again.

8. Pillar of Sesostris I,
from Karnak,
about 1956-1911 BC.
Cairo, Egyptian Museum.

9. Colossal bust
of Sesostris I, from Karnak,
about 1956-1911 BC. Cairo,
Egyptian Museum.

THE FUNERARY MONUMENTS: INNOVATION AND TRADITION

Thebes, which was about to become "the City" of Egypt and hold its dominant position for the whole of the 2nd millennium, does not preserve many signs of the earlier phase, when it must have been little more than a village. With the rise of the Theban royal house, which would eventually win supremacy over Heracleopolis and the entire country, more evidence and signs of change begin to appear. The western desert part of Thebes, traditionally reserved for necropolises, is characterized by the presence of rocky heights that rise, sometimes steeply, behind the cultivated fields. The Theban princes had their tombs carved in the cliffs, in the part further to the north, with broad, pillared façades. The man who became the legitimate ruler of the whole of Egypt in the middle of the 11th dynasty, Mentuhotep II,

chose a decidedly spectacular site for his extraordinary and innovative sepulchral monument, at Deir el-Bahri, inaugurating a new tradition. Today it is "overshadowed" by the more imposing and famous temple of Hatshepsut, but it is not hard to imagine the magnificent impression it must have made at the time, in the setting of the pinnacles of rock at the foot of al-Qurn, "the Horn," the sacred mountain overlooking the entire Theban necropolis. From a valley temple a paved road lined with sandstone statues of the king led through a garden of sycamores and tamarisks to two terraces surrounded by pillared halls, linked by a ramp. At the center, in the highest part, stands a square, compact building that was initially thought to be a pyramid, 72 ft or 22 m on a side, but which is more likely to have been a regularized mound, crowned by a projecting cap. Excavated in the mountain, behind it, a place of worship and a sepulchral crypt. But invisible, underground, yet another element formed an integral part of the complex: a long corridor running from

10

10. The Theban necropolis: Deir el-Bahri (on the right) and the hill of Sheikh Abd al-Qurnah, dominated by the Horn.

the part in front of the terraces as far as the square building. In it were found a statue of the king wrapped in a piece of linen and laid on a heap of sand, an empty sarcophagus and, at the bottom of two deep pits, offerings and models of boats. It is clear that the monument can be interpreted in several different ways: the mound set on top, which may have actually contained a heap of sand, has been seen as a reference to the primordial hill, as well as to the worship of the local and dynastic god, Montu. It is certain, however, that the underground "ritual tomb" is connected with the cult of the god Osiris and the identification of the dead pharaoh with him. With the advent of the 12th dynasty and the transfer of the capital to El-Lisht in the north, the rulers openly harked back to the traditions of the past, grafting new conceptions onto them in a dialectic relationship. All the kings of the dynasty chose pyramids as sepulchral monuments and raised these structures first close to the new capital, and then further north, at Dahshur, as if to pay homage to their great ancestor Snefru (who had built two of his pyramids there

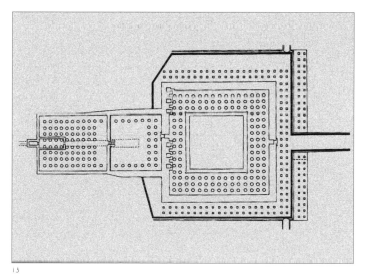

11. Overhead view of the funeral complex of Mentuhotep II next to the temple of Hatshepsut. Deir el-Bahri.

12. Funeral complex of Mentuhotep II, about 2055-2004 BC. Deir el-Bahri.

13. Plan of the mortuary temple of Mentuhotep II at Deir el-Bahri, about 2055-2004 BC (from D. Arnold, *Encyclopaedia of Ancient Egyptian Architecture*, London 2003, p. 150).

14. Reconstruction of the elevation of the mortuary temple of Mentuhotep II at Deir el-Bahri, 2055-2004 BC (from R. Schulz, M. Seidel, *Egypt*, Cologne 1998, p. 109).

15

and may have been buried in the "red" one), and in the vicinity of El-Faiyum, on which their economic policy relied so greatly. The choice of the pyramid is undoubtedly significant, yet the complexes were subjected to many modifications and revisions. In the first place no attempt was made to build on such a huge scale; indeed, apart from the first two, the pyramids were not constructed entirely of stone. The supporting structure consists of radial walls that were used to create compartments. These were then filled with rubble or mud bricks and then faced with stone. The biggest innovation was the internal structure: the rules of the Old Kingdom were broken once and for all in the Pyramid of Sesostris II at El-Lahun, whose entrance is no longer to the north, where it had always been. In addition, the complicated meanderings of the internal passages that surround the chamber of the sarcophagus as if it were an island were inspired by ideas about the tomb of the god Osiris. The complementary constructions tended to become simpler, but with Sesostris III and Amenemhet III, at the end of the dynasty, there was a new change, in the opposite direction. The latter pharaoh, after many centuries, appears to have again built two pyramids, one at Dahshur and one at Hawara, at the entrance to El-Faiyum. In a totally unexpected development, the Dahshur pyramid contained not only the king's funerary chamber, with a magnificent sarcophagus (that was not utilized), but two for queens: a royal pyramid had never been shared since the time of Djoser. Djoser's name must have been invoked again for the complexes of Sesostris III at Dahshur

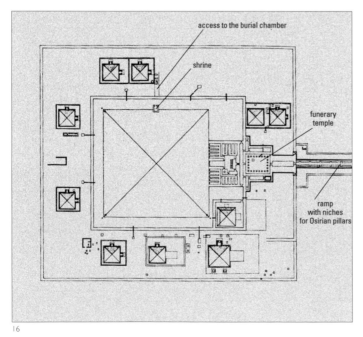

16

17

15. Relief with an image of Mentuhotep II with the god Montu, from the temple of Deir el-Bahri, 2055-2004 BC. British Museum, London.

16. Plan of the complex of the Pyramid of Sesostris I at El-Lisht, about 1956-1911 BC (from R. Schulz, M. Seidel, *Egypt*, Cologne 1998, p. 111, fig. 13).

17. Pyramid of Sesostris I, about 956-1911 BC. El-Lisht.

18. Facing page: Statue of Mentuhotep II in front of his temple and, in the background, the temple of Hatshepsut. Deir el-Bahri.

19

20

19. Pyramid of Sesostris III, about 1870-1831 BC. Dahshur.

20. Pyramid of Amenemhet III, about 1831-1786 BC. Dahshur.

and for Amenemhet III's second, definitive one at Hawara. Like the complex of Saqqarah, these are oriented north-south, rectangular and apparently divided into three parts, setting aside a great deal of space for other constructions. At Hawara the southern sector was occupied by the vast and famous "labyrinth", glorified by classical writers as a greater wonder than the pyramids. Built entirely of stone, and perhaps made up of an innumerable series of shrines for worship of the gods and the pharaoh, it harked back to the ideology devised by the Memphite monarchy, associating the ruler with the gods in a monumental residence for the afterlife.

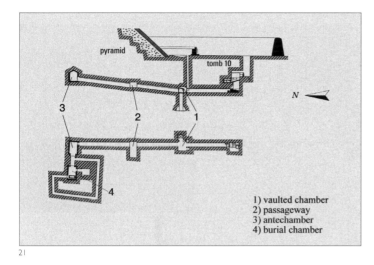

1) vaulted chamber
2) passageway
3) antechamber
4) burial chamber

21

22

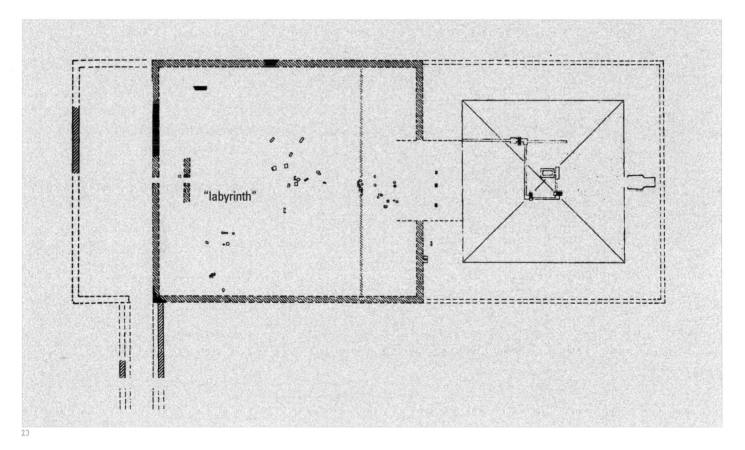

"labyrinth"

23

EGYPTIAN ART

21. Section and plan of the chambers inside the Pyramid of Sesostris II at El-Lahun, about 1877-1870 BC (from R. Schulz, M. Seidel, *Egypt*, Cologne 1998, p. 113, fig. 16).

22. Pyramid of Amenemhet III, about 1831-1786 BC. Hawara.

23. Plan of the Pyramid of Pharaoh Amenemhet III with the "Labyrinth" at Hawara, about 1831-1786 BC (from D. Arnold, *Encyclopaedia of Ancient*

Egyptian Architecture, London 2003, p. 15).

LIFE IN THE FIELDS

Life in the Nile Valley is heavily conditioned by the two natural elements that make it possible: the sun and the river. And it is that same natural environment which has suggested the dualism omnipresent in the civilization of the Nile, for the land is fertile, producing crops and life, and at the same time it is the barren desert, synonymous with death. The black earth and the red earth, as the fertile lands and the desert were called in ancient times, meet at the exact point reached by the water of the Nile and the silt brought by the river during the seasonal flooding. Here, in a clear-cut and abrupt manner, one passes from cultivated fields to the desert, and life depends not only on the level of the inundation, but also on the capacity of people to keep the canals that distribute water to all the cultivable land in a good state. It is thanks to the bas-reliefs decorating the walls of temples and private

I. Relief with scenes
of fishing and fighting,
about 2450 BC. Saqqarah,
Mastaba of Niankhkhnum
and Khnumhotep.

II. Fresco depicting
inspection of cattle, from
the tomb of Nebamun,
about 1350 BC. London,
British Museum.

tombs that we have a vivid and precious picture of the activities of agricultural life: plowing with oxen, the grain harvest, hunting, livestock at pasture, fishing on the river and even the slaughter of animals; in short every possible activity carried out in everyday life has been immortalized in scenes full of energy and realism. And it is movement that characterizes these images, breaking with the immobility typical of almost the whole of artistic production in Egypt and contrasting strongly with the majority of the decorations of royal tombs. In some cases these scenes, while filled with bustle, seem stiff, and the human figure, viewed in profile or from the front, often does not look well proportioned. Egyptian art had developed very precise canons for the representation of the human figure, standing or seated but always conceived as motionless: this is why in these scenes of movement the rules have broken down and are no longer completely applicable. Nevertheless, the artists did their best to tackle the subject, that of life in the fields, and find ways of communicating movement and filling the pictures with vitality.

New models were developed and even these subjects were in a certain sense canonized: among the most common, the work of plowing and sowing and the harvest of grain. The deceased works his field with a plow drawn by oxen while his wife walks behind him, scattering seed on the soil; the couple is then represented at a later time, gathering the ears of grain that are the fruit of their labor.

Animals are an integral part of the farming activities, as work aids and as a source of food. In addition to poultry, donkeys and oxen, even monkeys make their appearance in scenes of everyday life, climbing trees and stealing figs during the harvest.

The plants and environment of the river and marshes are also faithfully represented and with a wealth of details. Nilotic scenes, for example, are frequently portrayed in the decorations of palaces and temples and are filled with movement and spontaneity.

These images provide us with the information needed to fill the gaps relating to many aspects of the life of the lower social classes, and also present a fairly well-defined picture of the integration of human beings with the natural environment: looking at them, we gain a better understanding of how nature imposed its cyclic patterns on human life, determining its conditions. From this integration between the rhythms of nature and human activity stemmed the profound religious sense with which the Egyptians related to creation.

III

IV

III. Papyrus with scene of plowing and sowing, detail, 18th dynasty, about 1550-1295 BC. Cairo, Egyptian Museum.

IV. Fresco with birds amidst vegetation, from the palace of Amenhotep III at Malqata, about 1360 BC. Cairo, Egyptian Museum.

TEMPLES AND GODS: CULTS IN THE OASIS OF EL-FAIYUM

From the Middle Kingdom onward we begin to find more conspicuous vestiges of other kinds of buildings than tombs: of course there are records of such architecture from earlier ages, but very few remains. The first places of worship must have been built out of materials like wood and matting, but stone constructions are known from Djoser's time (3rd dynasty) in the great religious center of Heliopolis, the place where the cult of the sun was developed. At least sixteen obelisks were erected there, certainly from the reign of Teti onward (6th dynasty). They were the most characteristic monuments and can be interpreted, as we have seen, as representations of the *benben* stone (located at Heliopolis) or petrified beams of sunlight. The cusp in the form of a pyramid (pyramidion), which in some cases must have been clad in gold that gleamed in the sun, was once again an allusion to the idea of the primordial hill of earth, and thus to the concept of genesis and creation in which the sun played the leading part. However, the oldest obelisk to have been preserved *in situ* is that of Sesostris I (12th dynasty), sole survivor of the pair the pharaoh had set up in front of the temple dedicated to Atum. Building activity In the El-Faiyum area was intense, in celebration of both the local deities and the role of the pharaohs. It was only in the 1970s that the mystery of the "bare" temple of Qasr es-Sagha, completely devoid of inscriptions and clearly left unfinished,

was solved. A thorough investigation of the site has established a direct relationship with the settlement, to the west of Lake Qarun, which served as a base for expeditions to the nearby basalt quarries during the 12th dynasty. The dating of the remains of the houses, perhaps for the first time in Egyptology – which in general can count on different points of reference than classical archeology – has been based on the types of pottery found. The small sandstone temple has a row of seven shrines opening onto an oblong vestibule: the one in the middle is larger and probably contained a group of statues, perhaps including the ruler who dedicated the temple, while in the others were set statues of gods. Such an unusually large number suggests that all the deities of the region were venerated here. At Medinet Madi, the ancient city of Dja where the goddess of the harvest Renenutet, represented in the form of a cobra, was worshiped, it was an Italian mission that brought to light the small 12th-dynasty temple which had been incorporated into a new structure in the Ptolemaic period. Constructed by Amenemhet III and Amenemhet IV, it was preceded by an antechamber with two papyrus columns (almost *in antis*, as in certain classical temples) and consisted of three shrines for statues of gods sharing a common vestibule. The cult was also devoted to Amenemhet III himself, the ruler who had done most for the economic development of El-Faiyum and who celebrated himself and his deeds in an unusual double monument at Biahmu, a few miles to the north of the provincial capital of Medinet el-Faiyum (Shedet for the ancient Egyptians). The monument faces onto the lake:

25

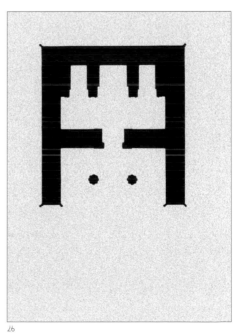

26

24. Facing page: Obelisk of Sesostris I, about 1956-1911 BC. Heliopolis.

25. *Pyramidion* of Amenemhet III, from Dahshur, about 1800 BC. Cairo, Egyptian Museum.

26. Plan of the temple of Amenemhet III and Amenemhet IV at Medinet Madi, about 1830-1780 BC (from *Il tempo delle piramidi*, Milan 1979, p. 317, fig. 421).

two separate courtyards, each enclosed by a thick wall and containing a base in the shape of a truncated pyramid and reaching a height of over 20 ft or 6 m, on which stood a colossal statue of the pharaoh seated on his throne, in red quartzite. It is very likely that Amenemhet III was deified here and worshiped as a creator god. The truly spectacular monument was described by the Greek historians Herodotus (about 450 BC) and Diodorus Siculus (1st century BC), who even spoke of two "pyramids" emerging from the waters of the lake.

27

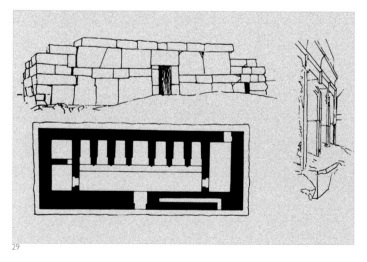

29

28

27. Reconstruction of the double monument of Amenemhet III at Biahmu, about 1831-1786 BC (from D. Arnold, *Encyclopaedia of Ancient Egyptian Architecture*, London 2003, p. 32).

28. "Bare" temple of Qasr es-Sagha, niches, 1870 BC.

29. Plan and elevation of the external façade and the niches of the vestibule of the "bare" temple of Qasr es-Sagha, about 1870 BC (from *Il tempo delle piramidi*, Milan 1979, p. 317, figs. 423-5).

AMON AND OSIRIS: THE LORD OF EGYPT AND THE LORD OF THE UNDERWORLD

The first kings of the 12th dynasty, and Sesostris I in particular, were the founders of what was to become the national sanctuary of Karnak, the great temple dedicated to Amon. Today a series of three thresholds are all that is left of the original, limestone construction, which was fronted by pillars with statues of the king in his aspect as the god Osiris set against them. The structure also comprised buildings of smaller size, such as stations for the procession of sacred boats carrying the divine image during festivities; one of these structures, the oldest religious monument to have come down to us complete from Egypt, is now known as the White

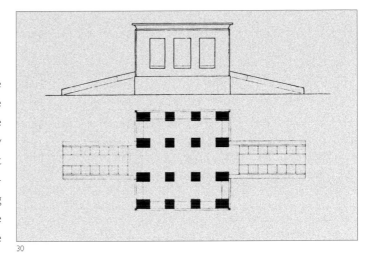

30

31

EGYPTIAN ART

30. Plan of the White Chapel of Sesostris I at Karnak, about 1925 BC (from *Il tempo delle piramidi*, Milan 1979, p. 317, figs. 419-20).

31. White Chapel of Sesostris I, side view, about 1925 BC. Karnak.

Chapel of Sesostris I. A true gem of elegance, it has proved possible to reconstruct in its entirety because during his enlargement of the temple of Karnak, Amenhotep III, an 18th-dynasty pharaoh who lived about 600 years later, had had it dismantled and reutilized in the foundations of the new monumental gate. A square kiosk, built of white limestone from the quarries at Tura, it has four rows of four pillars on a base and is accessible by ramps from the east and west. The very fine sculpted decoration, which plays on the alternation of intaglio, generally used for exteriors, and relief, for interiors, shows Sesostris I greeted by the gods on the occasion of his first jubilee. It has also been suggested that the kiosk was a stone version of the pavilion mounted for the jubilee celebrations. Sesostris I was also responsible for substantial works of renovation in the temple at

Abydos, which had existed since the Old Kingdom and was dedicated to the deity connected with the cult of the dead king, Khenti-Amentiu, who in this period was definitively identified with the god Osiris. Nothing remains to bear witness to the marvels described in some of the texts, but one of his successors, Sesostris III, built the first monumental complex that can be interpreted as a cenotaph, a structure that was to become typical of the New Kingdom. This "false" or ritual tomb had the function of magically ensuring the presence of the king to whom it was dedicated, along with Osiris himself, at his most important place of worship, and his participation in the festivities, the religious rituals and the benefits that stemmed from them. Although the monument of Sesostris III appears incomplete, it extends for an impressive distance underground, from the

33

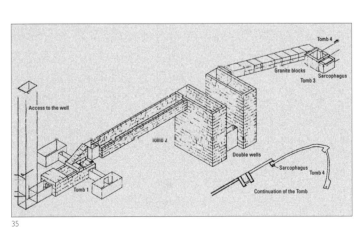

35

34

EGYPTIAN ART

32. Facing page: Osirian colossus of Sesostris I, originally set against a pillar in the Temple of Karnak, 1956-1911 BC. Luxor, Museum of Ancient Egyptian Art.

33-34. Sesostris I between the god Montu (on the left) and Amon, about 1925 BC. Karnak, White Chapel of Sesostris I.

35. Isonometric projection of the cenotaph of Sesostris III at Abydos, about 1870-1831 BC (from D. Arnold, *Encyclopaedia of Ancient Egyptian Architecture*, London 2003, p. 5).

bottom of two deep and converging shafts. There are four "nuclei," one of which (the third) seems to allude to the burial, given the presence of a splendid - empty - granite sarcophagus and a chest for Canopic jars (used to hold the viscera of the mummified body), while the fourth has been recognized as a reference to the tomb of Osiris. This amazing construction, an enigma for the first excavators, sanctioned the religious significance of the location. Already well established during the Old Kingdom (it should be remembered that the only statuette bearing Khufu's name, a small ivory object 3 in or 7.5 cm in height, comes from the temple at Abydos), its importance grew enormously in the Middle Kingdom, when it became a widespread practice for the faithful to make a "pilgrimage" to the sanctuary of the god, whose "tomb" was traditionally identified with that of one of the founders of the state, King Djer of the 1st dynasty. The ceremonies, at which the mythical story of the death and resurrection of the god was reenacted, drew crowds of people, especially from the

end of the Old Kingdom onward. From that moment on it is possible to discern the effects of a profound renewal of society. In the funerary sphere, this has been defined as a "democratization of the afterlife", since it extended to every stratum the aspiration to life after death, previously considered a privilege of the ruler and a favored few. Now the universally accepted moral standard and the idea of a judgment to which everyone would be subject put individuals on an equal footing, allowing all to hope for the destiny exemplified by the story of the god's death and resurrection. For this reason many chose to leave their mark at Abydos, in the form of a memorial tablet or a "false tomb," like the kings, or even a miniature shrine, so that their memory would not perish. The world's museums are filled with innumerable stelae, some of modest quality, that are carved with at least the scene of the funerary meal, magically valid for eternity, and sequences of names of the person and his relatives and colleagues, whether represented or not, all sharing the hope in an afterlife.

36

37

36. Statuette of Khufu, from Abydos, about 2570 BC. Cairo, Egyptian Museum.

37. Stele of Antef, from Abydos, about 1900 BC. Cairo, Egyptian Museum.

38. Facing page: Stele for the treasurer Ty, perhaps from Abydos, about 1750 BC. Florence, Egyptian Museum.

I. Seated statue of Amon
with Tutankhamun, about
1330 BC. Paris, Musée du
Louvre.

In the Egyptian conception of the world the divine permeated every aspect of reality, and nature was its prime living expression.

Thus all the deities represented a function or an aspect of natural reality, and the iconography of the gods summarized the role embodied by each through symbols or attributes that soon became canonical. If the gods of ancient Egypt were so numerous, it was due precisely to the fact that reality was perceived as being made up of a multiplicity of elements; the sense of the divine was so strong and so fully integrated into daily life that even chaos and violence had their divine personifications as constituent elements of the world.

Half human and half animal, Egyptian deities have always possessed an enigmatic symbolic fascination. Yet not all of them had this composite iconography: several had just a human form, while others were represented exclusively as animals, and others still had more than one totemic animal, like the god Thoth, for example, who could take the form of an ibis or a baboon. A number of deities were not associated with animal traits, but had their function expressed instead through symbolic representation of objects or plants. The iconography varied in relation to the specific role that the god or goddess assumed on each occasion. The New Kingdom saw an increase in a phenomenon typical of Egyptian religion, that of syncretism, a process in which two deities could "fuse" to become a new entity that combined the characteristics of both the original gods and their iconography. The best-known example of this phenomenon is the principal deity of the New Kingdom, Amon-Re, a syncretic union of Amon, the creator god, and Re, god of the sun. Another characteristic of divine iconography is the way that the hieroglyphic sign or signs of the god's name are placed above the head, turning them into an evocative symbol.

AMON: From the New Kingdom on he was the principal god of the Egyptian pantheon. He is at one and the same time the creator god and the preserver of order in the world. He can have a human appearance, and in this case is recognizable by his tall, double-plumed crown, or assume an animal form, either a ram or a goose, which is why he was also called the "Great Cackler."

ISIS: Goddess of the magic arts, sister and wife of Osiris and mother of Horus, she is always represented in the form of a woman. Like her sister Nephthys, she has above her head the hieroglyph indicating her name, a throne. She is presented in very different ways, as she is often linked with other deities. With her sister Nephthys, she performed the function of a protectress: in this case she is shown in the act of embracing the sovereign or his sarcophagus. Often her arms are winged, as if to protect the pharaoh better.

OSIRIS: He is the god of the underworld and is always represented in human form, with his mummified body wrapped in white bands. His attributes are the flail and the crook, symbols of kingship that may be linked to ancient pastoral traditions. Osiris represents the cyclic flow of nature in a continual process of death and rebirth. His skin is often black or green, for black was the color of the fertile silt brought by the inundation, whose regular cycle marked the passage of time more than any other event, while green was the color of the vegetation that died and was reborn with the cycle of the seasons.

HORUS: The son of Isis and Osiris, he is represented as a man with the head of a falcon, and often wears the two crowns of Upper and Lower Egypt. In fact the pharaoh was identified with Horus during his reign and with Osiris after his death. This god was linked to sovereignty because of his strong simultaneously solar and martial connotations: in fact among the principal requisites of the king were that of being illuminated by the divine light and having the capacity to defend and rule the country.

SETH: He is perhaps the hardest deity for us to understand, since he rep-

II

II. *Ushabti* chest with the god Anubis, about 1300 BC. Rome, Museo Gregoriano Egizio, Vatican.

resents the disorder, chaos and violence that opposed order. The god is depicted in an enigmatic manner with human features and the head of an imaginary animal, or simply as the latter, a being with a curved snout and two appendages above the head that probably represent ears, or perhaps horns. He is the only example of a deity whose iconography is not drawn from the natural world. Through his opposition to Horus and Osiris, he embodies the eternal struggle that goes on in the world between order and chaos.

MAAT: She is the personification of divine order on earth. According to Egyptian cosmogony the gods made the world on the basis of a universal order represented by the goddess Maat. She is depicted as a woman, wearing a band holding a feather around her forehead. In many votive images the pharaoh is shown offering a feather, symbol of the goddess Maat, to the gods, thereby demonstrating that he had been the guarantor of order on earth with respect to those who had established it.

III

IV

126

III. Statue of Isis nursing Horus, about AD 130. Rome, Museo Gregoriano Egizio, Vatican.

IV. Statue of Osiris, from the tomb of Psammetichus at Saqqarah, about 520 BC. Cairo, Egyptian Museum.

NUT: She is the goddess of the night sky. Nut is represented as a woman arched in a curve above the god of the earth Geb.

Her body is often covered with stars, and two solar disks are set in proximity to her mouth and her genital organs: according to some myths, in fact, the goddess swallowed the sun every night at sunset and then gave birth to it again at dawn. As goddess of the night sky she also assumed the role of protectress of the dead and was often represented under the lids of sarcophagi.

PTAH: The creator god of the mythology of Memphis is often shown with a human face and a body in the shape of a mummy wrapped in bandages. He holds a scepter and wears a skullcap; in many of the images he is placed inside a tabernacle. He is the embodiment of creation and consequently was regarded as the protector of all craftsmen

V

VI

V. Statue of Horus as falcon, about 664-332 BC. Rome, Museo Gregoriano Egizio, Vatican.

VI. Bas-relief representing the goddess Maat, New Kingdom. Florence, Museo Archeologico.

DECENTRALIZATION OF IDEOLOGY: THE PROVINCIAL NECROPOLISES

We have seen that during the Old Kingdom private burial grounds were usually located near the sepulchral monuments of the pharaohs. The decentralization of administration and the practice of handing the post of provincial governor down from father to son favored the development of cemeteries in the various regions. In Middle Egypt, between the First Intermediate Period and the Middle Kingdom, tombs for nomarchs (as the governors of the provinces, or nomes, were called) took on truly monumental proportions, showing how seriously central authority was being threatened by the power which the local lords enjoyed. It was not until the 12th dynasty that a shrewd domestic policy allowed the pharaohs to

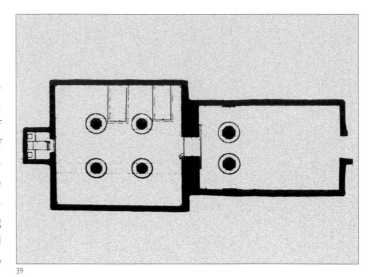

39

40

39. Plan of the tomb of Amenemhet at Beni Hasan, about 1950-1900 BC (from R. Schulz, M. Seidel, *Egypt*, Cologne 1998, p. 121, fig. 28).

40. Rock necropolis of Qubbet el-Hawa, Old-Middle Kingdom. Aswan.

suppress these tendencies to independence and put a stop to displays of power and wealth. The necropolises of Beni Hasan, El-Bersha, Meir and Qaw el-Kabir stand out for their truly "princely" rock tombs carved into the sides of hills, with several rooms decorated with scenes echoing the themes of the mastabas. Although badly decayed, the tombs at Qaw el-Kebir/Antaeopolis, the southernmost of these burial grounds, are distinguished by the grandeur of their layout, which is clearly inspired by the pharaonic models of the Old Kingdom in its sequence of a porticoed access below and a covered ramp leading up to a sort of terraced temple that recalls the mortuary one of Mentuhotep II at Deir el-Bahri. The architectural aspect is significant in some of the tombs at Beni Hasan too, which have façades *in antis* with fluted columns (defined as "proto-Doric" for their similarity to the Greek ones of nearly 1000 years later), and even

more spectacular in a tomb at El-Bersha, which stood at the end of a route of access with two palm-shaped columns painted pink in imitation of granite and had a vestibule with a ceiling painted blue with yellow stars. Most remarkable, however, is the decoration of the rooms inside, chiefly painted in relief on a plaster base. In the rows of images are depicted, as in the mastabas of the Old Kingdom, all the activities connected with the production of food, but what is striking here is the greater liveliness and the fascination with details, and above all the accent placed on the deeds and merits of the proprietor: two nomarchs at Beni Hasan receive delegations of foreigners bearing tributes; at Meir it is personifications of the Nile, the fields and the sea that bring their products to the lord, who in two cases is holding the *ankh*, symbol of "life" and prerogative of the gods and deceased pharaohs. At El-Bersha, incense is burned before

41

42

41. Façade of tombs BH 3, 4 and 5, about 1950-1900 BC. Beni Hasan.

42. Reconstruction of the tombs of Wahka and Ibu at Qaw el-Kebir/Antaeopolis, about 1900-1800 BC (from K. Michalowski, *L'art de l'ancienne Egypte*, Paris 1968, p. 375).

43

**43. Scene of hunting birds
in the marches, about
1900 BC. Beni Hasan,
Tomb of Khnumhotep III.**

Djehutihotep and he is purified like a sovereign. His tomb contains the famous scene showing the greatest deed of his career: he had a colossal statue of himself carved from alabaster, about 23 ft or 7 m high, in a regal pose on a throne, and then had the artists depict its epic transport by his fellow citizens, whom he describes as "joyful." The ropes of the sled carrying the statue are pulled by 172 people, while on the statue itself a man pours water onto the ground so that the sled will move more easily and another beats out the rhythm to the pullers with his hands; the nomarch's sons and notables and the entire population look on in wonder. These are new themes, inconceivable in an earlier age, which reflect a change in attitude toward the central authority: the kings of the Middle Kingdom chose to rely on decentralization and assigned responsibility to the provincial lords, ensuring their loyalty but evidently recognizing their merits and the honors that ensued from them.

44

45

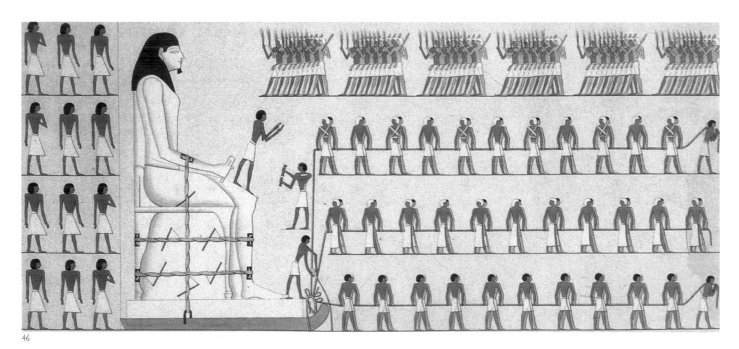
46

44. Scene of the raising of antelopes, drawing after a painting in tomb BH 3, about 1900 BC. Beni Hasan.

45. The arrival of Asians with gifts, drawing after a painting in tomb BH 3, about 1900 BC. Beni Hasan.

46. Transport of the statue of the nomarch Djehutihotep, drawing after a painting in his tomb at El-Bersha, about 1900 BC (from K. Michalowski, *L'art de l'ancienne Egypte*, Paris 1968, pp. 572-3).

STATUE OF THE *KA* OF HOR

about 1750 BC
Cairo, Egyptian Museum

SUBJECT

The wooden statue, perhaps the largest to have come down to us from ancient Egypt, was found at Dahshur by the archeologist Jean-Marie de Morgan during the excavations carried out by the French mission in 1894. Preserved in an excellent condition thanks to the dry climate of Egypt, it is still inside the wooden shrine that housed it.

The statue does not represent the pharaoh Hor, a ruler of the 13th dynasty, but his *ka*, or vital energy. To make this distinction clear the hieroglyph used for the word *ka*, formed of two arms reaching for the sky, has been reproduced above the head.

The king appears to be nude but traces of a painted belt can still be seen. It is possible that there was also a painted *shendyt* kilt, but more likely that the statue was girded with a real piece of linen. The statue held objects in both hands, presumably a scepter, emblem of power, and a weapon symbolizing command and victory over the enemy, both now lost.

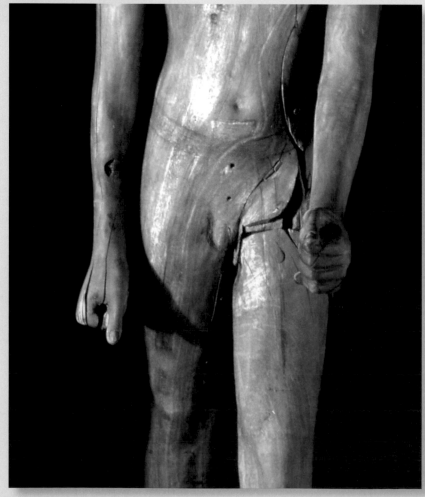

COMPOSITION

The effect created by the eyes, made out of crystals and stones bordered with bronze, is very suggestive and, as in other cases, gives the statue the appearance of being alive.

The figure is slender and agile, largely due to the fact that, unlike stone which made the sculptures much heavier and therefore more difficult to work, wood allowed the artist to create empty spaces between the arms and the bust. The false beard is also unusually thin and "free," while the slight smile on the lips conveys a sense of serenity.

The figure is made to look even lighter by the increase in its height resulting from the hieroglyphic sign reproduced above the head. The *ka* is the part of the deceased that survives after death, his vital energy or "double," and is the entity to which offerings are made. The hieroglyph serves to turn the material and visible statue into the immaterial and invisible ka, and allows it to perform all its functions. In the view of the artist the identification is total.

ROYAL STATUARY

It is perhaps in the production of statues that we can best appreciate the changes that took place at the end of the 3rd millennium. One consequence of the period of autonomous local governments was the setting up of workshops far from the court's influence, and thus free to seek their own means of expression. The impact of the first royal statue reproduced here, the one of Mentuhotep II located in the "ritual tomb" beneath the mortuary temple at Deir el-Bahri, is disconcerting, so remote is it from the lofty perfection of the Memphite school. Massive, with heavy, almost "barbaric" forms, it depicts the pharaoh with a fixed stare,

wrapped in his jubilee cloak and wearing the Red Crown of Lower Egypt. The special conditions under which it was preserved have allowed the original coloring to survive almost intact: the contrast is elementary, with the red crown and white robe set against the black skin, which by convention alludes to regeneration (the skin of Osiris is black, or green, just as the fertile soil bathed by the flood is black). The funerary use of this stone "surrogate," which immortalizes the king in the ceremony renewing sovereignty, is in keeping with the rules, but the language has changed a great deal. So it is no wonder that the term "neoclassicism" has been invoked for the series of ten statues found in the mortuary temple of the Pyramid of Sesostris I at El-Lisht: here the desire for a return to tradition,

47

48

47. Statue of the pharaoh Mentuhotep II, from Deir el-Bahri, 2055-2004 BC. Cairo, Egyptian Museum.

48-49. Statue of Sesostris I, from El-Lisht, viewed in profile and from the front, 1956-1911 BC. Cairo, Egyptian Museum.

50

**50. Statue of Sesostris I,
detail of the relief on the
throne, from El-Lisht,
1956-1911 BC. Cairo,
Egyptian Museum.**

about 80 years after the reign of Mentuhotep II, is evident in the canonical handling of the figure and in an execution so accurate it seems aloof. Hence the message is clear: the definition of royalty depends on the revival of stylistic modules of the past. The word "propaganda" has often been used in relation to not just statuary but many other aspects of Egyptian art, and not exclusively that of the pharaohs: the term should be understood in the sense of a "persuasive message," a form designed to convey an idea and make it convincing.

The comparison between the two royal statues described above is revealing, so sharp is the contrast in the way the same subject is tackled. It has to remembered, however, that the first statue was never seen again, owing to the use to which it was put, and perhaps neither was the second series, except by a small number of priests. In the latter case, the repetition of a form with a few slight variations may have constituted part of the message, but this still requires evaluation.

How subtle the arts of persuasion have always been can perhaps be even more clearly demonstrated by the splendid statues representing two pharaohs from the end of the 12th dynasty.

For this period we can be certain of one innovation (with respect to the lack of data for earlier periods): many royal statues were displayed in temples dedicated to the gods, and therefore visible to large numbers of people. Sesostris III and Amenemhet III had

51

51. Head of Sesostris III, from Madamud, 1870-1831 BC. Cairo, Egyptian Museum.

52

53

52. Statue of Sesostris III, from Deir el-Bahri, 1870-1831 BC. Cairo, Egyptian Museum.

53. Statue of Amenemhet III, from Karnak, about 1831-1786 BC. Cairo, Egyptian Museum.

54. Facing page: Head of Amenemhet III, 1831-1786 BC. London, British Museum.

themselves depicted with features that have been described as typical of a realistic portrait: heavy eyelids, marked shadows under the eyes, folds at the sides of the mouth, narrow lips.

Perhaps it would be more correct to speak of another kind of idealization: the king is no longer presented as an inaccessible god, but as a human being who takes problems on himself, feels the responsibility of his role and even suffers. There are many texts from this period that reflect on the sovereign's role. To some extent the "positivity" of his function is no longer unquestionable, but is subject to judgment, and by a yardstick that everyone recognizes and considers applicable to all. The emaciated faces which some have seen as an expression of the king's role as "good shepherd,"

concerned about the well-being of his people, are unlikely to have been realistic. Rather they communicate a political vision, and without doubt one intended to persuade. More overt perhaps is the message that is powerfully delivered by some sculptures of Amenemhet III, who must have really had a forceful personality.

From El-Faiyum, the place this ruler had made the center of his economic planning, comes the bust that is all that remains of a larger than life-size statue (the torso alone, reaching to just under the breast, is over 3 ft or 1 m high); the head is emphasized by a large, heavy wig with twisted locks, never seen before. The strongly modeled features of the face are framed by a natural beard and the ritual, false one.

55

56

55-56. Bust of Amenemhet III dressed as a priest, from El-Faiyum, viewed from the front and in profile, 1831-1786 BC. Cairo, Egyptian Museum.

57

58

A leopard skin is draped over his shoulders and two divine insignia at the sides of the bust show that the pharaoh (identified, unequivocally, by the hole in the forehead for attachment of the cobra diadem) is represented in the function of a priest presiding over rituals.

Found at Tanis, but perhaps originally from El-Faiyum again, another sculpture usurped at a later date undoubtedly represents the same ruler making an offering: a double figure, with "barbaric" wigs and

full beards, supporting containers overflowing with produce of the lakes: fish, birds and lotus stems.

Thus the king is presented as legitimate officiant of rites and dispenser of food, and we have already seen that he was celebrated as such in the monuments at Biahmu as well.

The divinity of the king is not now in an abstract sphere, hard to conceive for most people, but presented in a version that has to be decoded, certainly, but effective in its impact.

57-58. Double statue of Amenemhet III with containers of offerings, from Tanis, front and rear view, 1831-1786 BC. Cairo, Egyptian Museum.

COLOSSAL HEAD OF SESOSTRIS III

about 1850 BC
Luxor, Museum of Ancient Egyptian Art

SUBJECT

The fragment, undoubtedly part of a large statue of the king on his feet, was unearthed on February 25, 1970, in front of the 4th pylon of the temple at Karnak. As well as the head, some small pieces of pink granite were recognized as belonging to the dorsal pillar, on which the titles of Sesostris III were engraved.

The colossal statue must have measured about 10 ft 4 in or 3 m 20 cm. At the time of its discovery it still bore traces of paint — yellow on the border of the crown, red on the diadem and several parts of the face — a coloring that must have produced a very different effect to the one we see today. A hole at the base, with traces of stucco, may be the sign of a restoration carried out in antiquity, or of an attempt to usurp the monument.

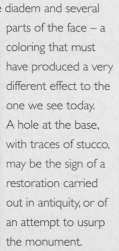

The eyebrows are the only stylized element, unusually represented by a "herringbone" pattern. The innovation, made at the pharaoh's behest, consists in the carving of the eyelids, weighing heavily on the narrow and tired eyes; there are deep lines under the eyes and at the sides of the nose, while the thin lips are tightly closed. It is a "realistic style" that interprets the concept of tormented kingship, of a human being appointed to play the role of a god, contrasting with the vision of harmony and perfection of the gods incarnate of the past.

COMPOSITION

The head is well preserved, except for the points that stuck out: the plaited divine beard, the nose, the cobra's head. It can already be deduced from the beard alone that the missing part of the statue should be pictured as representing Sesostris dressed for his Sed festival or as Osiris, with his arms crossed on his breast.

It is dominated by the *pschent* crown, formed of the two crowns emblematic of Upper and Lower Egypt, the white, ending in a bulb, and the red, a flared tiara that blends into the dorsal pillar in a very elegant way.

Set low on the forehead, it makes the sturdy ears stand out, along with the small quadrilateral of the face, in which all the expressiveness is concentrated.

SPHINX OF AMENEMHET III
about 1800 BC
Cairo, Egyptian Museum

SUBJECT
In a good state of preservation, it belongs to a group of sphinxes found at the Tanis site in 1863. Given its characteristics, it has long been considered a "barbarian" product, perhaps attributable to the Hyksos rulers who did in fact have their capital near Tanis. For over than a century now, comparison with other works, especially the face, has made it clear that the pharaoh represented here is Amenemhet III, even though his name does not appear in the inscriptions.

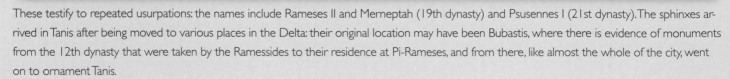

These testify to repeated usurpations: the names include Rameses II and Merneptah (19th dynasty) and Psusennes I (21st dynasty). The sphinxes arrived in Tanis after being moved to various places in the Delta: their original location may have been Bubastis, where there is evidence of monuments from the 12th dynasty that were taken by the Ramessides to their residence at Pi-Rameses, and from there, like almost the whole of the city, went on to ornament Tanis.

COMPOSITION

The Greek term "sphinx" may derive from the Egyptian word for "living image" and is applied to composite figures, mostly with the body of a lion and the head of a king, like the gigantic one at Giza (4th dynasty). They are openly symbolic, identifying the power of the sovereign with the animal that has always been associated with the concept of kingship: the lion.

This work, along with the rest of the group, introduces a new type of sphinx: no longer the head of the ruler with his headdress, but just the human face framed by the mane, giving it a truly "barbaric" energy.

The surface seems to vibrate, presenting itself in an innovative way to the light and shade, and the face is imperious, characterized by prominent cheekbones and fleshy and almost sneering lips. Amenemhet III carried on with the "message" of his father Sesostris III, that of an "explained" sovereignty linked to actions, but amplified it with vigor and force.

THE INDIVIDUAL AND THE SACRED: THE CUBE STATUE

In comparison with the vestiges of the Old Kingdom, it can certainly be said that even the statues of private individuals had now become more visible: the practice of "pilgrimage" to the sanctuary of Osiris at Abydos, along with the desire to leave a memorial there, encouraged the production of "surrogates" that, while not of the highest artistic quality, served their purpose. Abydos and other sanctuaries in the country have yielded a great deal of evidence of religious practices, signs of homage to personages of the past, deified for their merits and considered to still exercise an active influence. Pilgrims would often leave behind sculpted images of themselves as a token of faith or gratitude, along with memorial tablets whose inscriptions sometimes include phrases appealing directly to the piety of passersby.

Among them are numerous statuettes, some of modest size and quality, representing the essential features of a person, at times simplified into a cloaked body, as well as a peculiar type of effigy: the so-called cube statue. This should be interpreted, to judge by certain examples that seem to explain its genesis, as a squatting figure, sometimes looking as if it were being carried on a litter, with the arms crossed above the knees. Such a representation of the person at rest left ample room for inscriptions, bringing it to "life" by identifying it clearly and making it a participant in every aspect of the religious life of the place where it was located.

59

60

59. Statuette of Khety, from the northern necropolis at Abydos, about 1900-1800 BC. Cairo, Egyptian Museum.

60-61. Two cube statues of the treasurer Hetep, from his tomb at Saqqarah, about 1900 BC. Cairo, Egyptian Museum.

SOVEREIGNTY

Sovereignty in ancient Egypt had a very special character due to its dual significance, religious and temporal, which made the ruler a figure intermediate between men and gods. Even images of sovereigns had the same dual value: some works, intended for veneration and rituals, were not made to be displayed but to perform a magical function; others, located in central places of administration like temples or palaces, served to create an image of authority and act on popular feelings. The pharaoh was a superior man and had to provide a model for his subjects. Representations of the sovereign are always idealized and abstract, with no concessions to the naturalistic portrait; he is depicted in accordance with an ideal of perfect beauty and physical vigor. The bust is bolt upright, a position that is a sign of dignity and strength; the shoulders are powerful and the legs, support of the man and therefore of the state, are highly muscular. The pharaoh can wear different types of headdress and crown, depending on the function for which the statue has been made. The headdress of striped cloth, the *nemes*, is very common, but in the majority of statues that were put on public display the pharaoh wears the double crown, a symbol of his authority over the whole of Egypt. Inevitably on the forehead appears the uraeus, the cobra, universal emblem of kingship, often flanked by the vulture, both of which are symbols of the two protecting deities of the Delta and the Nile Valley. For each of the sovereign's different functions there is a specific iconography: the representation of the pharaoh devoted to his people is different to the one in the guise of warrior, priest or offerer. The purpose of the image, votive or propagandistic, also strongly conditioned the choice of attributes and dress. The role of the pharaoh on earth was not limited to ruling Egypt: it was his

I. Statue of Rameses II, about 1275 BC. Luxor, Temple of Amon-Re.

II. Rameses IV in triumph, from Karnak, about 1150 BC. Cairo, Egyptian Museum.

task to guarantee and defend the order brought to the earth by the gods at the moment of creation, the gods to whom he had to answer for his actions. Thus the sovereign on earth was identified with Horus, god of the sun who according to myth fought and overcame the forces of chaos. After death, however, he became Osiris, mythical ruler of Egypt and god of the underworld, with the attributes (the body wrapped in linen bandages, or with a scepter and flail, or with black or green skin) with which the deceased pharaoh is portrayed in royal tombs. After death, the sovereign finally joined the gods and took his place alongside them. This function of go-between with the deities, assigned to the pharaoh since the Old Kingdom, gave a touch of the divine to him even in life, and led his subjects to venerate and fear him. In the New Kingdom this tendency became overt and universally accepted, and the sovereign, now a god

incarnate, was venerated in the same way as the traditional deities: this is what happened in the shrine of the temple of Abu Simbel, for example, where Rameses II was worshiped along with Amon, Ptah and Horus. However, the pharaoh performed other functions too, of which the most important was that of priest. In fact he was the high priest and it was his role to officiate the rites in such a way as to establish contact with the divine world and guarantee, with his authority, the stability of the country. In reality all the other priests who carried out rites in the country's many temples did so as his representatives. In the exercise of his priestly function he is represented with specific attributes and wears a leopard skin over his shoulders. In a theme attested since the time of Pepi I, the pharaoh is portrayed in votive statues used for veneration as he kneels in the act of presenting two containers filled with offerings to the gods.

III

IV

III. Statue of Sesostris III, about 1870-1831 BC. Paris, Musée du Louvre.

IV. Statue of Thutmosis III kneeling, about 1430 BC. Cairo, Egyptian Museum.

SARCOPHAGI, CUSTODIANS OF LIFE AFTER DEATH

Naturally the contents of tombs varied widely in this period. As far as the sarcophagi are concerned, specialist studies of the provincial workshops have made it possible to identify characteristics that allow us to broaden our understanding of the evolution of religious beliefs and thought. Among the stone sarcophagi, those of the ladies of the court buried in the mortuary temple of Mentuhotep II stand out for the quality of their execution, even though they date from as far back as the end of the 3rd millennium: on display in the Cairo Museum are the sarcophagi of Ashayt and Kauit, made of slabs of white limestone decorated on the outside with what appear to be scenes from the daily life of a noblewoman. In contrast with the style of Mentuhotep's statue, the skillful sculptors of these scenes displayed a sense of equilibrium and elegance combined with a taste for description. The royal sarcophagi of the 12th dynasty, especially those from the second half, can be considered unrivaled in their combination of magnificence, purity of forms and quality of material. Many of them have a socle at the bottom, resembling the molding of a monumental façade, or the base of a boundary wall. On the smooth walls of pink granite of the sarcophagi found in the Pyramid of Amenemhet III at Dahshur are set plaques with a pair of eyes carved in relief to ward off evil.

A few private individuals were buried in outer sarcophagi made of stone, some of which had a structure inspired by the wooden ones. But these last are the most common, painted on the inside and outside

62

62. Sarcophagus of Kauit, detail with offerings to the deceased, from Deir el-Bahri, about 2030 BC. Cairo, Egyptian Museum.

with friezes of objects that should be regarded as evocations and recreations of reality, and covered with inscriptions that are intended to help the deceased overcome all the difficulties they will face in the other world. The form and some elements of the decoration of these sarcophagi are echoed in the chests used to hold the so-called Canopic jars, which have already been mentioned and are found more frequently in this period.

There are always four of these vessels (and so the chest containing them is divided into four compartments), since the embalmed viscera they were intended to contain were placed under the protection of the four funerary deities called the "Sons of Horus." In this period, and up until the beginning of the New Kingdom, the lids were modeled in the shape of human heads.

63

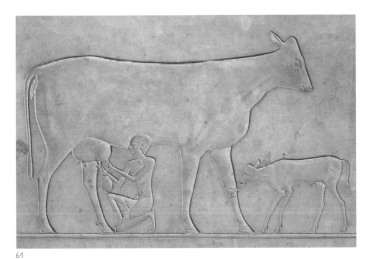

61

66

65

63. Canopic jars of Inpuhotep, from Saqqarah, about 1900 BC. Cairo, Egyptian Museum.

64. Sarcophagus of Kauit, detail with scene of the milking of a cow with her calf, from Deir el-Bahri, about 2030 BC. Cairo, Egyptian Museum.

65. Sarcophagus of Ashayt, detail with the deceased receiving offerings, from Deir el-Bahri, about 2030 BC. Cairo, Egyptian Museum.

66. Painted wooden coffin of Sepi, about 1900 BC. Cairo, Egyptian Museum.

JEWELRY AND AMULETS: THE SPLENDOR OF ETERNITY

A lucky series of finds were made between the end of the 19th century and the first few decades of the 20th in the tombs of princesses inside the funerary enclosures of Amenemhet II and Sesostris III at Dahshur and Sesostris II at El-Lahun (although the burials may be of a later date, perhaps from the 13th dynasty). They consisted of extremely elegant pieces of jewelry that are now the pride of the Cairo Museum and the Metropolitan Museum in New York. As well as allowing us to admire their beauty, the discovery yielded important scientific results: in the first place it revealed the typical contents of a tomb, and that pieces of jewelry were produced specifically as grave goods, and thus not intended to stand up to use. Only in a few cases may jewelry worn in life have been buried with its owner, as is suggested by signs of wear. The various elements of the grave goods were deposited on the mummified body and between the bandages, where they were supposed to provide magical protection, through the preciousness of the material used and through the significance of the form and symbolic value of the colors (white as light, black as eternal life, green as "luxuriance", yellow as gold...). Alternatively (and these were perhaps the "real" jewels) they were placed in a separate recess in the tomb, alongside the Canopic chest. The most typical element is the "broad" *usekh* collar, with many rows of beads and ending in two falcon's heads that rested on the shoulders. Other parts of the body "protected" by jewelry and amulets were the wrists and ankles, the waist and the cut made in the side for embalming. The most refined pieces of jewelry, however, are the

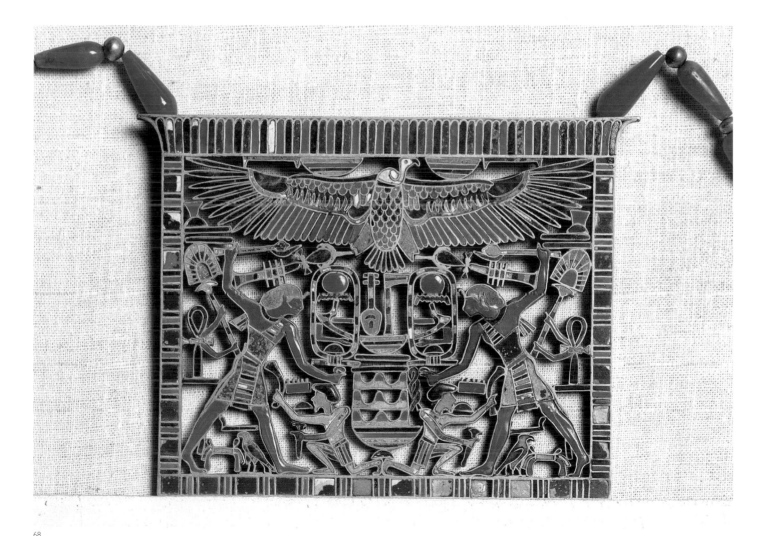

68

67. Facing page: Diadem of Princess Sat-Hathor-Yunet, from El-Lahun, about 1850-1800 BC. Cairo, Egyptian Museum.

68. Pectoral of Mereret, from Dahshur, about 1850-1800 BC. Cairo, Egyptian Museum.

ones which were probably worn by the princesses when they were alive. The belts of shells (cowries made of gold in the example illustrated here) have a very modern appearance; as does the combination of amethyst and gold in a belt made up of panther heads facing one another on a double row of beautiful purple spheres, also to be found in an anklet with a claw hanging down on one side. One necklace consists of bivalve shells and starfish made by the technique of granulation, perhaps of Aegean origin. Some typically Egyptian pendants that were later to become popular throughout the Mediterranean must have been attached to armlets. They "declared" their significance in auspicious mottoes composed of hieroglyphs: "happiness," "all life and protection" or "the heart of the two gods (= Horus and Seth) is at peace."

But above all it was the hair that must have glittered: it could be plaited into dense braids ringed with gold tubes or adorned with rosettes. An attempt was even made to capture "nature" itself to decorate the forehead: the incomparable diadem of Khnumit, a very light coronet made up of ten rows of gold beads held together by elements of four crossed lotus calyces, on which beads of turquoise and cornelian alternate with granules of lapis lazuli.

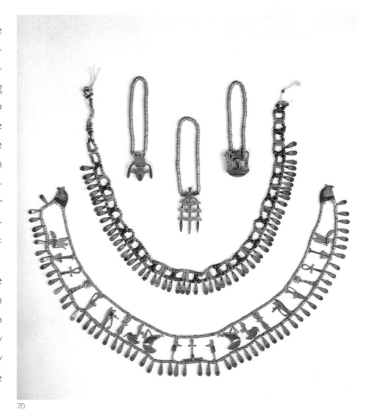

70

71

69. Facing page: Mirror of Princess Sat-Hathor-Yunet, from El-Lahun, about 1850-1800 BC. Cairo, Egyptian Museum.

70. Jewelry of Princess Khnumit, about 1850-1800 BC. Cairo, Egyptian Museum.

71. Gold belt of Princess Sat-Hathor-Yunet, from Dahshur, about 1850-1800 BC. Cairo, Egyptian Museum.

4. The New Kingdom: the Splendor of the Empire

ontinuity with the 12th dynasty was the hallmark of the 13th, which even kept the same capital. While in the south of the country there was nothing to suggest a new period of instability, this is exactly what was brewing in the north, and was to culminate in domination by the Hyksos. These "rulers of foreign lands" were Asiatic peoples who may have completed their subjugation of Northern Egypt in a violent manner, but before that had coexisted peacefully with the Egyptians for a long time. The counterattack, launched once again from Thebes, was motivated by a sense of nationalism. After the war of liberation from the invaders, a policy of expansionism led to the foundation of an empire. The victorious Theban royal house ushered in the age of Egypt's greatest splendor, an era in which it enjoyed immense wealth and great prestige. The long period of the New Kingdom, lasting for over 500 years, saw the realization of grandiose projects and profound cultural developments; Egypt was no longer isolated from the world and encountered other countries and cultures that were its equals. Art increasingly became a means of communication.

2

3

1. Facing page: Tutankhamun's throne, detail of the back with the pharaoh and his queen Ankhesenamun, about 1330 BC. Cairo, Egyptian Museum.

2. The pharaoh Amenhotep II on a chariot displaying his skill with the bow, 1427-1400 BC. Luxor, Museum of Ancient Egyptian Art.

3-4. Bust of Rameses II from Tanis and, on following pages, detail, 1279-1213 BC. Cairo, Egyptian Museum.

THE SECOND INTERMEDIATE PERIOD: FOREIGN RULE

When the 12th dynasty came to an end the power of the pharaohs went into progressive decline, until they once again lost control of the country. The diminishment in the prestige and authority of the figure of the pharaoh was such that the 14th and the 15th dynasties were made up of a large number of short-lived reigns. Of some of them no memory persists, and a few of the surviving statues do not even bear names. These rulers were local governors and their authority was in no way universal: just as during the First Intermediate Period, the unity of the country had been lost. The weakening of central power favored the infiltration of new Semitic populations from the area of Syria and Palestine, who moved into the land of the pharaohs from the eastern Delta. The Egyptians had reacted to this immigration during the Middle Kingdom by raising a wall to stem the tide of foreigners, but with the collapse of central authority it was no longer possible to control their influx. Semitic groups settled in the Delta and became so powerful that their rulers were able to declare themselves pharaohs: they constituted Manetho's 15th and 16th dynasties, and later Egyptian historians called them the Hyksos. They absorbed Egyptian traditions, assimilating their gods to the local ones and copying the iconography of the kings. The most significant contribution made by these Asians to the civilization of the Nile was the introduction of the chariot and some hitherto unknown weapons. In the broad sense even the image of sovereignty that emerged in the New Kingdom was the fruit of Hyksos domination. It was from Thebes, in fact, that the effort to reestablish national unity was launched. The image of the ruler as warrior hero and defender of the country's unity was a new one. A marked sense of nationalism emerged, and would be reinforced when Egypt came into contact with the other great civilizations of the Near East.

5

6

5. Lid of the sarcophagus of King Sekhemre-Heruher-Maat Antef, detail, about 1560 BC. Paris, Musée du Louvre.

6. Lid of the sarcophagus of King Sekhemre-Up Maat Antef, detail, about 1560 BC. Paris, Musée du Louvre.

7. Facing page: Bas-relief representing Rameses II with prisoners, from Memphis, about 1270 BC. Cairo, Egyptian Museum.

FUNERARY AND RELIGIOUS ARCHITECTURE

Foreign rule brought an abrupt interruption in the traditions dating back to the origin of the state. The 13th dynasty was still closely linked to the Middle Kingdom, and there is no longer any reason to include it (as has been done hitherto) in the Second Intermediate Period, separating two phases of political stability: the rulers went on building pyramids in which they emphasized the inaccessibility of the burial chamber, which had now come to resemble an immense sarcophagus. The sanctuary at Abydos continued to draw vast numbers of the faithful, with the result that regulations had to be imposed to prevent their votive shrines from encroaching on the processional route. The provincial workshops were active, suggesting that they received many orders. While foreigners settled in the north of Egypt (the results of excavations at the site of their capital, Avaris, in the eastern Delta, are increasingly exciting, revealing very close contacts with the Aegean world), Thebes succeeded in

recreating a tradition. This time the success of the Theban royal house did not lead to a reconnection with the foundations of the state. Thebes favored the dynastic god Amon-Re and began to erect an extraordinary series of monuments in his name. The god Amon, certainly known since the Old Kingdom, had grown in importance during the Middle Kingdom, largely thanks to the rise of the 12th dynasty. His role as a national deity was enhanced by fusing him with the ancient god of the sun (whose cult was centered on Heliopolis), as Amon-Re. The strength of established tradition, especially during the first half of the 18th dynasty, found expression in an alternation between recognition of the Heliopolitan priesthood (devoted to the Sun, Re or Atum) and the Theban one, worshiping a "solarized" Amon. The tombs of their predecessors, the rulers of the 17th dynasty, were in the slopes of the western mountain, as had been those of the 11th dynasty. The early pharaohs of the 18th dynasty may have continued the practice, until Thutmosis I inaugurated the Valley of the Kings, definitively separating the place of royal burial from the temple for worship.

8

8. Relief with Queen Hatshepsut, represented as a man (on the left), celebrating the erection of a pair of obelisks in honor of Amon at Karnak, **from the Red Chapel of Hatshepsut at Karnak, about 1460 BC. Luxor, Museum of Ancient Egyptian Art.**

9. Painting with Thutmosis
III offering incense and
libations to the god Amon-
Re, about 1430 BC.
Deir el-Bahri,
Temple of Hathor.

THE VALLEY OF THE KINGS

Dominated by the Horn (the highest peak, immediately recognizable by its pyramid shape, a fact probably of significance for the ancient Egyptians), the Valley of the Kings (Wadi el-Biban el-Muluk) is made up of the East Valley, where fifty-eight tombs have been discovered, and a smaller branch, the West Valley, with four tombs. Up until the end of the 20th dynasty, with a few exceptions, the pharaohs chose to be buried in galleries that sometimes penetrated a long way into the mountain. The entrances may have been concealed on the outside, for example with stones, but a number of elaborate structures appear to have been left visible: support for this may come from the fact that inspections were carried out – as is well documented in

10

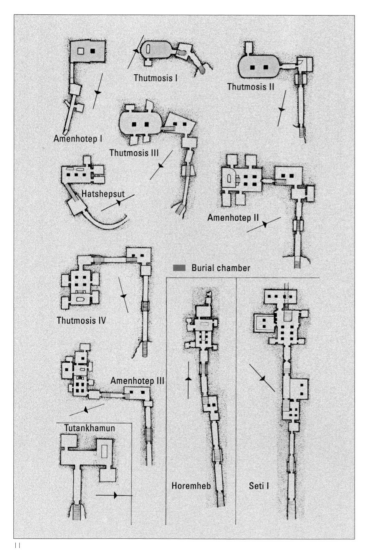

Thutmosis I

Thutmosis II

Amenhotep I

Thutmosis III

Hatshepsut

Amenhotep II

Thutmosis IV

Burial chamber

Amenhotep III

Tutankhamun

Horemheb

Seti I

11

12

10 and 13. Paintings imitating a papyrus scroll that describe the journey of the Sun in the other world during the hours of the night, about 1430 BC. Thebes, Tomb of Thutmosis III, Valley of the Kings.

11. Drawing showing the evolution in the plans of royal tombs during the New Kingdom, 16th-12th century BC (from C. Aldred, P. Barguet, C. Desroches Noblecourt, J. Leclant, H.W. Muller, *L'impero dei conquistatori*, Milan 1985, nos. 419-20).

12. View of the Valley of the Kings. Thebes.

the texts – or at least that precise data were kept on their location. The internal structure of the tombs, over the long period in which they were constructed, went through three stages of development, roughly corresponding to the three dynasties of the New Kingdom (18th, 19th, 20th). During the 18th the tombs had a sharp bend or curve of the axis in their plan, which may have derived from the complicated internal organization of the pyramids of the Middle Kingdom and thus retained the same significance. With Horemheb, last king of the 18th dynasty, a change took place: the plan became rectilinear, but the corridor was "broken" and continued along a parallel axis, with a "bayonet joint." During the 20th dynasty the plan tended to grow simpler and was rectilinear.

13

SETI I AND THE GODDESS HATHOR
about 1290 BC
Florence, Museo Archeologico

SUBJECT

Still in excellent condition, this painting was one of several that decorated the tomb of Seti I in the Valley of the Kings at Thebes, discovered in 1815 by Giovanni Battista Belzoni from Padua. It was detached from the wall and taken back to Italy by the joint Tuscan-French mission.

Goddesses are usually shown following the pharaoh and resting one hand on his shoulder, to protect him: in this painting the same concept is expressed through a different iconographic scheme, as the king and the goddess are unusually facing one another and looking into each other's eyes. Hathor, a deity strongly associated with femininity, joy and love, is offering the pharaoh her necklace, a symbol of protection and life, while holding his hand to indicate their union.

The pharaoh and the goddess are the same height, and yet the female figure is made to look taller by the fact that the king is not wearing his crown, while the goddess has on the headdress adorned with the symbols that identify her.

COMPOSITION

Fully respecting the canons of Egyptian art, this scene is dominated by a profound sense of symmetry, broken by small details that serve to enliven the composition.

The attention is focused on the points of contact between the two figures, represented by the meeting of their hands. In fact, they are at the center of the scene, exactly on the vertical axis of symmetry.

The male and female figures are reflected as if in a mirror.

During the New Kingdom the craftsmen in the service of the court attained extraordinarily high levels of artistic quality, as can be seen here in the representation of the pharaoh's linen robe: transparent, the long garment reveals the shape of the arms and legs beneath, but at the same time the folds of the drapery are perfectly reproduced with denser brushstrokes.

DECORATIONS AND SYMBOLOGIES OF THE TOMBS

The decorative themes provide confirmation that the architecture was saturated with symbolism. The tomb was the place where preparations were made for regeneration of the dead king, seen in terms of an analogy with the nocturnal course of the Sun as he passes through the underworld of the god Osiris and, overcoming attacks from hostile forces perennially seeking to undermine the order of the universe, is restored to life at dawn. The words and pictures on the walls describe the Sun's journey at night, with the gods assisting him on his boat, hour after hour, through those dark worlds that are the necessary "counterpart" of the day. Thus, for example, a deep pit that was dug in the initial part of the tomb and thought to be a deterrent for plunderers or a means of collecting rainwater, may allude symbolically (without invalidating the other hypotheses) to the cavern of the mortuary god Seker and Osiris's tomb. If it filled with water, this could be interpreted in another sense: for theologians, this would be a direct allusion to the primordial waters, in which the dead must be immersed in order to be reborn. The funerary texts are full of references to tortuous routes in the afterlife, which may help explain the changes of direction of the passageways, while the straight ones seem to have been inspired by monuments to the sun. In addition, independently of its real direction, determined by the site chosen on the sides of the valley, each tomb should be seen as ideally oriented from south to north, as the north is the zenith of the sun's journey at night, just as the south is that of the day. And yet, the orientation of the sarcophagus inside the burial chamber has changed in different periods, set first parallel to the axis, then at right angles to it and finally in line with it again. There are many elements that still require explanation, such as the shape of the chamber housing the sarcophagus, which was oval in the first part of the 18th dynasty (according to some a representation of the hereafter, for others an allusion to the twelfth hour of the night, the last, when the Sun, in the form of a scarab, gets ready to be reborn and is thrust onto the semicircular horizon); or the significance of the symmetries and proportions. Elements that only go to show the profound and elaborate planning of a monument we tend to see as "static," but which may actually have been conceived as filled with "dynamic" potentialities or energies.

14

**14. Painting with gods
in attitude of jubilation,
about 1295 BC. Thebes,
Tomb of Rameses I,
Valley of the Kings.**

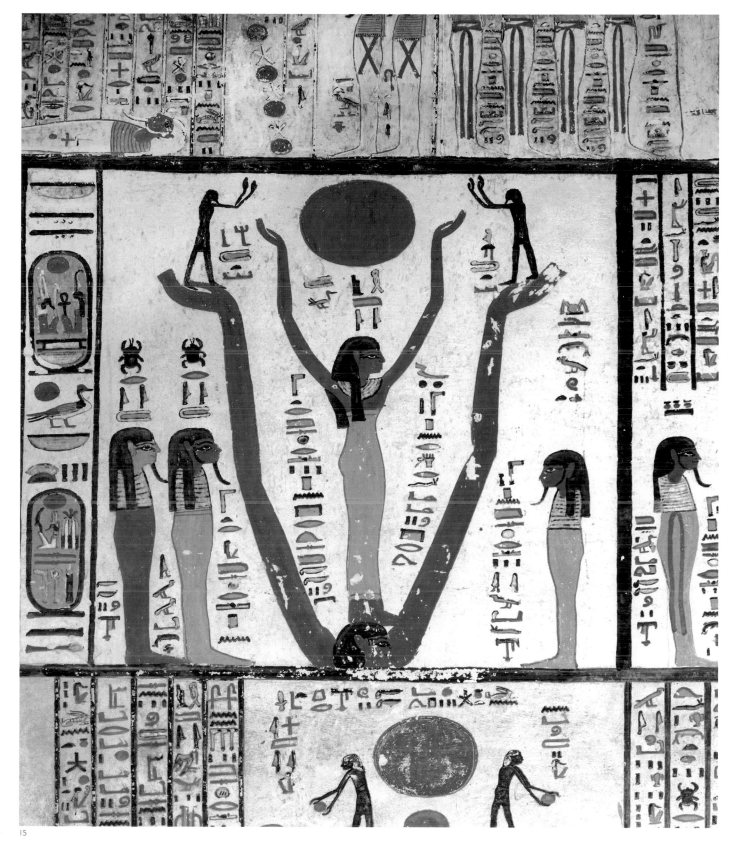

**15. Painting representing
the regeneration of the
Sun, about 1140 BC.
Thebes, Tomb of Rameses
VI, Valley of the Kings.**

**16. Following pages:
Painting with the pharaoh
Thutmosis IV greeted by
gods, about 1390 BC.
Thebes, Tomb of Thutmosis
IV, Valley of the Kings.**

TOMBS OF MEMBERS OF THE ROYAL FAMILY IN THE VALLEY OF THE KINGS

A privileged few were admitted to the Valley of the Kings without having been pharaohs, and so a number of not specifically royal tombs have been found, mostly dating from the 18th dynasty. Tomb no. 46, for example, belonged to Amenhotep III's parents-in-law, Yuia and Tuiu. Its spectacular contents caused a sensation that anticipated the discovery of Tutankhamun's tomb, which now bears the last number assigned in the valley (62) and may itself have been an adaptation of a private tomb already under construction.

Still awaiting evaluation is the rediscovered tomb no. 5: one of the first to be identified (at least as far back as 1825), it had not been thoroughly excavated or investigated owing to its very poor state of preservation. When its exploration was resumed in 1989, it proved to be an extraordinary structure with several underground levels, unparalleled either in the valley or elsewhere: for the moment, the data recovered suggest it was a tomb-memorial for the sons of the great Rameses II, whose tomb (no. 7) stands not far away, opposite it. Thus Rameses, who showed his pride in his numerous offspring on more than one occasion, may have decided to create a monument for them that would be equally exceptional.

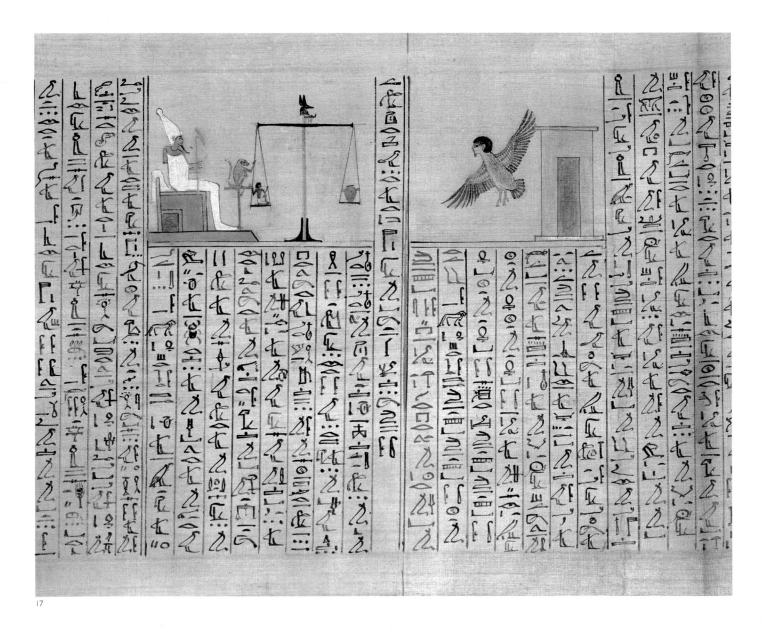

17

17. Papyrus with the *Book of the Dead of Maiherperi,* "Royal Fan Bearer of the Right-Hand Side," one of the privileged few whose tombs are located in the royal necropolis in Thebes, in the Valley of the Kings. Perhaps of Nubian origin (he is represented with dark skin), he must have been a member of the ruling family in the first half of the 18th dynasty and may have been the son of a concubine; detail, about 1450 BC. Cairo, Egyptian Museum.

18

19

20

THE VALLEY OF THE QUEENS

To the southwest of the Valley of the Kings, another valley opens at the foot of a sort of gorge, recognizable from a distance because the rocks above seem about to fall into it: here the rainwater sometimes forms a cascade and is collected in a basin. Perhaps because this fact was regarded as symbolic of the feminine principle, the valley was chosen as the "Seat of Beauty." Known as the Valley of the Queens today, it was a necropolis for queens and princes, mostly from the 19th and 20th dynasties. The tombs are similar to those of the kings, but with a simpler plan and a different repertoire of decoration, preferring images of the deceased in front of gods. Outstanding for their vivid colors are the tombs of two of Rameses III's sons, and above all that of Rameses II's wife Nefertari, with its intense chromatic contrasts. The boundary between the desert and the cultivated fields is lined with the sometimes monumental remains of temples associated with the royal tombs, the "castles of a million years" as the Egyptians called their mortuary temples.

18. Painting with the queen playing senet, about 1250 BC. Thebes, Tomb of Queen Nefertari.

19. Valley of the Queens, Theban necropolis.

20. Chamber of the sarcophagus with pillars supporting a star-spangled ceiling, about 1250 BC. Thebes, Tomb of Queen Nefertari.

TOMB OF NEFERTARI
about 1250 BC
Luxor, Valley of the Queens

SUBJECT

In 1904, during the excavations carried out by the Italian Archeological Mission in the Valley of the Queens at Luxor, the Italian archeologist Ernesto Schiaparelli discovered the tomb of Queen Nefertari, "the Lovely One, Beloved of Mut," Great Royal Bride of Rameses II. Although already violated and stripped of its contents, the tomb, with its 5400 sq ft or 500 sq m of decorated walls, is a treasure in itself.

The paintings that cover the whole of the inside of the tomb are the product of a moment of great splendor in Egyptian history and bear witness to the very high artistic level attained by the craftsmen working in the Theban necropolis. The scenes represent the magic accompaniment to the burial and portray the main deities of the New Kingdom and the queen in the act of officiating their rites.

These are framed by splendid painted hieroglyphs that recite the magical spells of the funeral ritual and at the same time decorate the walls, providing a backdrop to scenes that would otherwise look as if they were suspended in the air.

COMPOSITION

The colors used are vivid and bright and stand out against the white plaster of the walls, reflecting a deliberate attempt to create an extreme chromatic contrast. Their recent restoration has revealed just how colorful and luminous even tombs could be.

Great care is taken over the representation of the queen, with the aim of emphasizing her beauty and regality, qualities to which her name already alludes.

For this reason the artist who painted Nefertari's tomb chose to portray her with a pink complexion instead of the ocher one generally used for women, while her cheeks are flushed and the carefully drawn lips are tinted a more intense pink. On her head the queen wears a crown formed of two tall plumes set on top of a headdress in the form of a vulture, symbol of the goddess Mut.

THE ABODES OF THE GODS

In this period Egyptian temples, whether devoted to the gods or used for the funerary cult of the pharaoh, shared numerous elements that were required by the symbology of the time. The temple was considered the abode of the deity on earth, who inhabited it in the form of a statue kept in a shrine in the most inaccessible part, the inner sanctum. The external appearance of the abode of the gods and the elements of which it is made up allude to the most divine location of all, that primordial mound which, according to the accounts of the genesis of the world, emerged from the waters of chaos and was the place where creation began. Thus the rear of

the temple is raised slightly above its monumental entrance, the pylon, a gateway with two towers that reproduces the hieroglyph for the horizon, from which the creator Sun rises. The dense pillars of the colonnades and the hypostyle hall allude to the plants that, growing every year after the retreat of the floodwaters, repeat the "first time" of creation. In fact the most common type is the papyrus column, with an open or closed capital. Entering, you pass from brilliant sunlight into the semidarkness of the pillared halls, illuminated by beams of light from openings high up on the walls. The ceilings represent the sky: the sacred atmosphere of the place increases as you move into the total darkness of the sanctum, abode of the god. The east-west orientation of the majority of temples is intended

21

22

21. The great colonnade, Temple of Luxor, about 1360-1330 BC.

22. Pillars with the heraldic plants of Upper and Lower Egypt, Temple of Amon-Re, abuot 1430 BC. Karnak.

23

to echo the daily course of the Sun. Given their function, temples were accessible to the public only as far as the first courtyard, while the inner part was reserved for the priests to whom the king, nominally the sole executor of religious rites, delegated the task of representing him. But the exterior was visible to all and was in fact the part set aside to house images that underlined the role of the sovereign: the pylon was dominated by the scene in which he ritually destroys the enemies of Egypt, seen as a threat to the order established by the gods which the pharaoh was committed to preserve. And, especially in the Ramesside period (19th-20th dynasties), the accent was placed on real events, on deeds that actually demonstrated the necessity of the king's role and bore witness to his divine superiority, presented almost as "manifestos."

**23. Pylon, Temple of Luxor,
about 1260 BC.**

24

24. Closed papyrus capital,
Temple of Amon-Re,
about 1260 BC. Karnak.

**25. Columns of the hypostyle
hall, Temple of Amon-Re,
13th century BC. Karnak.**

THE MORTUARY TEMPLE OF HATSHEPSUT AT DEIR EL-BAHRI

Of the mortuary temples on the west bank, whose fronts naturally face onto the Nile, to the east, and which are dedicated to the pharaoh accompanied by gods and goddesses, the best known is undoubtedly the great temple of Hatshepsut. She was the woman who, daughter of a king and widow of a king, ruled Egypt for twenty years in lieu of her stepson, later to become Thutmosis III. The architect Senenmut (his name too has been preserved: among other things he was perhaps the most prominent official of his day) was probably brought in to com-

plete the work begun by Hatshepsut's husband, Thutmosis II. Taking his inspiration from the sepulchral monument of the 11th dynasty at Deir el-Bahri, he built a complex of very modern appearance alongside it. As usual the access consisted of a "valley temple" and a broad paved road, leading to a spectacular area of level ground occupied by a garden and two pools of water in the shape of a T, planted with papyrus. And in front lay the impressive scene of the two upper terraces, with colonnades at the front and ramps for ascent. This was an idiosyncratic reinterpretation of the succession of courtyards and monumental gateways traditional in the Egyptian temples of the time. At the foot of the rocky cliff, a large courtyard surrounded by deep porticoes with two

26

26. View of the valley of Deir el-Bahri.

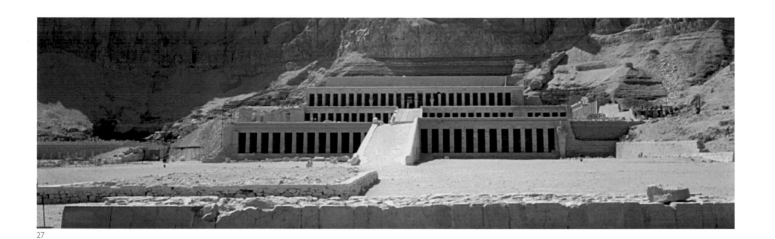

27

28

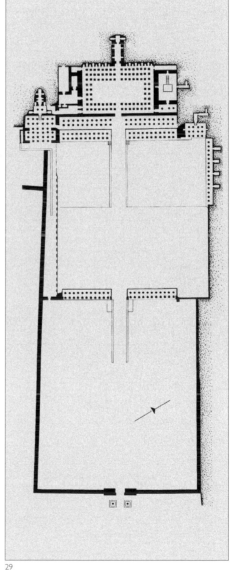

29

**27. Mortuary temple
of Hatshepsut, about
1460 BC. Deir el-Bahri.**

**28. Scene of offering
to the god Horus.
Mortuary temple
of Hatshepsut, about 1460
BC. Deir el-Bahri.**

**29. Plan of the mortuary
temple of Queen Hatshepsut
at Deir el-Bahri
(from C. Aldred, P. Barguet,
C. Desroches Noblecourt,
J. Leclant, H.W. Muller,**

L'impero dei conquistatori,
Milan 1985, p. 310, fig. 393,
updated).

30

31

and three rows of columns preceded the shrine for the holy images. In addition to the main deities, Hatshepsut honored her father Thutmosis I in her temple with a chapel for offerings. Her intent was clearly to legitimize her decision to occupy the throne not as a mere regent, but as a female Horus. The same intent lay behind famous scenes that escaped Thutmosis III's *damnatio memoriae*, or attempt to cancel out all memory of Hatshepsut: her divine birth, for example, generated by the god Amon in the guise of Thutmosis I and "turned" on the potter's wheel by the god Khnum. Equally celebrated are the reliefs that commemorate one of the salient episodes of her reign, the return of the expedition to the country of Punt (probably the area of Eritrea-Somalia), with images that depict that far-off world with a curious eye. Later on the queen had a shrine devoted to herself in the guise of the goddess Hathor added to the southern side of the upper terrace, with a pronaos of elegant pillars whose capitals are carved to represent the goddess's face, with cow's ears and lyre-shaped horns.

30. Temple of Hathor, containing the statuary group of the goddess, in the form of a cow, protecting Pharaoh Thutmosis III, from Deir

el-Bahri, 1430-1400 BC. Cairo, Egyptian Museum.

31. Pillar of the sanctuary of Hathor annexed to the mortuary temple of Hatshepsut, about 1460 BC. Deir el-Bahri.

THE TEMPLE OF AMENHOTEP III: A PAEAN TO GRANDEUR

The motif of the terrace of the temple at Deir el-Bahri seems to have been used again in later temples. But the ruler who must have awed his contemporaries with the magnificence of his monuments, Amenhotep III, wanted something quite different: he had a complex of unimaginable grandeur built for himself, although only a few ruins survive. Surrounded by a wall measuring 765 × 600 yd or 700 × 550 m, it was destroyed by an earthquake, perhaps just after the reign of Rameses II as many of the blocks and statues were reused in the temple built by his successor Merneptah. Centuries of plunder and flooding by the Nile have almost leveled the area but have left stand-ing two vestiges of its splendor: the so-called Colossi of Memnon. The two monolithic statues of red quartzite represent the ruler to whom the temple is dedicated and were set in front of its first monumental gateway, or pylon. Another pair of colossal statues stood in front of a second pylon and a third was linked by an "avenue" of sphinxes to a fourth passageway, leading to a colonnaded court. This court must have had no equal, with statues of the pharaoh 26 ft or 8 m high on the east and west sides, carved from quartzite in the north half and pink granite in the south half. The temple must have contained a profusion of statues, representing the king and a large number of deities, some with unusual iconographies that emphasized their animal aspect (crocodile-sphinxes, Anubis-sphinxes), and almost the whole pantheon, of which Amenhotep III was certainly part.

32

33

32-33. The Colossi of Memnon: colossal statues of Amenhotep III in front of his mortuary temple, about 1360 BC. Thebes.

HATSHEPSUT AND THE FEMALE PHARAOHS

Over the course of ancient Egypt's three thousand years of history at least two women bore the title of pharaoh. The first was Nitocris, at the end of the Old Kingdom, a time when, after the extremely long reign of Pepi II, central authority had weakened. There is little trace of Nitocris either in written history or in art. We know that she probably ascended the throne as a result of a power vacuum, that she was the last ruler of the Old Kingdom and that after her the unity of the country broke down. Unfortunately, however, there is nothing to tell us how the queen chose to

have herself represented in public images and in the statues that portrayed her. Hatshepsut, daughter and wife of kings, ascended the throne of Egypt as temporary regent of Thutmosis III, but ended up reigning as a pharaoh in her own right. The daughter of Thutmosis I and wife of her half brother Thutmosis II, she took over the reins of government following the premature death of her husband, acting in the name of her stepson Thutmosis III, still a child.

To shore up her authority Hatshepsut made herself as similar as possible

I

II

I. Statue of Queen Hatshepsut, about 1460 BC. New York, Metropolitan Museum.

II. Statue of sphinx with the head of Queen Hatshepsut, about 1460 BC.

III

IV

to a male pharaoh, even in her appearance. The queen's iconography is twofold: in some votive statues, while the clothing and posture are typically male, the features of a woman can be discerned. Hatshepsut wears the *shendyt* kilt and the *nemes* headdress, the typical attire of the king, but it is just possible to make out the shape of her breasts.

The arms and the overall structure of the body also retain a feminine delicacy. In some cases alabaster was used so that the color of the skin was extremely pale, while men were represented with their skin burned by the sun. In other figures, however, the queen chose to have herself portrayed in a wholly male guise: this is the case with the Osirian colossi that adorned the pillars of her mortuary temple at Deir el-Bahri. The enormous face in the Cairo Museum represents the queen with the double crown of Upper and Lower Egypt, as actual ruler of the country. As if she were a male pharaoh, she is identified with Osiris and wears the false beard emblematic

of sovereignty. Her skin is ocher and the lineaments are those characteristic of the royal statues of the 18th dynasty. Although depicted as a man to all intents and purposes, there is still a fineness of features and expression that gives away the fact that the person portrayed is a woman: the hint of a smile, the high and sharp cheekbones, the large, made-up eyes and the overall shape of the face suggest, perhaps intentionally, the character and femininity of the queen. The statues of male appearance include numerous sphinxes with the features with which the queen preferred to be portrayed. The headdress, the beard and even the typology of these statues are male, and in them, as in the colossi at Deir el-Bahri, it is not possible to discern that subtle contrast between the subject and the face that artists often sought to create. When Thutmosis III gained power, his *damnatio memoriae* fell on the queen's works: her name was chiseled off the statues and the temples and replaced by that of her stepson.

III. Head of Queen Hatshepsut, from Deir el-Bahri, about 1460 BC. Cairo, Egyptian Museum.

IV. Statue of Queen Hatshepsut kneeling, from Deir el-Bahri, about 1460 BC. Berlin, Staatliche Museen.

EGYPTIAN ART

191

THE MORTUARY TEMPLES OF RAMESES II AND III

The monuments of the great figures in Egyptian history have been unevenly preserved: there are evident similarities in the structure of the temple of Rameses II, called the Ramesseum, and that of Rameses III at Medinet Habu, but only the latter has been spared by time. The ruin of the Ramesseum, and above all the shattered colossal image of the pharaoh, inspired the gloomy verses of Percy Bysshe Shelley's poem "Ozymandias."

The two complexes, separated by some 60-70 years, adopt the structure most characteristic of Egyptian temples, with a succession of pylons and courtyards, a hypostyle hall, secondary rooms and antechambers, culminating in the shrine. In the Ramesseum the "canonical" structure seems to be punctuated by the looming presence of Rameses himself, who creates a suggestive aura with his images – however mangled by time – and with the emphasis given to the historical events in which he was a participant and protagonist. Laid out from east to west and somewhat oblique in plan, the temple immediately offered the visitor a vision of the colossus of pink granite representing the king seated on his throne, set at the back of the courtyard after the first pylon and flanked by an only slightly less imposing image of his wife. The second pylon (with two more enormous statues, one transported in almost epic fashion to the British Museum in London by the Paduan Giovanni Battista Belzoni at the beginning of the 19th century) was decorated with the scene of the most famous episode of Rameses II's reign, the battle against the Hittites at Kadesh, and the text of the peace treaty that put an end to hostilities between the two great powers after fifteen years. Of the other parts of the temple, the hypostyle hall leaves a lasting impression

34

192

34. Mortuary temple of Rameses II, called the Ramesseum, about 1220 BC. Thebes.

35

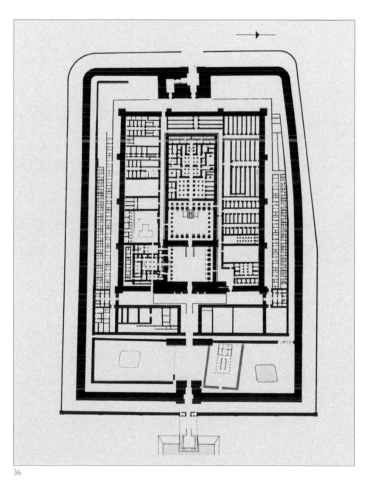

36

37

35. Fallen colossus
in the first courtyard
of the mortuary temple
of Rameses II, Ramesseum,
about 1220 BC. Thebes.

36. Plan of the mortuary
temple of Rameses III
at Medinet Habu, about
1160 BC (from C. Aldred,
P. Barguet, C. Desroches
Noblecourt, J. Leclant,

H.W. Muller, *L'impero dei
conquistatori*, Milan 1985,
p. 315, fig. 409).

37. Central columns of the
hypostyle hall, Ramesseum,
about 1220 BC. Thebes.

38

39

38. First pylon, mortuary temple of Rameses III, about 1160 BC. Thebes, Medinet Habu.

39. Inner court, mortuary temple of Rameses III, about 1160 BC. Thebes, Medinet Habu.

with its monumentality and the remains of its original coloring: there is an obvious allusion to the better-known pillared hall at Karnak, which we shall examine below. The sense of romantic decadence which is inescapable at the Ramesseum gives way to wonder before the well-preserved temple at Medinet Habu, which remained in use for a long time, right up to the Christian era. Rameses III's temple has the look of a fortress, with a keep inspired by Syrian military architecture but which appears to have been used for not very warlike pastimes, judging by its interiors. Then a large space is left open from which to appreciate the temple proper with its classical pylon. This has four niches for flagstaffs and is decorated with scenes of the ritual massacre of enemies by the king, while the god Amon looks on with approval. The succession of colonnaded courtyards and the layout of the following rooms corresponds to that of the Ramesseum, but here it is possible to imagine the

original effect since the colors are extraordinarily well preserved. The great depth to which the inscriptions on the walls and heavy columns are incised strengthens the already forceful impression. While the decoration inside is devoted to religious themes, a relief on the northern outside wall celebrates the king's victory over the "Sea Peoples" (a group of seafarers from the Near East who had attempted to invade Egypt), in an emulation of the exploits of Rameses II: the position clearly indicates a desire to publicize the ruler and underline his superiority. The palace, to the south, is relatively well preserved (whereas few traces of it remain in the Ramesseum); while it was probably also used as a residence, its main purpose was for worship. The palace communicated with the first courtyard through the so-called "Window of Appearances," which replicated the one from which the king showed himself to the public but here may have been purely ritual.

40

40. Mortuary temple of Rameses III, detail with prisoners, about 1160 BC. Medinet Habu, Thebes.

STATUE OF MERYTAMUN

1250 BC
Cairo, Egyptian Museum

SUBJECT

This fragment of what must have been a statue of not much less than life size comes from Thebes. Representing Merytamun, Great Royal Bride of Rameses II who took the place of Queen Nefertari after her death, it was found in 1896 by Flinders Petrie in the sanctuary dedicated to the queen that the pharaoh had had built in the Ramesseum.

Merytamun is portrayed in a manner intended to exalt her youthful beauty and her role as queen of the country: in keeping with the fashion of the New Kingdom, she has a large wig with tightly curled ringlets, a band around her forehead with two uraei, symbols of sovereignty, wearing the crowns of Upper and Lower Egypt, and a beautiful modius of uraei and solar disks on her head. Only the more prominent extremities, the nose and part of the uraei, have been lost, and this does not mar the beauty of the statue, which still bears traces of the polychrome decoration with which it was finished.

COMPOSITION

The power of suggestion exercised by the statue is due to the skill shown by the artist in giving it a character and a particular expression that identifies the face of the queen, while adhering to the rigid rules that governed statuary and favored an idealization of the subject.

The chubby face is splendidly framed by the blue wig and the gold pectoral, and vividly conveys the girl's youth and striking beauty;

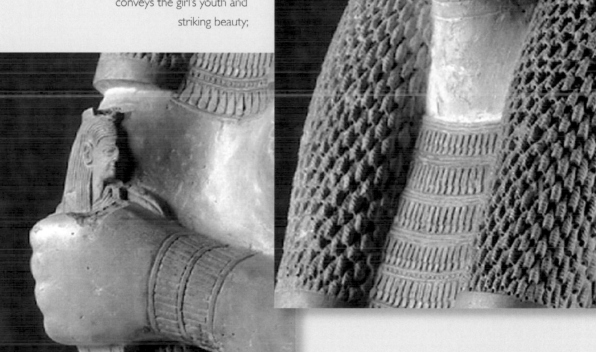

she clutches to her breast the *menat*, the counterpoise of the necklace typical of the goddess Hathor.

The color that has been preserved helps to bring the image to life: the pale red of the lips, which are parted in a faint smile, and the eyes, with their slightly darker pupils, which create the impression of a faraway gaze.

THE TEMPLE OF AMON-RE AT KARNAK

On the east bank of the Nile, where the city of Thebes had grown up, the sanctuaries dedicated to the great dynastic god Amon-Re have survived to bear witness to the grandeur of the past. The "national" temple at Karnak, of immense proportions, was linked by Amenhotep III to what can be described as the most harmonious temple in Egypt, the one at Luxor. Its orientation, with the front facing toward Karnak, and the long paved road lined with sphinxes reveal the connection between the two complexes. Luxor was in fact the point of arrival of the festive procession of Opet, which every year brought the statues of the gods from Karnak, their barks carried on the shoulders of priests, to the "Southern Opet," the Egyptian

41

**41. View of the temple
of Amon-Re. Karnak.**

name of the Temple of Luxor. Here were held the ceremonies connected with the celebration of the pharaoh's divine birth, as the progeny of Amon Re. The structure we see today is the one that was enlarged at the end of the 18th dynasty and again by Rameses II. Some buildings from the Middle Kingdom and the beginning of the 18th dynasty certainly stood in the area, but Amenhotep III's project swept them away completely. The main nucleus is the present back of the temple (i.e. the part opposite its entrance), with the stations for the sacred barks. It is faced by a hypostyle hall filled with slender papyrus columns and opening onto a vast porticoed courtyard that gives it an even more evocative atmosphere. It was probably Tutankhamun (perhaps implementing a plan of Amenhotep III's) who decided to enlarge this part by adding a double row of papyrus columns with open capitals (70

ft or over 21 m high). The result was almost a kiosk, illuminated by windows with gratings in the side walls which Horemheb later had decorated with scenes of the Opet festival. Rameses II then completed it with another colonnaded court containing his colossal statues, along with several statues usurped from Amenhotep, and the pylon, with two obelisks and flagstaffs set in front. The pylon provided another large surface on which to celebrate his victory over the Hittites at Kadesh, doubtful in reality but absolutely indisputable in the eyes of the Egyptian people. The "avenue" of sphinxes, extending further north, led to the precinct of the goddess Mut, companion of Amon-Re, and then, after 1.5 miles or 2.5 kilometers, to the great enclosure of the god, whose "historic" temple had existed since at least the Middle Kingdom, and perhaps even longer. In Amenhotep III's time the main block, oriented west-east, had already been extended to

the south, a sign that the sanctuary had been included in the system of celebrations that connected it with Luxor. After the Middle Kingdom, it was the rulers of the 18th dynasty who devoted the greatest attention to the national sanctuary, enlarging it with a series of pylons (now numbered from the outside to the inside, and thus not in chronological order). It can be said that Amenhotep III "sanctioned" the so-called southern propylaea with the construction of the 3rd pylon, to the west, which formed an L-shaped structure with the courtyards and the 7th and 8th pylons from the Thutmoside period. An original contribution was made by Thutmosis III, who had a rectangular structure built at right angles to the axis of the temple at the eastern end of the complex, with a double row of columns of an unusual form, resembling giant stakes. This structure, perhaps alluding to the pavilions for celebration of the royal jubilee, seems to have been

42

42. Ruins of the temple
of Amon-Re and sacred
lake. Karnak.

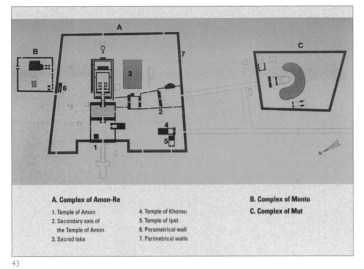

43

dedicated to the cult of the pharaoh as a manifestation of Amon-Re. In the Ramesside period there were further notable renovations, comprising extensions (the 2nd pylon) and restorations in the southern propylaea, which in the meantime had been expanded as far as the 10th pylon. The most spectacular addition was the celebrated hypostyle hall, a forest of 134 papyrus columns whose central passageway, along the axis, is made up of twelve taller columns with open capitals. Seti I and his son Rameses II, who were responsible for the construction of the spectacular hall (the central colonnade may date back to Amenhotep III), focused their attention on this zone. Both father and son used the outer walls, to the north and south, to commemorate their military exploits in Asia or Nubia. On the west side of the southern extension is inscribed the most complete surviving version of the peace treaty agreed with the Hittites after the battle of Kadesh.

44

45

43. Plan of the complex of the temples of Amon-Re, Montu and Mut at Karnak.

44-45. Central colonnade of the hypostyle hall, Temple of Amon-Re, about 1260 BC. Karnak.

EGYPTIAN ART

46

47

**46-47. Avenue lined with
sphinxes with ram's
heads and detail,
Temple of Amon-Re,
13th century BC. Karnak.**

48

49

48. Sacred lake, Temple of Amon-Re. Karnak.

49. Hypostyle hall, Temple of Amon-Re, about 1260 BC. Karnak.

50. Facing page:
Obelisk of Thutmosis I,
Temple of Amon-Re,
about 1500 BC. Karnak.

51. Relief with Thutmosis
III triumphing over his
enemies, Temple of
Amon-Re, about 1450 BC.
Karnak.

52. Following pages:
Colonnade of the Temple
of Luxor, dating from
Amenhotep III's reign,
about 1360 BC.

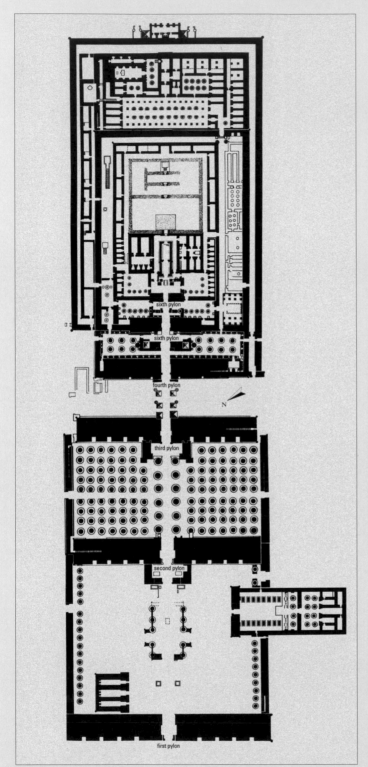

The complex of Karnak, or *Ipet-Isut*, "Chosen of Places," as it was called in ancient times, is the largest group of temples of the New Kingdom. It was dedicated to the Theban triad made up of Amon-Re, the principal sun god of the New Kingdom, Mut, goddess of the night sky, and their son, Khonsu, god of the moon. Karnak bears witness to millennia of Egyptian history: the oldest part of the sanctuary, now completely lost, dated from the reign of Sesostris I, in the Middle Kingdom. Subsequently, right through the New Kingdom and into the Late Period, every ruler wished to make a contribution, making modifications or additions to the complex to enlarge and embellish it, until it attained its final complicated structure. Of the three temples that make up the complex it is Amon-Re's that has undergone the biggest changes. It is now laid out along two perpendicular axes that were formed over the course of time through the construction of numerous pylons, which constitute the typical architectural element of the Egyptian temple. In this case there are ten that bestow majesty and grandeur on the structure, marking out its rhythms. Even though it was constructed on the basis of a coherent plan, the temple retains a remarkable uniformity of layout thanks to its succession of built and empty spaces. The entrance located in the west provides access to the temple through the first pylon, built by Nectanebo I and Nectanebo II and then finished in the Ptolemaic period. This links up with the wall of mud bricks that encloses the whole temple, called the "Wall of Amon." The second and third pylons are among the most imposing and richly decorated ever constructed. The second, begun by Horemheb but completed by Seti I and Rameses II, was decorated with scenes of devotion in which the two pharaohs play a leading role and with a celebration of their victories over their enemies. At the sides of the entrance two colossal statues of Rameses II seated were erected to guard the temple. To build the pylon Horemheb utilized many small blocks of stone salvaged from the demolition of Akhenaton's constructions as filling materials, thereby sparing them from the *damnatio memoriae* to which they had been condemned. The second pylon led into the great hypostyle hall, containing 134 columns roofed with enormous stone architraves. The hall was illuminated through the difference in height between the two ceilings: the nave, in fact, consisted of two rows of columns that were taller than the others, allowing the rays of the sun to enter from above and create a play of light and shade. Next we come to the third pylon, built by Amenhotep III and originally decorated with gold, while the floors were embellished with silver. Blocks from other build-

**I. Plan of the central
temple of Amon-Re
(from R. Schulz,
M. Seidel, *Egypt*,
Cologne 1998, p. 157).**

ings were used to fill this pylon as well, and this has now permitted the complete reconstruction of the White Chapel of Sesostris I. The fourth pylon, erected by Thutmosis I, was preceded by four obelisks and formed the entrance to the oldest part of the temple, the one dating from the Middle Kingdom. In the space between the fourth and fifth pylon Queen Hatshepsut had raised obelisks that were nearly 100 ft or 30 m high, made of pink granite from the quarries at Aswan. They had been partially covered with gold to reflect the rays of the sun: in Egyptian symbology, in fact, the obelisk was a representation of the rays of light descending from the sky. At the rear of the oldest temple stood the Festival Hall or Akh-Menu, constructed by Thutmosis III and used to hold the ceremony

for the king's jubilee. One of the shrines of the Akh-Menu is known as the "botanical garden" because the pharaoh had it decorated with exotic plants and animals seen on his Asian expeditions, symbolically offered here to the god. Along the north-south axis stand four more pylons, separated by the same number of courtyards, which are much larger than the others. The eighth pylon was built by Hatshepsut and the famous Karnak Cachette was found in one corner of the courtyard that precedes it: an enormous deposit of statues that had been used in worship throughout the history of the sanctuary up until the Late Period. Partially damaged or surplus to requirements, they were buried in the sacred ground of the temple so that they would not be lost.

II

III

II. Heraldic pillars of Thutmosis III, Temple of Amon-Re, about 1430 BC. Karnak.

III. The colossi of Thutmosis III near the north front of the seventh pylon, Temple of Amon-Re about 1430 BC. Karnak.

SETI I'S CENOTAPH AT ABYDOS

At the beginning of the 19th dynasty the religious center of Abydos saw one of the most significant constructions of the era, and one that fell within the tradition of the "cenotaph," still alive in the New Kingdom. Seti I built a temple for funerary use that was completed by his son Rameses II, who went on to erect a temple for himself near his father's to serve the same purpose. Less imposing in appearance, Seti I's temple is laid out on terraces, following the slope of the ground. It was approached from a basin of water set in front of the 1st pylon, which

53

54

55

212

53 and 56. Temple of Seti I, about 1280 BC. Abydos.

54. Inner colonnade, Temple of Seti I, about 1280 BC. Abydos.

55. The god Anubis and Seti I, drawing after a painted bas-relief in the Temple of Abydos, about 1280 BC.

led to the 1st court and the 2nd pylon, porticoed in an unusual manner, like the façade of the main building behind. Inside, two transverse pillared halls have seven openings corresponding to the seven sanctuaries at the rear, dedicated to the pharaoh in the guise of seven different deities: Osiris, the national gods Ptah, Re-Harakhty and Amon-Re, and the triad of Abydos, Osiris, Isis and Horus. Behind this structure, decorated with reliefs of rare refinement depicting religious subjects, is the most significant part, the actual cenotaph of the king in the form of the tomb of Osiris. The Osireion, as it is incorrectly called, is the most complete example to have come down to us of the architectural motif derived from the mythical account of the scattering of the god's dismembered body, whose parts were then found and buried under a hill covered with trees. A long corridor leads underground from the north side of the precinct and then turns through a right angle before reaching a sort of island, surrounded by a moat that was supplied with water by an underground channel. On the island, beneath a ceiling supported by ten pillars of pink granite, stood the empty sarcophagus representing the identification of the dead king with the god. This underground part was in all probability protected by the hill or mound referred to in the myth, and lodgings for the trees have been identified on the surface.

THE RULER AS GOD: ASPECTS AND TRANSFORMATIONS OF SACRED ARCHITECTURE

In every age the pharaoh was considered divine, the representative on earth of the god Horus, son and legitimate heir of Osiris. There is less evidence, however, of a cult surrounding the person of the living ruler, except in the New Kingdom, when at least Amenhotep III, Amenhotep IV-Akhenaton, to whom we shall return, and Rameses II did receive such worship. Amenhotep III has left numerous indications of his desire to be considered equal to the gods, living image of the highest deity, "Bright Disk of the Sun." A long way from Thebes, at Sulb and Sadinga, over 300 miles or 500 kilometers to the south of Aswan at the far end of Lower Nubia, he had a pair of temples built for himself and his wife Tiy; here the rulers were identified with Amon and Hathor-Isis respectively. Rameses II accentuated the theocratic character of the

kingdom, and the devotion shown to him in life is particularly evident in the series of temples he had erected, once again in Lower Nubia. The area, coveted since the Old Kingdom for its wealth of minerals, metals and exotic goods, was then firmly in the hands of the Egyptians, who administered it and spread their own culture, using the building of temples as a means of communication with the population, without of course forgetting their economic potential. Rameses had a total of seven built there, completing the most imposing of them first, in the twenty-fourth year of his reign. The name of Abu Simbel is familiar to all after the feat of the dismantling of the two rock temples, the larger one dedicated to Rameses II and the smaller to his wife Nefertari, to save them from being submerged by Lake Nasser. In the large temple it can be said that the concept of deification is truly expressed in visual form: the monumental façade is a clear allusion to the form of the temple pylon, but in this case two pairs of colossal statues of the seated pharaoh, 72 ft or 22 m high, have been carved out of the rock

57

214

57. The two temples of Rameses II and Nefertari, about 1250 BC, after reconstruction. Abu Simbel.

face, flanked by figures of members of his family on a much smaller scale. In a niche above the entrance is set a statue of the sun god Re-Harakhty, to whom two figures of Rameses at the sides pay homage. The god is resting his right hand on an object that corresponds to the hieroglyph *user* and has a statuette of the goddess Maat under his left hand. This can be read, as in a rebus, as the throne name of Rameses II (*User-Maat-Re*), who is thus presenting himself as an incarnation of the sun god and in the act of worshiping himself. In the depths of the mountain, the canonical elements of a temple are reproduced as if "in negative": a large hall with pillars against which are set Osirian figures of the king, then a hypostyle hall, a vestibule and a sanctum flanked by shrines. At the back of the sanctum, there are four divine images, on the same level: the Memphite Ptah, Amon-Re, Rameses himself and Re Harakhty. The insistence on sun worship is underlined by a particular phenomenon that has been observed: at two times of the year the rays of the rising sun shine straight into

the sanctum. It is not unlikely that one of these moments, around October 20, corresponded to the anniversary of the pharaoh's first jubilee, which was thus commemorated in extraordinary fashion. The figure of Rameses also dominates the small temple. Its façade is made up of buttresses that follow the inclination of the rock face and form deep niches from which emerge six standing statues. The niches at each end house the royal couple, of very similar dimensions (care has been taken to make the top of their crowns reach the same height), the two in the middle, at the sides of the entrance, hold statues of Rameses, on a slightly smaller scale; the proximity of the figure of his wife, again slightly shorter, produces an impression of uniformity. The interior consists of a hall with pillars crowned by heads of the goddess Hathor, a vestibule and the sanctum. Here Nefertari, "for whom the sun shines," is identified with the goddesses Hathor and Isis, who are shown crowning her in a scene of great beauty. Horus and Seth do the same with her husband.

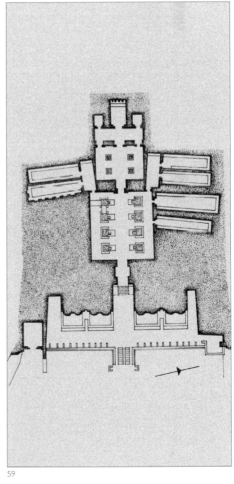

58. Louis Haghe, *The Temples of Aboo-Simbe*, from the Nile, 1845. London, British Library.

59. Plan of the large temple of Rameses II at Abu Simbel, about 1250 BC (from C. Aldred, P. Barguet, C. Desroches Noblecourt, J. Leclant, H.W. Muller, *L'impero dei conquistatori*, Milan 1985, p. 314, fig. 408).

60

61

62

60-63. Details of some colossal statues on the façade, large temple of Rameses II, 1250 BC. Abu Simbel.

64

65

**64. Large temple
of Rameses II,
about 1250 BC.
Abu Simbel.**

**65. Osirian pillars
representing the pharaoh
in the large entrance hall,
large temple of Rameses
II, about 1250 BC.
Abu Simbel.**

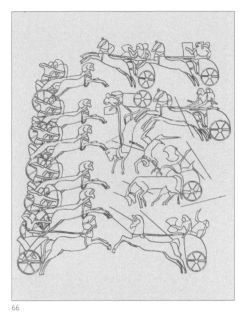

66

67

68

66. Drawing of the painted
relief depicting the battle
of Kadesh, about 1250 BC.
Abu Simbel, large temple
of Rameses II.

67. Louis Haghe,
*Sanctuary of the Temple
of Aboo-Simbel*, 1845.
London, British Library.

68. Façade of the small
temple, about 1250 BC.
Abu Simbel.

STATUE OF RAMESES II
about 1270 BC
Turin, Egyptian Museum

SUBJECT

This statue, which comes from Thebes, is perhaps the most famous of the many effigies of himself that Rameses II had made, and undoubtedly deserves the admiration that has been lavished on the refinement of its celebratory representation of the ruler on his throne.

The statue arrived in Turin in 1824, when the city's Egyptian Museum, perhaps the most important in the world after the one in Cairo, was officially founded following King Charles Felix's acquisition of the collection of Bernardino Drovetti, the French consul in Egypt. The museum had not even been mounted yet when Jean-François Champollion rushed there to see the rich collection, "hungry" for Egyptian monuments ever since he had succeeded in deciphering the hieroglyphic script just two years earlier. An example of this script giving the titles of the pharaoh can be seen in the vertical strip in the middle of the kilt. The statue of Rameses enchanted Champollion, who described it as the "Egyptian Belvedere Apollo" and even devoted a couplet to it: "For six whole months I've seen it every day / and always think I'm seeing it for the first time!"

The sandaled feet rest on the Nine Bows, symbolizing all the enemies of Egypt, while subjugated Nubians and Asians are represented on the base.

COMPOSITION

Rameses' face, roundish and with youthful features, wears a faint smile and his gaze, full of divine superiority, is turned slightly downward. His clothing is complicated, ceremonial attire. On his head is set the so-called blue crown, a military parade and war helmet with flanges at the sides and plates of blue faience. Over the forehead the concentric coils of the cobra frame the typical royal diadem, the uraeus.

Rameses is dressed in a long pleated tunic with short flared sleeves. Only the one on the right arm is visible, as the whole of his left side is covered by a cloak. This is also pleated and knotted on the breast, under the broad collar with many rows of beads and pendants. The front part of the kilt spreads out to form a trapezoid.

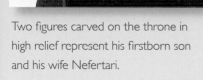

Two figures carved on the throne in high relief represent his firstborn son and his wife Nefertari.

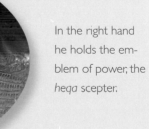

In the right hand he holds the emblem of power, the *heqa* scepter.

PAINTING IN THEBAN PRIVATE TOMBS

Alongside the mortuary temples of the pharaohs in the Theban necropolis, tombs of private individuals multiplied, carved in the low spurs of the hill at Sheikh Abd-al Qurnah and Dra'Abu'n-Naga. These were the tombs of officials and priests, the "middle class" that shared in the prosperity of the time. They communicated a new sense of life and of expectations for the next world through the decoration of their own tombs. Their aspirations, reflected in the tomb paintings give us an idea of the changes underway. The idyllic impression created by the sight of the Egyptian villages on the west bank at Luxor today cannot be very different from the view of the

same hills almost 3500 years ago, except that the dwellings one would have seen then were intended to last for eternity.

The appearance of the tombs can be reconstructed from their frequent representation in the painted scenes inside: in general the external structure has been destroyed. There was often a walled courtyard that left a clear view of the façade carved out of the rock, with the funerary stele in front. Structured in various ways, the façade could resemble a temple and be crowned with a projecting molding.

If space allowed, the roof behind the façade could take the form of a pyramid: now that the pharaohs had entrusted the message of their divine survival after death to other means, that powerful

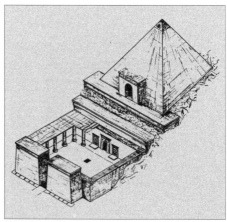

69

71

70

69. Reconstruction of a tomb from the Ramesside period, 13th-12th century BC (from R. Schulz, M. Seidel, *Egypt*, Cologne 1998, p. 250, fig. 198).

70. Painting representing the governor Sennefer and his wife, 1410 BC. Sheikh Abd-al Qurnah, Tomb of Sennefer.

71. Plan of a private tomb at Thebes, about 1300 BC (from R. Schulz, M. Seidel, *Egypt*, Cologne 1998, p. 251, fig. 199).

72

symbol was appropriated by their subjects. The internal structure maintained the distinction between underground crypt, accessible through a shaft inside the shrine that was blocked after the burial, and the place of worship on the surface, partly or wholly carved from the rock. Once through the entrance, the temple usually had a plan in the shape of an upside-down T, made up of a transverse atrium leading into a longitudinal shrine with the statue of the deceased at the back.

The friability of the rock determined the choice of the technique used for decoration. Here the painted relief, traditional in all previous periods, was unsuitable, and so the artists painted directly in tempera on a plaster base: the paints, as archeological finds have revealed, were in the form of solid cakes of pigment mixed with binders. And it proved a "liberation": the conventions of the relief, which at least in our eyes seem to have acted as a constriction up until that moment, were not abandoned but adapted without hesitation to a freer style of drawing, in search of an expressiveness that relied on contrasts of colors and correspondences, while new

solutions were also tried out. Generally speaking, it can be said that the decorative program assigned the religious themes proper to the shrine, while subjects more closely related to "real life" were tackled in the vestibule or atrium.

What is striking, however, is the different approach taken to themes that could be defined as canonical, and present since the Old Kingdom. Here the aim was not to grasp the characteristic aspects and fix every activity so that its benefits could be enjoyed for eternity; instead every aspect of ordinary life was in some way related to the occupant of the tomb, as if it were an episode from their actual experience. The accent was placed on individual experiences, on the functions carried out, the posts held. What had once been the indispensable scene of the "taking possession" of offerings was now barely hinted at in the still obligatory panel of the traditional false door. It was explored instead in scenes representing feasts and merrymaking, with guests listening to the music of a harpist or entertained by dancing women. The necessities of survival on earth and forever in the afterlife were certainly produced in

72. Scene of offering,
about 1300 BC. Thebes,
Tomb of Roy.

the master's fields, but the artists got to linger over every aspect, lively or typical or curious, and the whole thing was related to the experience of the individual, who was presented as a privileged, influential person. However, the extent to which the decoration was part of a program and to which its motifs need interpreting, almost decoding, is demonstrated by the use of themes that dated from the most ancient times and had an already highly symbolic significance: the scenes of hunting and fishing in the marshes, for example, were inspired by representations of the pharaoh almost as the master of nature. In one of the Theban tombs we seem to be looking at a festive boat trip, with the scene dominated by the proprietor, surrounded by his wife and daughters who, dressed up and bejeweled (and thus not in attire very suitable for the occasion), demonstrate that the image retained a ritual value. The

accompanying inscriptions appear to make this clear: "gladdening the heart by seeing the beautiful in the abode of the eternity of existence." Themes and symbols that are not always easy for us to understand are projected into the dimension of the other world and the guiding thread, or rather the goal that is sought, is the idea of rebirth. Such a riot of colors certainly exalts the beauty of the creation that the Egyptians hoped to enjoy in the afterlife, but it also reflects the joy of "creating" that is characteristic of art.

The rules of representation are all respected, but the artists also wanted to experiment with three-quarter and frontal views, while the once pure colors are now shaded, both to accentuate details and to give the figures a sense of depth. Rows are still used to organize the scenes, but they are interrupted or adapted to meet the needs of the "narration."

74

75

73. Facing page: Interior of the tomb of the governor Sennefer, about 1410 BC. Thebes.

74. The parents of the deceased in front of a table of offerings, 15th century BC. Sheikh Abd-al Qurnah, Tomb of Benia-Pahekamen.

75. Painting with officials, about 1450 BC. Sheikh Abd-al Qurnah, Tomb of Rekhmire.

76

77

76. Scene of fishing, 19th dynasty. Deir el-Medina, Tomb of Ipuy.

77. Procession of Cretans bearing offerings, 1450 BC. Sheikh Abd-al Qurnah, Tomb of Rekhmire.

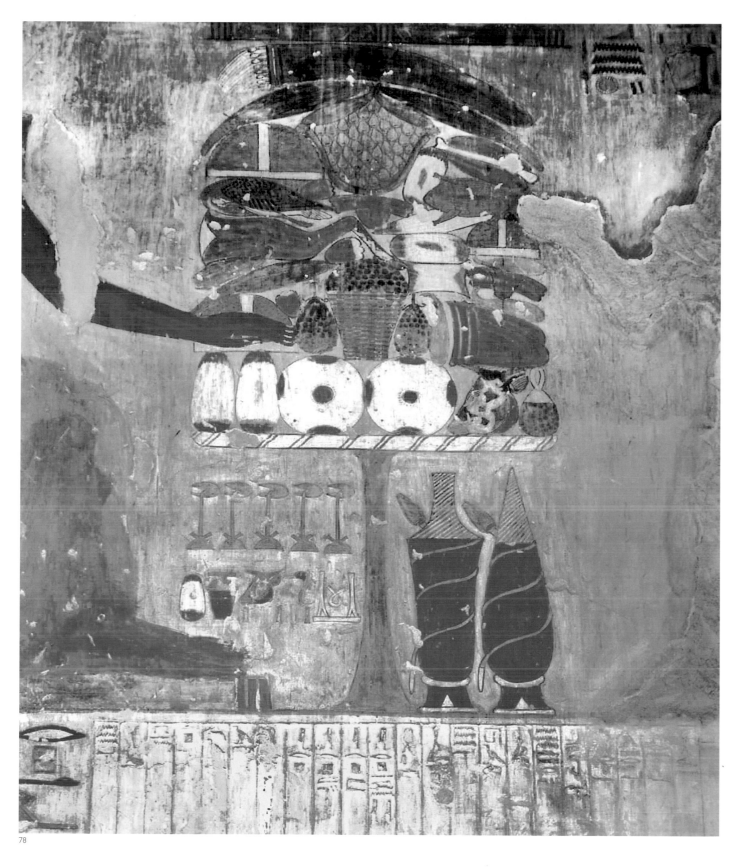

78. Table richly laid with offerings, 1450 BC. Sheikh Abd-al Qurnah, Tomb of Rekhmire.

RELIEF FROM THE TOMB OF RAMOSE

about 1360-1350 BC
Thebes, Necropolis of Sheikh Abd-al Qurnah

SUBJECT

Tomb no. 55 in the necropolis of Sheikh Abd-al Qurnah belonged to a very high-ranking official, the "Governor of the City and Vizier" Ramose. He lived at an extremely delicate moment in history, at the end of the reign of Amenhotep III and the beginning of the ascent of Amenhotep IV-Akhenaton, and thus in the early phase of his religious reform. Ramose's tomb was left unfinished; it is thought he may have followed the pharaoh to the new city of Akhetaton that he had founded in Middle Egypt, at what is now Tell el-Amarna.

Only the tomb's courtyard and large hypostyle hall are decorated, partly with paintings but mostly in relief, and the effect is both stunning and instructive: the walls next to the entrance and on the left (the only ones painted) show the perfection of the refined style of Amenhotep III's time. In the following scenes, opposite, we see the transformation: there is an Amenhotep IV represented in perfect keeping with the traditional canons, and therefore distinguishable only by the name; but nearby the new style appears and it is clear that the "reforming" ruler had already introduced his artistic rules, which broke with all tradition.

COMPOSITION

This banqueting scene belongs to the part in "classical" style, which certainly reaches the height of virtuosity. We can see the guests and members of the family, arranged in couples; the first on the right is Lady Urel with her husband Mai, "Controller of Horses," certainly an important post.

They are taking part in traditional ceremonies, consisting of offerings and banquets. Relaxed and confident, they hold bunches of lotus flowers and are adorned with garlands and rich necklaces, which are also marks of honor: Mai is wearing a double collar and armlets awarded "for valor."

The effect of the white limestone, against which the eyes outlined in black stand out, the softness of the very low relief and the rippling of the surface produced by the representation of the elegant hairstyles cannot be surpassed by even the most elaborate painting.

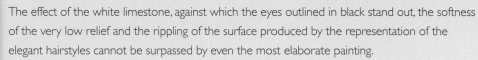

NAKHTMIN AND HIS WIFE
about 1325 BC
Cairo, Egyptian Museum

SUBJECT

The two fragments undoubtedly come from the same group of statues, in which the married couple was represented standing, the man on a larger scale, and connected to a supporting slab with inscriptions at the back. All that has been salvaged from the group are these pieces, whose faces have been deliberately damaged and whose origin is unknown. Nakhtmin was a "royal scribe" and "generalissimo" and may even have been the son of a king, probably Ay, the successor of Tutankhamun. This means he must have come from the city of Akhmim, center of the worship of the god Min. His wife, portrayed resting her right hand on his shoulders, remains anonymous.

The gauzy mantle is stretched over her arm: under her hand is the bundle of beads of the *menat* necklace, typical of the goddess Hathor, and the rosette engraved on the disk of its counterpoise.

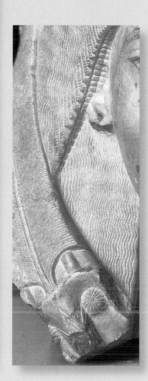

COMPOSITION

The faces of the couple, framed by elaborate headdresses, suggest a transposition of the reliefs in Ramose's tomb into sculpture. The man's wavy wig parts to reveal a perfectly smooth oval face, with large slanting eyes whose makeup is represented in color.

We can see the pierced lobes of his ears (an important clue for the dating of the statue) as well as the plume of the fan that Nakhtmin carries as a mark of his role, receding on the right side.

In the figure of the woman, with eyes "lost in dream" (as Jacques Vandier has described them, a scholar succumbing to emotion), the soft lines revealed by the folds of the dress, which show the influence of the Tell el-Amarna style of a few years earlier, contrast with the wistful face and opulent wig that looks like a piece of chasing: curly locks, twisted together at the bottom. A garland of flowers rings the head and is held down, in the middle, by the band with a bunch of lotuses that hangs over the forehead; another band under the ears, perhaps of precious metal, keeps the wig in place.

THE NECROPOLIS OF DEIR EL-MEDINA

Religious themes predominate in the tombs of the necropolis of Deir el-Medina, next to the village of the workers, artists and craftsmen who built the tombs of the pharaohs in the Valley of the Kings. They are of modest size, decorated by artists of proven ability used to working for the most exacting clients, who thought about their own eternal abodes when not fulfilling their rulers' demands. Most of the decorations are in the underground chamber, which has favored their preservation. Yellow is the preferred color for the background, mak-

ing the scenes stand out. These are executed with skill, but lack the inventiveness we see in many tombs of notables of the New Kingdom. The subjects the artists were accustomed to depicting (the nether regions bristling with dangers that the Sun had to face at night) seem to determine their choice of themes, and there are numerous scenes drawn from the illustrations of papyrus copies of the *Book of the Dead*, the most common collection of mortuary texts. This predilection may also be a sign of a growing tendency to introspection, more evident still in the Ramesside period, an underlying insecurity that made people more fearful of the afterlife.

79

81

80

79. Longitudinal section of the typical tomb of a worker-craftsman, 15th-12th century BC (from C. Aldred, P. Barguet, C. Desroches Noblecourt, J. Leclant, H.W. Muller, *L'impero dei conquistatori*, Milan 1985, p. 318, fig. 425).

80. The shade of the deceased and his *ba* "soul," represented as a bird with a human head, 1150 BC about. Deir el-Medina, Tomb of Arinefer.

81. Sennedjem and his wife at the senet board, about 1250 BC. Deir el-Medina.

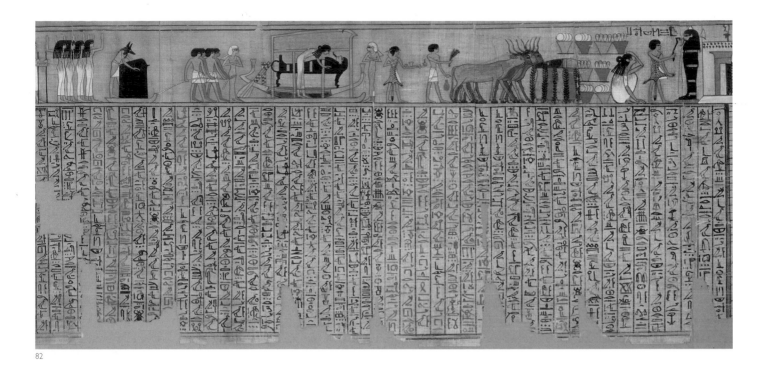

82

83

82. Papyrus with the *Book of the Dead* of the scribe Nebqed; at the top, the continuous illustration with the scene of the funeral, about 1300 BC. Paris, Musée du Louvre.

83. The architect Kha with his wife worshiping the god Osiris, in a scene painted on the papyrus with the *Book of the Dead*, from Deir el- **Medina, about 1420 BC. Turin, Egyptian Museum.**

STATUARY: FORMULATION OF AN "ICONOGRAPHY OF POWER"

A number of statues for funerary and religious purposes, mostly of colossal size, have already been described in our discussion of architecture. This close link between statuary and architecture was the most typical aspect of the age, or at least very well documented in comparison with earlier periods. The statue certainly retained its role of "surrogate" for the deceased and support for the spiritual entity of the *ka*, which made necessary its presence in the tomb, but to this funerary function was added a votive one. It became increasingly common for statues to be placed in temples, by concession of the king. The arts of persuasion referred to in connection with the royal statues of the Middle Kingdom certainly did not remain discreetly hidden in the age of the Egyptian empire. The tendency to gigantism was almost inherent in the universal role assigned to the figure of the pharaoh, but it was openly declared by the colossal figures portraying the protagonists of a period that had opened with a series of military successes. Egypt was now able to count on a well-organized army, and this constituted an indispensable and reliable reserve of labor even when no campaigns of conquest were being waged. The first rulers of the 18th dynasty seem to have chosen to hark back to the models of the Middle Kingdom, with the same intent of reviving tradition that their predecessors had displayed with regard to the Memphite era at the end of a period of crisis. But there was an increasing insistence on the heaven-sent role of the king, and the idea of first the ruler-hero and then the divine sovereign was asserted, literally, by gigantic images that demanded attention and recognition. Identification of the pharaohs was still entrusted to the iconography, i.e. to the attitude, to particular emblems and to inscriptions. But certain features also seem to have been typical of each king. These may even have been elements of portraiture, but were adopted for stylistic reasons: the Thutmoside nose, the eyes and lips of Amenhotep III. In addition, there are el-

84

85

84. Statue of Thutmosis III, from Karnak, about 1450 BC. Cairo, Egyptian Museum.

85-86. Colossal head of Amenhotep III, from Sheikh Abd-al Qurnah, 1390-1352 BC. Luxor, Museum of Ancient Egyptian Art.

87

88

ements that appear to have been stylistic guidelines issued by the court workshops and that can be used to identify and date other sculptures, including a genre that now showed great respect for the past: statues of the gods. Not the ones used in rituals, which were kept out of sight in the sanctuary and were probably made from precious materials, but the ones displayed in the shrines of temples, and in large numbers in certain mortuary temples. We only have a few images of deities from earlier periods, but now they come in all shapes and sizes, including compositions of figures and above all triads. These combine the tendencies to introduce order into the pantheon by grouping the deities in families of father, mother and son and to link the pharaoh to the gods, usually as their son. Consequently, with the ruler transferring his characteristics to divine images, in keeping with the style of his time, it is not always easy to distinguish figures of the gods from pharaohs in divine form.

87. Statue of the god Amon with the features of Tutankhamun, from Karnak, 1336-1327 BC. Luxor, Museum of Ancient Egyptian Art.

88. Amenhotep III and the god Sobek, from Dahamsha, about 1390-1352 BC. Luxor, Museum of Ancient Egyptian Art.

MASTERPIECES OF STATUARY FROM THE REIGN OF AMENHOTEP III

As has already been pointed out, the deification of the ruler became more overt around the middle of the 18th dynasty, under Amenhotep III. More statues of this pharaoh are known than for any other, whether represented as a ruler or a god. One of the most emblematic of all was brought to light in 1989, in the most recent of the extraordinary discoveries to which Egypt has almost made us grow accustomed.

A pit in the temple of Luxor was found to contain twenty-six very well-preserved statues, buried there to make room on the surface, perhaps in the Roman era. The reign of Amenhotep III is well represented, and by some true masterpieces. One in particular, 8 ft

or almost 2.5 m high and carved from the favored red quartzite, might almost be said to be a representation of Amenhotep as a sun god, the "Bright Disk of the Sun of All the Lands."

The figure of the king is set against a dorsal pillar and stands on a base that is in turn set on a sled on top of the real plinth.

At the top of the pillar, the winged solar disk blends with the rounded tip of the royal crown, the same as the one worn by the god Atum.

Sleds were often used to carry images of deified dead kings in procession behind the statue of the god during festivities.

But the statue of Amenhotep may have accompanied the statue of the god even while the pharaoh was still alive, presenting him for worship as Sun of the Lands, a real power and "fruitful to he who has generated him (Amon)," as the inscription declares.

89

90

89. Relief with Amenhotep III in front of Amon, detail, 1390-1352 BC about. Temple of Luxor.

90. Larger-than-life-size statue of the deified Amenhotep III, standing on a sled, about 1390-1352 BC. Luxor, Museum of Ancient Egyptian Art.

STATUE OF THE GODDESS IUNIT

about 1400 BC
Luxor, Egyptian Museum

SUBJECT

Dating from the 18th dynasty, the statue of the goddess Iunit belongs to a group of twenty-six statues found at the Temple of Luxor in 1989. All in an excellent state of preservation, they had been hidden in a *favissa* (the Latin word for a hiding place for sacred objects), under one of the temple's floors. The hiding place was in all likelihood created in the Roman era and the majority of the works found in it can be dated to the New Kingdom: among them were statues of important rulers like Rameses II and Amenhotep III, sphinxes and effigies of gods. The latter included a statue, still in a perfect state of preservation, of a little known goddess called Iunit.

The goddess is represented devoid of any divine attribute apart from the *ankh*, the sign of life that she holds in her right hand, which has the double significance of an identifying element and an offering made to men.

COMPOSITION

Owing to her fine and elegant
features, her enigmatic and
almost total lack of attributes
and in particular her ineffable
smile, this statue has been
nicknamed the Mona Lisa of
Luxor. Her peculiarity, in fact,
lies in a disarming simplicity, as
she is presented without any
of the symbols and attributes
that usually accompany Egyptian works, and are indeed an
integral part of their artistic
composition.

In this case it is solely the proportions of the statue that make it an
expression of the divine essence,
and not symbols, attributes or hieroglyphic inscriptions.
The elegant figure, moreover, has
a slender and extremely feminine
body, covered by nothing more than
a clinging robe. All the surfaces are
perfectly smooth and the working of
the gray granite is marvelous; very
hard and little used in sculpture, this
material produces suggestive effects
thanks to the paler inclusions that
enliven its appearance.

In the temples, numerous private individuals also participated in the rites in the form of statues, displaying their privileged status. It was not infrequent for the right to a statue to be granted by the pharaoh, and so it will bear his cartouche on the breast or one shoulder. Then there were people who made their privileged roles clear in a distinctive way: numerous statues exist of Senenmut, Hatshepsut's steward, but they all underline the function that brought him closest to the queen, as tutor of her daughter, the princess

Nefrura. He is also seen holding the little girl on his lap in a curious type of sculpture that harks back to the cube statue of the Middle Kingdom: all that we see of the little girl is her head emerging from the cubic block. The tradition of statues of scribes and of reviving motifs of the past was maintained by the great Amenhotep son of Hapu, the most prominent of Amenhotep III's officials: the sculptures that represent him, like many of those of his contemporaries, are of outstanding artistic quality, with an aura of idealization and a masterly execution, although it is at times an "academic" perfection. The votive function of the statues is underlined by new

91

92

91. Cube statue of the architect Senenmut holding the princess Nefrura on his lap, from Karnak, 1470 BC. Cairo, Egyptian Museum.

92 and 95. Statue of the governor Sennefer and his wife Senay with their daughter, and, on following pages, detail, from Karnak, about 1410 BC. Cairo, Egyptian Museum.

93

94

iconographies: there are images of worshipers, of people making offerings carrying statuettes of gods, sometimes located inside a shrine behind which the offerer himself is kneeling. The accentuation of private religiosity was particularly marked in the Ramesside era, perhaps even at the expense of the emphasis usually assigned to the function exercised by the individual.

There are also numerous groups of statues, for instance of married couples, a type well known since the Old Kingdom for funerary use. But when the statuary group of a couple was admitted to a temple, it stood out and communicated other meanings, sanctioned by the concession of being located in the place of worship, like the value assigned to the family.

247

93. Statue of the architect Amenhotep son of Hapu, from Karnak, about 1360 BC. Cairo, Egyptian Museum.

94. Statue of the architect Amenhotep son of Hapu, from Karnak, about 1360 BC. Cairo, Egyptian Museum.

THE REVOLUTION OF THE AMARNA PERIOD

Toward the end of the 18th dynasty, over a period of less than twenty years, Egypt almost saw the overthrow of the foundations on which it had based its very identity: the reign of Amenhotep IV-Akhenaton produced effects of upheaval in every aspect of the civilization, even though it took the form of an attempt at religious reform. Succeeding his father Amenhotep III, he stuck to tradition at the beginning, but in the fifth year of his reign decided to abandon Thebes and found a new capital at an uninhabited site in Middle Egypt (now Tell el-Amarna); he dedicated the city to the worship of a single god, Aton, the sun disk, excluding any other deity. As is well known, the reform was a failure, but the repercussions of the "revolution" were to last a long time and affect many fields, despite the fact that the rulers who followed tried to wipe out all

memory of that moment in history and its protagonists. In every aspect, the art of that period is seen today as a phase of great innovation and a genuine break with the conventions of the past. It seems that it was the pharaoh himself who directed the artists and laid down the new rules. Before leaving Thebes, he produced an awe-inspiring "manifesto" in the form of a series of colossal statues (about 13 ft or 4 m high) erected in a building to the east of the sanctuary at Karnak, only part of which has survived the destruction wrought by his successors. No one can remain unmoved before those images of the king, with slit eyes, emaciated face, delicate bust and feminine hips with swollen thighs. It is pointless to ask whether they are realistic: the provocative effect is deliberate. They must have seemed almost blasphemous in a country whose basic principle was the veneration of tradition. Yet here was a totally new language used to convey a new vision of divine sovereignty, as well as to create, and in this it did follow tradition, a style for representing members of the royal

96

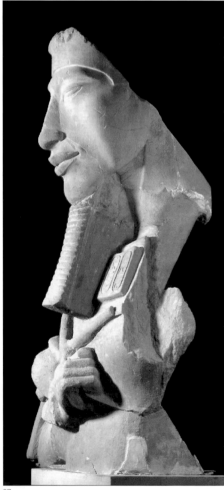

97

98

250

96. Colossal head of Akhenaton wearing the double crown, profile, about 1350 BC. Luxor, Museum of Ancient Egyptian Art.

97. Bust of Akhenaton, about 1350 BC. Paris, Musée du Louvre.

98. Fragment of colossus of Akhenaton, from Karnak, about 1350 BC. Cairo, Egyptian Museum.

99

100

family; a style that gradually spread to the monuments of private indi-viduals. By a happy chance the workshop of a sculptor called Thutmosis has been identified in the center of the city of Tell el-Amarna, along with the models and statues on which he was working, such as the famous bust of the king's wife Nefertiti. The finds show that different styles of expression coexisted: the series of heads with elongated skulls, believed to be those of the royal couple's daughters, adhere to the same con-ventions as statues of the king, who had deliberately chosen a different "ideal" from that of the past. But there are also the splendid heads of Nefertiti (who in certain reliefs cannot always be distinguished from her husband) and plaster casts of statues that show how the "exaggerated

canon" (as it has been called) could leave room for a more understated approach, which the artist took independently. We have begun with statues, but innovations were made in every field, and the abandonment of Tell el-Amarna, despite its destruction, allows us to evaluate what has survived without it having been subjected to alterations. For the one god, Aton, a great sanctuary was created that was completely open to the sky, with a series of six courtyards where nothing blocked the light, not even the lintels of doors, for which no provision was made between the pylons; even the architraves in the colonnaded courts were broken. The darkness of the inner sanctum was replaced by an altar facing the eastern horizon, perhaps surrounded by statues of the royal couple,

99-100. Copy of the bust of Queen Nefertiti in Berlin, about 1340 BC. Florence, Egyptian Museum.

legitimate officiants of the rites. Other places must have been intended for the exaltation of nature and creation, and so presumably had the pleasing appearance of a temple-garden. Tombs for the courtiers who had followed the king were cut in the rocky slopes around the new city; not unlike Theban tombs in structure, some had rooms with papyrus columns carved out of the rock and painted. But the decorative themes for the walls were completely different: all reference to the Osirian afterlife was banished and the emphasis placed on the figure of the king instead, both in his relations with the tomb's owner and in his role as guarantor of his survival. Akhenaton's own tomb (never used) was excavated in a valley to the east, about 6 miles or 10 kilometers from the city: unlike the royal tombs of the 18th dynasty, its rooms are arranged in a straight line, perhaps in keeping with solar ideology. As we have seen, this is a layout that would be adopted in the Valley of the Kings. At Tell el-Amarna, and earlier at Karnak, a new technique of con-

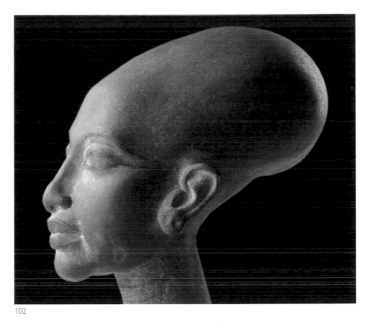

102

103

104

101. Facing page: Fragmentary head of Nefertiti, from Memphis, about 1340 BC. Cairo, Egyptian Museum.

102. Head of a princess from Tell el-Amarna, profile, about 1340 BC. Cairo, Egyptian Museum.

103. Relief with Akhenaton and Nefertiti making offerings to the god Aton, from Tell el-Amarna, about 1340 BC. Cairo, Egyptian Museum.

104. Figurine representing Akhenaton making an offering, from Tell el-Amarna, about 1340 BC. Cairo, Egyptian Museum.

struction was introduced that entailed the use of blocks of limestone or sandstone of standard size (about 21 × 10 in or 53 × 25 cm) that were easy to transport, but which had to be laid with abundant mortar. Today they are known as talatat, and thousands have been found, reutilized in other buildings after destruction of the monuments. Study of the decorations they bear still has to be completed, but an entire wall has been reconstructed in the Luxor Museum. The division into rows was eliminated and replaced by compositions with scenes that include details of daily life and curious observations in their depiction of temple activities. Striking above all, in the material recovered at or near Tell el-Amarna and in the decoration of the rock-cut tombs of officials, is the insistence on and omnipresence of the royal couple, Akhenaton and Nefertiti, sometimes accompanied by their daughters, while they perform rites or show themselves to the joyful populace, or in the intimacy of the family. They are even turned into icons for worship, in reliefs inside shrines in the courtyards of people's homes. And here we see the limitations that prevented the success of a reform for which the ground had already been prepared during Amenhotep III's reign. While Akhenaton used quite different means from his father to promote the divinity of the king, they remained centered solely on his person.

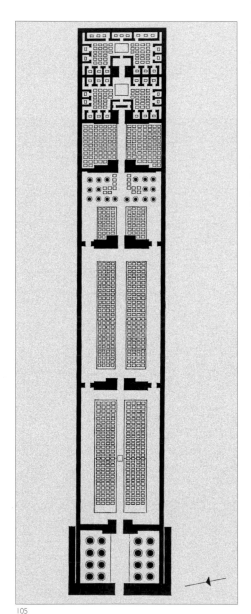

105

106

254

105. Plan of the temple of Aton at Tell el-Amarna, about 1340 BC (from C. Aldred, P. Barguet, C. Desroches Noblecourt, J. Leclant, H.W. Muller, *L'impero dei conquistatori*, Milan 1985, p. 303, fig. 379).

106. Stele with Akhenaton's family under the solar disk, 1340 BC. Cairo, Egyptian Museum.

107

108

107. Scenes in painted relief from the Temple of Akhenaton, Karnak, about 1350 BC. Luxor, Museum of Ancient Egyptian Art.

108. Relief representing Ay and Ti receiving rewards of gold from Akhenaton, from Tell el-Amarna, about 1340 BC. Cairo, Egyptian Museum.

COLOSSAL STATUE OF AKHENATON
about 1350 BC
Cairo, Egyptian Museum

SOGGETTO

Perhaps the most controversial ruler in the history of ancient Egypt was still called Amenhotep (IV for us) when he began the construction of a temple dedicated to the god Aton, outside the national sanctuary of Amon-Re at Karnak. It faced east, toward the rising sun. Destroyed by Horemheb at the end of the dynasty and by his successors, it must have had a court surrounded by twenty-eight colossal statues of the pharaoh backing onto pillars and 13-15 ft or 4-5 m high: a true "manifesto" of a new vision of divine kingship.

Deliberately shattered when it was thought that even the memory of that time had to be banished, they must have almost surpassed people's capacity to understand: the ruler once again placed himself in a superhuman dimension, as manifestation and sole interpreter of the one god, who had replaced all the others. It may have been Akhenaton himself who dictated the rules in this phase of "exaggeration," and Bak was the artist to whom he entrusted its execution.

COMPOSITION

All the colossi represent Akhenaton standing and in the guise of a living man. In only one case is he nude and sexless, androgynous. Every emblem of sovereignty is underlined. Crowns and headdresses are combined: the *nemes* with the double crown, or the bulky *khat* headdress, or the four feathers of the god Shu, firstborn of the Sun according to myth. On the forehead the uraeus, on the chin the royal beard; the hands are crossed to hold the scepters; the cartouches on the wrists and the arms repeat, like a sign of affiliation, the royal names of the god Aton.

To embody the divine dimension, his features are distorted: the eyes are turned into slits, the light erodes the gaunt face with its prominent lips and chin.

The bust is emaciated, the belly swollen and the thick thighs are supported by scrawny legs: it is a striking and sensational negation of the traditional ideal in Egypt. It is likely that the definition of divine sovereignty derives from the whole series of statues and rests on the primordial creative force embodied in the king, in this king.

UNFINISHED HEAD OF NEFERTITI
about 1340 BC
Cairo, Egyptian Museum

SUBJECT

Speaking of Nefertiti means taking on a legend: no woman of antiquity, except perhaps Cleopatra, has been so celebrated and is so familiar to the public, solely by virtue of the works of art that are assumed to portray her. She was designated by her husband as his indispensable female counterpart in the program of religious reform he had launched and was imposing on his followers.

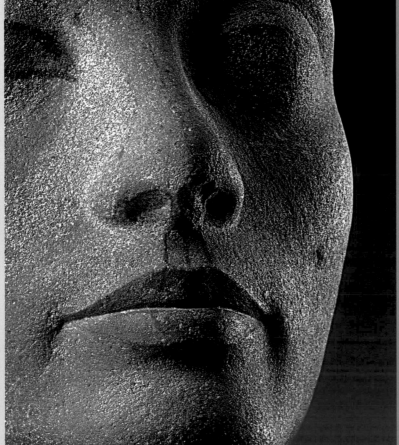

This head was found in 1932 at Tell el-Amarna, the city founded by Akhenaton as a center for worship of the Aton, the solar disk. It was in the workshop of the sculptor Thutmosis, who may have been Bak's successor in the far from simple task of putting the principles elaborated by the pharaoh into concrete form.

COMPOSITION

We do not know for certain who Nefertiti's parents were: she may have had ties with the influential family of Ay, Tutankhamun's successor. She was the mother of Akhenaton's six daughters, and perhaps of Tutankhamun too. The quartzite head may have been kept as a model for other statues. It was intended for a composite statue, made out of different materials, which was an innovation of that time.

The effort to create a harmonious effect, in contrast to the "exaggerated" part of the program, is evident. The protuberance on the head must have held the crown, probably the one typical of Nefertiti, a tall tiara that spread out at the top and that few could afford. Two lines mark its edge on the forehead,

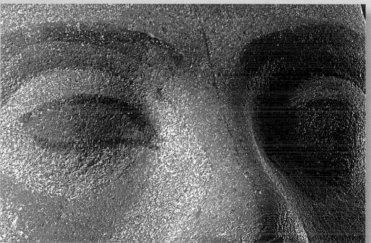

while others mark the center of the face and the shape of the eyes and eyebrows.

The oval of the face is perfect and, even though the eyes are not there, she already seems to be gazing into unknown depths.

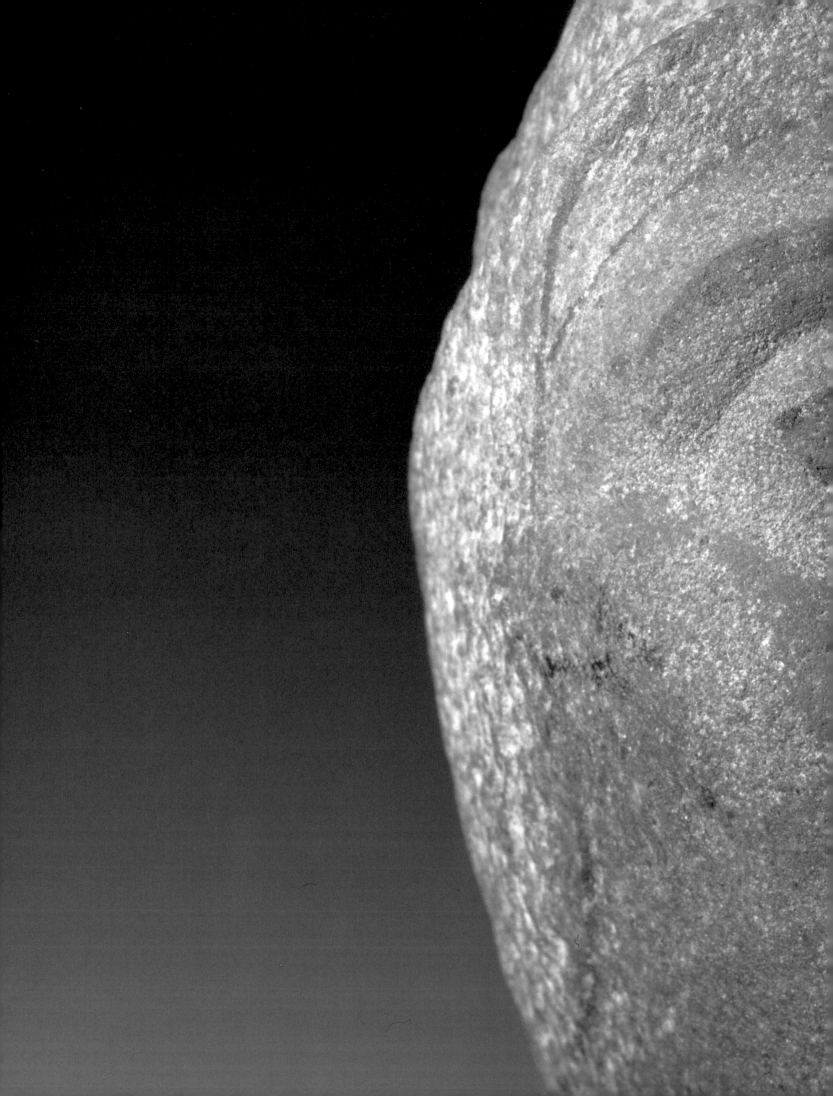

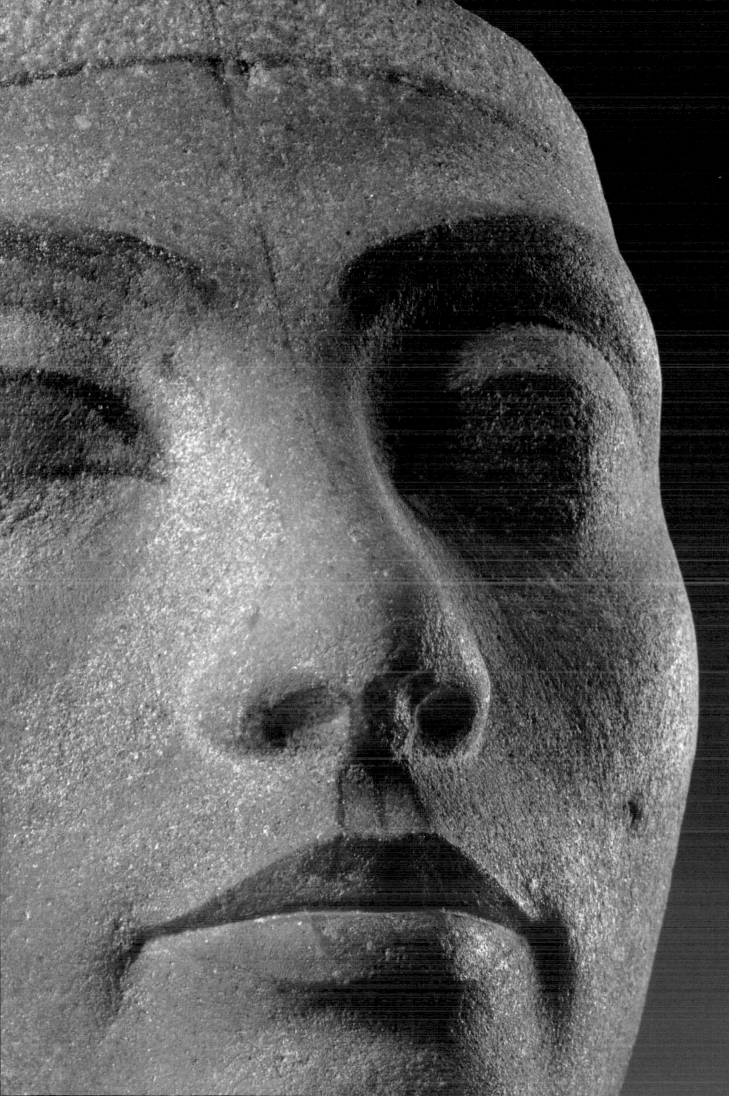

GRAVE GOODS AND JEWELRY

The Theban necropolis has yielded numerous finds that often reflect an exquisite taste in the production of objects intended for burial in tombs.

As we know, the range of these objects could be very wide, and they were associated with an equally varied symbology.

The fundamental element was of course the sarcophagus, or in some cases the series of wooden caskets in human shape, one set inside the other: known as anthropoid coffins, these symbolically identified the deceased with the god Osiris.

At the end of the 18th dynasty the lids of Canopic jars assumed the form that was to become standard, with each reproducing the head of the son of Horus with which it was identified and under

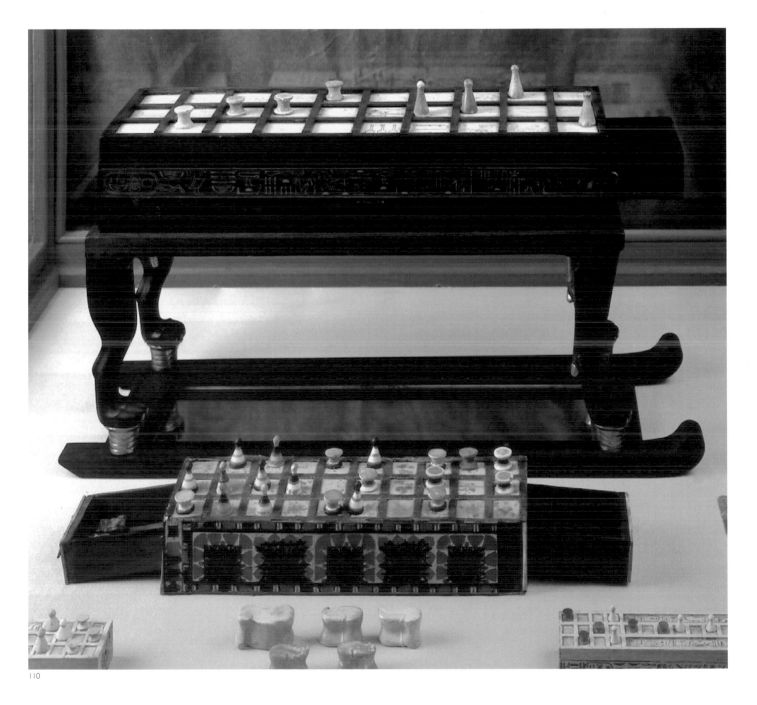

110

109. Facing page: Chest with Canopic jars, from Tutankhamun's tomb, about 1330 BC. Cairo, Egyptian Museum.

110. Board game, from Tutankhamun's tomb, 1330 BC. Cairo, Egyptian Museum.

whose protection it was placed (the head of a man, jackal, falcon or baboon).

Outstanding in their variety were the amulets, intended to provide magical protection for the parts of the body on which they were placed; they were believed to have the same effect on the living. Made out of semiprecious stones or faience, usually of a turquoise color, they were sometimes fitted with a ring so they could be hung around the neck.

Among the most common was the *udjat* or sacred eye, reproducing a human eye and eyebrow along with the markings of a hawk's eye; its meaning ("whole, intact," which is also what the amulet guaranteed) refers to the myth of Thoth's healing of the eye of the falcon Horus, after Seth had torn it out in their fight for dominion of the earth.

The power of the scarab stemmed from solar mythology: in the hieroglyphic script it was equivalent to the verb "to become, to come into existence," and was used to represent the new sun rising in the morning.

It is probably not correct to regard these objects as a form of art, however fine they may be. Looking at the intact grave goods of the architect Kha and his wife Merit, now in the Egyptian Museum of Turin, the allusion to everyday life is so immediate, and even moving, that it is not hard to appreciate the decorative qualities of each element; qualities we are able to grasp even without understanding their significance.

Perhaps the aims and the intensity of art are more evident when we examine some more complicated sets of grave goods as a whole: while trying to analyze them, we also have to consider their

111

111. Sarcophagus of the pharaoh Thutmosis IV in his tomb in the Valley of the Kings, about 1390 BC.

112. Pendant, from
Tutankhamun's tomb,
1330 BC. Cairo,
Egyptian Museum.

113. Facing page: The god
Anubis on a litter in the
form of a shrine, from
Tutankhamun's tomb,
1330 BC. Cairo,
Egyptian Museum.

114. Gilded shrine, from
Tutankhamun's tomb,
1330 BC. Cairo,
Egyptian Museum.

115

115. Lid of a Canopic jar, from Tutankhamun's tomb, about 1330 BC. Cairo, Egyptian Museum.

116. Facing page: Lid of a Canopic jar, perhaps made for Kiya, Akhenaton's second wife, and then used for someone else's burial in **the Valley of the Kings, about 1340 BC. Cairo, Egyptian Museum.**

117

118

117. Perfume jar
reproducing the emblem
of the union of the Two
Lands, with the heraldic
plants of Upper and
Lower Egypt, from

Tutankhamun's tomb,
about 1330 BC. Cairo,
Egyptian Museum.

118. The goddess Selkis
protecting the side
of a casket, from
Tutankhamun's tomb,
1330 BC. Cairo,
Egyptian Museum.

119

overall effect. Faced with the contents of Tutankhamun's tomb, for example, our admiration may be immediate, but our understanding needs support. Starting with an "interpretation" of the jewelry, we uncover a dense mesh of symbologies that prepare the pharaoh for regeneration; the message is entrusted not just to the value assigned to the colors (as has already been pointed out), but also to the use of precious, unalterable metal, to the choice of motifs and to further levels of interpretation based on their combination. The "density" of the significance of many pieces is easy to guess: it is plain that no detail is purely decorative. And yet is often equally easy to forget about the meaning and let ourselves be captivated by the mastery of the work, by the unusual compositions, by the evocative or simply delightful images, like the small figure of a gilded protective goddess who has her back turned to us.

119. Casket decorated with scenes of battle, showing the pharaoh on his chariot, from Tutankhamun's tomb, 1330 BC. Cairo, Egyptian Museum.

MASK OF TUTANKHAMUN
about 1330 BC
Cairo, Egyptian Museum

SUBJECT

The spectacular discovery of Tutankhamun's tomb, which bears the last number (62) in the Valley of the Kings, is perhaps the most famous adventure in archeology. The richness and splendor of the grave goods of the young pharaoh, who favored a return to traditional religion after Amenhotep IV-Akhenaton's attempt at "monotheistic" reform, filled the pages of newspapers for a long time after that momentous day of November 4, 1922, stirring people's imagination and triggering a revival of enthusiasm for ancient Egypt.

That tomb with its abnormal layout was heaped with an incredible quantity of objects, the goods that were to accompany him on his journey of regeneration. A set of four gilded shrines held the sarcophagus, which was made of yellow quartzite and contained three anthropoid coffins, the last one of solid gold, the substance of which the flesh of the gods was made.

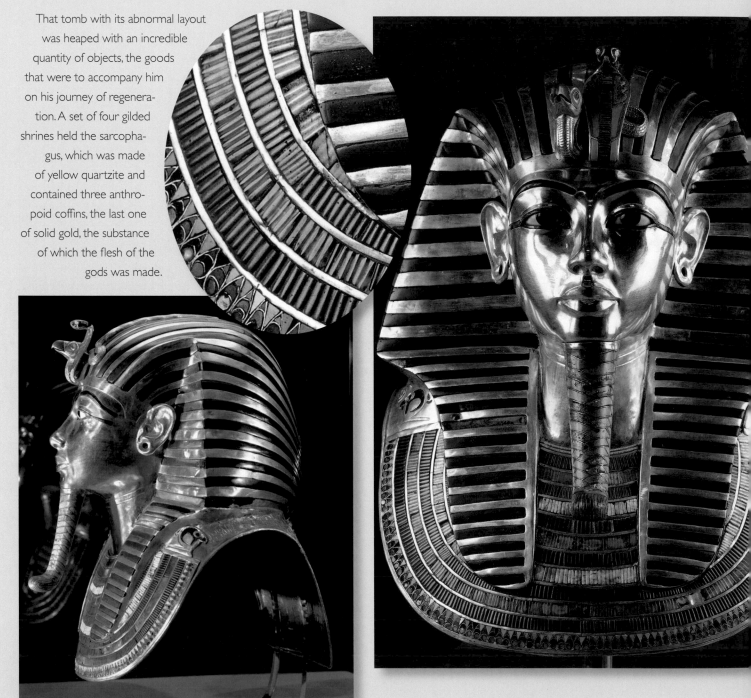

Inside it lay the mummified body of Tutankhamun, its head covered by the mask.

COMPOSITION

Very hard to photograph because of its gleaming surfaces, the mask represents Tutankhamun's youthful face in an idealized style that indicates a return to tradition in the world of art as well. The *nemes* headdress, wrapped tightly under the nape of the neck, has blue stripes.

The diadem consists of goddesses in the form of a vulture and a cobra, representing Upper and Lower Egypt respectively; the gold is inlaid with cornelian, lapis lazuli, quartz and turquoise glass paste.

The eyebrows and outlines of the eyelids are made of lapis lazuli while the eyes are reproduced in obsidian and quartz, with a touch of red at the corners.

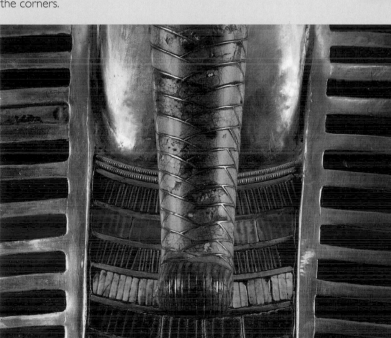

The divine beard, resembling that of the god Osiris, is an inlay of turquoise glass paste in gold; the collar is composed of elements of lapis lazuli, quartz and green feldspar. The text of a chapter from the *Book of the Dead*, specifically dedicated to protection of the head, is engraved in the gold on the back.

TUTANKHAMUN'S THRONE
about 1330 BC
Cairo, Egyptian Museum

SUBJECT
Among the marvels that Howard Carter found in tomb no. 62 of the Valley of the Kings in 1922 was this wooden chair, covered with gold and inlaid with silver, glass paste and semiprecious stone.

The legs are in the shape of feline paws and two lion's heads are set in front of the arms, to guard the pharaoh.

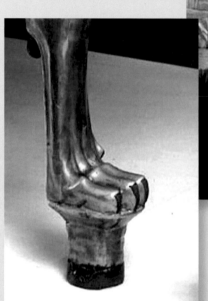

On the side panels two winged cobras wearing the double crown of Upper and Lower Egypt protect the cartouche bearing the name of the king.

On the side panels two winged cobras wearing the double crown of Upper and Lower Egypt protect the cartouche bearing the name of the king. The back is decorated with a scene in the Amarna style: the pharaoh is seated on a chair in a relaxed manner, with his arm resting on the back, while his wife spreads ointment on his shoulder from a pot. Above them is set Aton, the solar disk. Its rays, terminating in hands, are bearers of life: in fact they are holding out the hieroglyphic symbol of the *ankh* to the pharaoh and his queen.

COMPOSITION

The scene of the main panel is perfectly in keeping with the style of the Amarna period: the pharaoh is shown in a moment of his private life. Even the representation of movement is typical of the style of this period: the bands that hang down from the king's crown, as well as the queen's belt and the bands behind her back, are undulated to convey the idea of cloth stirred by the wind. The level of accuracy attained in the definition of even the smallest details is astonishing.

The king's clothing and jewelry are faithfully reproduced by means of an inlay of tiny and perfectly shaped pieces of semiprecious stone. Silver has been used for the fabric of the clothes, producing a highly luminous effect. Even with materials like metal the artist has succeeded in conveying the softness of the forms: the sinuous body of Queen Ankhesenamun is visible between the folds of the drapery, as if glimpsed through a linen dress.

GRAVE GOODS

For the Egyptians the next world was a fundamental dimension of existence and required detailed planning during their lifetime. Guaranteeing survival after death through the provision of whatever might be needed in the other world was a concern from the days of their youth; thus those who could afford it took care to prepare their tomb and its contents in such a way that everything would be ready when required.

The Egyptians believed that what awaited them at the moment of death was another life in the next world, as real in every sense as the one they lived on earth, and much longer. This is why materials thought to last forever, like stone, or extremely precious and pure substances like gold were used for graves and their contents.

CANOPIC JARS

During the process of mummification some of the internal organs removed from the body were embalmed separately and only the heart was put back in its place. The other organs regarded as fundamental (liver, lungs, stomach and intestines) were preserved inside cylindrical vases, known as Canopic jars. The protectors of the organs were the four sons of Horus, and so the lids of the jars were often given the form of the heads of these four gods, in their zoomorphic or anthropomorphic aspect.

USHABTI

These are small statuettes of servants represented with their bodies wrapped in bandages and their arms crossed on their breast. The ushabti had a magical value because they acted as a substitute for the deceased in the menial tasks required of them in the afterlife.

In fact their bodies were inscribed with a spell from the *Book of the Dead* with which the deceased charged the statuette to answer for him whenever he was asked to perform particular tasks: in fact the word *ushabti* means "answerer." Some of the statuettes hold hoes or baskets, the implements needed to carry out their duties.

I. Lid of Canopic jar, from Tutankhamun's tomb, about 1330 BC. Cairo, Egyptian Museum.

II. *Ushabti* statuettes, from Tutankhamun's tomb, about 1330 BC. Cairo, Egyptian Museum.

EGYPTIAN ART

III.

III. Canopic jar with the head of Imset, one of the four sons of Horus, detail. Cairo, Egyptian Museum.

AMULETS

Amulets were an integral part of the set of magical objects buried with the deceased: they were symbols of the forces that were supposed to protect them and guarantee their health. The majority of these amulets were placed between the bandages during mummification.

Their specific function, as protectors of a particular part of the body, was often clarified by hieroglyphic inscriptions that increased their efficacy. They could take various forms: the talismans considered most powerful were in the shapes of a scarab, of the *djed* pillar, a symbol of permanence and durability, and of the *ankh*, symbol of life.

JEWELRY

The grave goods included jewelry that was often of great aesthetic value, but whose primary role was to perform a magical function.

Necklaces and pectorals served to protect some parts of the body of the deceased that were considered weak, like the neck, or particularly important organs like the heart. The most precious jewelry was made from gems, gold, silver and enamel, and the most common forms were the symbol of life and health and the scarab. Frequent among royal jewelry were the cartouche of the ruler or the cobra and vulture, emblems of kingship.

PERSONAL EFFECTS AND FOOD

Along with offerings made to the *ka* of the deceased, pots and dishes for food and actual provisions, like bread and grain, were placed in the tomb. Other objects of everyday use were included in the grave goods, such as containers for cosmetics, often finely engraved, boxes of writing implements or pots for ointments made of semiprecious stone.

IV

IV. Scarab of Amenhotep
III, about 1360 BC. Rome,
Museo Gregoriano Egizio,
Vatican.

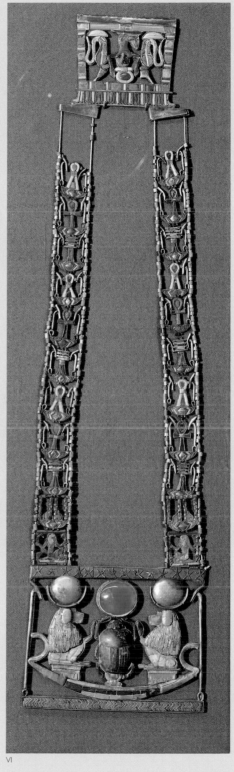

V

VI

V. Unguentarium in the form of a lion, from Tutankhamun's tomb, about 1330 BC. Cairo, Egyptian Museum.

VI. Necklace with scarab and baboons, from Tutankhamun's tomb, about 1330 BC. Cairo, Egyptian Museum.

EGYPTIAN ART

5. The Late Period: in Search of the Origins

I n the last phase of the history of ancient Egypt, the Nile Valley lost political ground to the Delta, where the Ramessides had already had their residence. Various locations were embellished with monuments in what was a genuine state, with its capital at Tanis, separate from the southern realm of Thebes. In the confused situation created by dynastic disputes, Nubia also gained its independence. But then, profoundly Egyptianized, it set out to conquer the country that used to rule it and succeeded in reunifying it. Not for long though: in the Near East the Assyrian state was on the rise, and its hordes seized control of Egypt. However, they were driven out by the prince from Sais they had chosen to act as their governor: the Saite dynasty ushered in the last era of independence and prosperity before the country fell under the rule of the Persians, who were only to lose control of Egypt for short periods until it was conquered by Alexander the Great. Egypt would then share the same destiny as his empire. Amidst these confused and dramatic events the production of art continued at a high level, looking to the past for its models.

2

3

1. Facing page: Statuary group of the official Psamtik protected by the goddess Hathor in the form of a cow, from his tomb at Saqqarah, about 520 BC. Cairo, Egyptian Museum.

2. Outer wooden sarcophagus of Tjesreperet, wet nurse of the daughter of the pharaoh Taharqa, 690-664 BC, from her tomb at Thebes. Florence, Museo Archeologico.

3. Head of a statue, perhaps of the Kushite pharaoh Shebitku, 702-690 BC. Cairo, Egyptian Museum.

FUNERARY AND RELIGIOUS ARCHITECTURE AT TANIS AND THEBES

After the 20th dynasty the "legitimate" rulers left Thebes in the hands of the powerful high priests of Amon, who soon assumed the prerogative of pharaohs, and moved their court to Tanis in the eastern Delta, turning it into what was almost a museum city. They built a large temple for Amon, to serve as a northern counterpart to Karnak. Today its ruins, the only part of the immense hill to have been explored by archeologists, offer a spectacular view of crumbled obelisks, fallen colossi and broken columns. The name of Rameses II is everywhere: in fact about 12 miles or 20 kilometers away there was a lot of material waiting to be reused, at the city of Pi-Ramesse which may have been abandoned because of a shift in a branch of the river. Rameses himself had brought monuments of the past from important centers of the Delta, like Bubastis and perhaps even Heliopolis, to beautify his capital. Archeological exploration has now confirmed the destruction of

Pi-Ramesse, but it can be said to have been "transferred" to the new capital at Tanis. Statues and sphinxes from the Middle Kingdom, twenty-three obelisks from the New Kingdom and gigantic statues of Rameses were reutilized in the Temple of Amon. At the beginning of the Second World War, the tombs of several rulers were found inside the temple precinct. A new type of royal tomb had been introduced following the abandonment of the Valley of the Kings, and it is presumed that it remained in use. The archeological evidence stops at Tanis, in the Third Intermediate Period, but the Greek historian Herodotus confirms its use by the Saite 26th dynasty. The superstructures, perhaps used for worship, have vanished, and the underground part (just beneath the surface, to avoid the infiltration of water) is reduced to small burial chambers, used for members of the family or notables as well. The fact that in some cases the walls of the chamber are finely decorated with scenes from the classical repertoire for a king, and that there is evidence of precious materials used for the preservation of his body, cannot conceal the truth that the vision of the ruler had changed

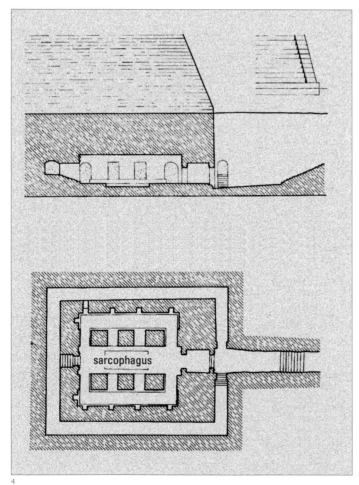

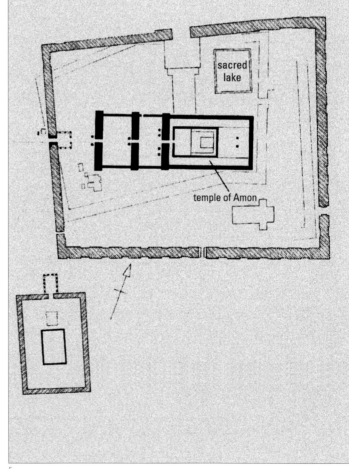

4

5

4. Plan and section of the chambers inside the Pyramid of Taharqa at Nuri, 690-664 BC (from D. Arnold, *The Encyclopaedia of Ancient Egyptian Architecture*, London 2003, p. 237).

5. Plan of the sacred area of Tanis (from D. Arnold, *The Encyclopaedia of Ancient Egyptian Architecture*, London 2003, p. 238).

284

profoundly. The Nubian kings of the 25th dynasty adopted the epitome of royal monuments, the pyramid, in the necropolises of El-Kurru and Nuri near Napata, their distant capital located almost at the fourth cataract of the Nile. King Taharqa even gave his burial chamber the shape of an Osirian tomb: it was a reference to the origins that may well have been understood, but now seemed empty of content. At Thebes too there are examples of the new funerary tradition: in the precinct at Medinet Habu, the Temple of Rameses III, shrines were constructed for the cult of the "divine worshipers," the priestly title of queens and princesses of the 25th and 26th dynasty, buried not far away in chambers deep underground. However, they could not have rivaled the astonishing tombs that the administrators who served the "divine worshipers" had built for themselves in the Assasif necropolis, opposite Deir el-Bahri. There are about ten of these structures: considered among the most amazing ever to have been constructed in Egypt, they have been described as palace tombs. Only in a few cases has part of the superstructure been preserved: built of unfired brick, this had a

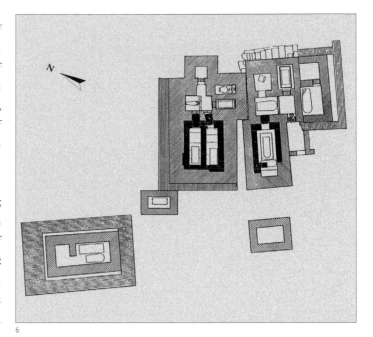

6

7

6. Plan of the royal tombs of Tanis (from R. Schulz, M. Seidel, *Egypt*, Cologne 1998, p. 281, fig. 15).

7. Tomb of Sheshonk, superstructure of unfired brick, about 575 BC. Assasif, Thebes.

pylon and high walls surrounding the opening onto the surface of the solar court, the only room in the underground complex open to the sky. The underground part of these tombs is often immense, sometimes on more than one level, and comprises at least one vestibule, the porticoed solar court and a pillared hall as well as the burial chambers. The decoration, as might be expected, is rich and carefully studied: it clearly reflects a desire to return to tradition through an approach that can be called antiquarian, and that focuses in particular on the choice of the texts, drawn from all the funerary literature created by priests up to then. The decorative program makes skillful use of internal references, correspondences, and even the possibilities offered by the Egyptian script, which can be oriented in the direction opposite to that in which it is read, taking those who know how to follow it on a suggestive and sophisticated journey.

8

9

8. Tomb of Sheshonk, boundary wall of unfired brick with niches, about 575 BC. Assasif, Thebes.

9. Tomb of Montuemhat, solar court, about 660 BC. Assasif, Thebes.

THE ENLARGEMENT OF THE SANCTUARY AT KARNAK AND THE FLOURISHING OF THE TEMPLES

The sanctuary at Karnak underwent substantial enlargements during the reign of Sheshonk I, the ruler from Bubastis who founded the 22nd dynasty. He laid out the first courtyard, adorned with porticoes to the north and south and incorporating a small temple from the end of the 19th dynasty and the front part of that of Rameses III. The sphinxes of Rameses II, which formed the "avenue" in the middle, were moved to the sides, where they can still be seen. The pylon, the temple's entrance, may have been commenced during the last indigenous dynasty, the 30th (when the whole complex was surrounded by a wall with monumental portals), but was never completed. The Nubian rulers, devoted to Amon, could not fail to leave their mark on his main temple: during his long reign Taharqa had a building constructed for the cult connected with the sacred lake, as well as a monumental kiosk for the processional boat in the first courtyard, with elegant open papyrus columns, linked at the bottom by screens and perhaps unroofed. Building activity was intense everywhere, but time has not always spared even imposing structures, especially in the Delta, and so our knowledge remains patchy. In addition, systematic archeological exploration is still in its early stages. For example, the city of Sais, capital of the 26th dynasty but of ancient origin, must have had a large temple for the goddess Neith, housing the sepulchral crypts of the rulers (as at Tanis), but today we can hardly do more than indicate the place where the city once stood. Only a little better is the situation at

10

**10. Bubastis Portal
in the first courtyard
of the temple,
about 925 BC. Karnak.**

**11. Kiosk of Taharqa in
front of the second pylon,
Temple of Amon-Re,
690-664 BC. Karnak.**

Bubastis, where it is possible that some structures for the cat goddess Bast had already been built by Khufu. Here at least we can recognize the projects of the Late Period, carried out by the pharaohs of Bubastis and all the way up to the last native king, Nectanebo II (30th dynasty). Isolation has favored the preservation of a small temple of Amon in the Kharga oasis that may have been built in the late 26th dynasty but was decorated by the Persian "pharaoh" Darius I, in the 27th dynasty. The original construction presented several innovations: a pronaos of papyrus columns linked by screens, then a hypostyle hall onto which opened the sanctuary and lateral shrines and the stairs leading to the roof. A set of rooms on the upper floor was also used in worship. During the 29th dynasty another hypostyle hall was added at the front and then Nectanebo I (30th dynasty) built the surrounding wall,

12

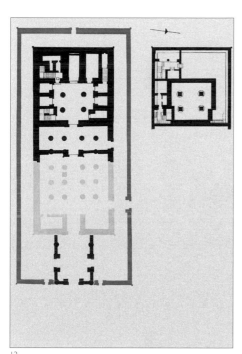

13

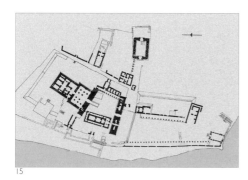

15

14

12. Temple of Ibis, 6th-4th century BC. Kharga Oasis.

13. Plans of the Temple of Ibis at Kharga from the Persian to the Ptolemaic period, 6th-3rd century BC (from C. Aldred, F. Daumas, C. Desroches-Noblecourt, *I Faraoni. L'Egitto del crepuscolo*, Milan 1981, p. 305, figs. 356-7).

14. Kiosk of Trajan, 2nd century AD. Philae (now moved to the island of Agilkia).

15. Plan of the complex of temples at Philae (from C. Aldred, F. Daumas, C. Desroches-Noblecourt, *I Faraoni. L'Egitto del crepuscolo*, Milan 1981, p. 309, fig. 371).

as he had done at Karnak. This had an access kiosk whose columns, like those inside, had capitals of the composite type, with a variety of decorations (different kinds of papyrus, palmettes), on a bell-shaped base. This type was to prove popular in later major constructions in Egypt, during the Greco-Roman era. Nectanebo I himself used a wide range of capitals in the pavilion he had built in what may once have been the most striking location in the whole of Egypt, the Temple of Isis on the island of Philae. This is the oldest construction to have survived in one of the most sacred places, and one that subsequently became a stronghold of Paganism. It was not until 535 that the temple was turned into a church, dedicated to St. Stephen.

The Greek Ptolemies and after them the Roman emperors, first Augustus and then the Antonines, added their own constructions to the temple at Philae, dismantling the earlier ones built by the Nubian and Saite rulers. Indeed one Roman building, the so-called Kiosk of Trajan, was regarded as an example of Egyptian art until the beginning of the 19th century. In Nectanebo I's pavilion capitals with a variety of ornaments are surmounted, in daring fashion, by another capital with the faces of Hathor-Isis. It is worth mentioning another place of worship whose history was to extend beyond the age of the pharaohs, reflecting changes in religious beliefs and practices: the Serapeum at Saqqarah. The sacred place already existed at the time of Amenhotep III, with large catacombs used for the burial of the Apis bulls, animals sacred to Ptah of Memphis but also associated with Osiris and, like the god, mummified on their death. Between the 19th and 26th dynasty the so-called "small gallery," 223 ft or 68 m long, was in use here, while Psamtik I inaugurated the large gallery, 650-ft or 198-m long, onto which open the crypts with gigantic granite sarcophagi for the bulls, deposited in them until the end of the Ptolemaic age.

On the outside, it was Nectanebo I (30th dynasty) who built important structures, not yet completely investigated, that were extended with a long avenue of sphinxes.

16

**16. Temple of Isis,
colonnade and first pylon,
4th century BC - 2nd
century AD. Philae
(now moved to the island
of Agilkia).**

17

18

EGYPTIAN ART

17. Temple of Isis,
4th century BC - 2nd
century AD. Philae
(now moved to the island
of Agilkia).

18. Temple of Isis,
columns with capitals
with the faces of Hathor-
Isis, 4th century BC.
Philae (now moved
to the island of Agilkia).

STATUE OF ISIS
about 520 BC
Cairo, Egyptian Museum

The seated statue of Isis be-longs to a series of schist stat-ues from Saqqarah, found by Auguste Mariette in the tomb of the scribe Psamtik in 1863.

Isis, wife of the god of the underworld Osiris, is the goddess of magic, but here is also repre-sented in the guise of queen, as the uraeus on her forehead testifies.

The goddess usually carries on her head the hieroglyphic symbol of her own name, the throne. However, she is frequently assimilated with the goddess Hathor and assumes her attributes, as is the case with the headdress formed of two cow horns framing the solar disk.

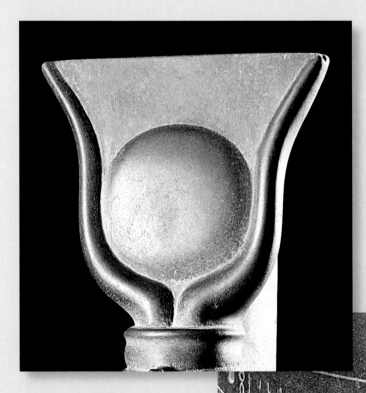

The position is the typical one, since the Old Kingdom, for statues of seated women, with the hands placed on the knees, the right one holding the *ankh*, the symbol of life.

On the base, slightly rounded at the front, is inscribed the votive formula of the deceased Psamtik, client of the work.

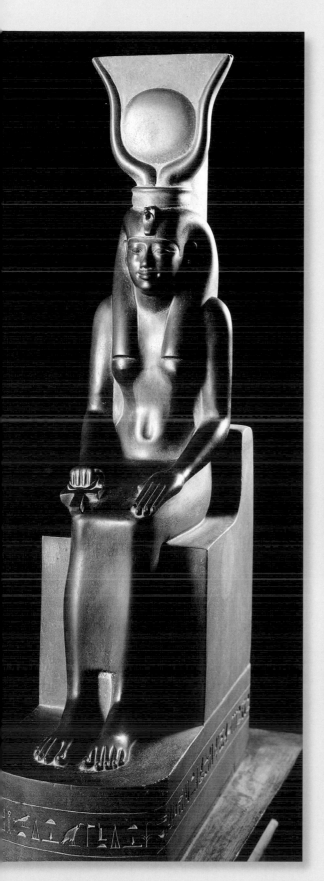

COMPOSITION

The intact statue, found exactly as it had been left 2500 years ago, is unique in its excellent state of preservation but highly representative of the production of statuary in the 26th dynasty. The way the black stone is worked is designed to produce a precise aesthetic effect: the curves are perfectly smooth, while the handling of the surfaces almost creates the impression that the stone is soft. The forms are outlined by the light which, reflected by the shiny surface, looks as if it is given off by the stone itself.

The choice of schist, and even the particular technique, were not accidental but harked back to works from an earlier age which the artist was certainly trying to emulate. Thus the perfection of this statue is worthy of a goddess; even the expression on the graceful and delicate face is aloof, gazing beyond the human sphere.

THE CHANGE: THE NEW CANON OF PROPORTIONS

For twenty centuries, from the threshold of the Old Kingdom up until the Late Period, Egyptian artists had adhered to a canon of proportions in their two-dimensional representations of the human figure that required them to comply with a strict mathematical relationship. Only in the most difficult phases of the country's history had contact been lost with this tradition: in particular this had occurred at moments of breakdown of its political unity, the so-called Intermediate Periods. The Amarna period had also seen a change in style, at the behest of Akhenaton. In each of these cases, however, on the reestablishment of political and social calm artists had gone back to the past to recover the techniques, the inspiration and the rules that had been temporarily lost.

It was during the 26th dynasty that the first and only substantial change in the system of reference created at the time of the Old Kingdom took place. The canon of proportions laid down that the standing human figure had to be inserted in a grid eighteen squares high, from the base of the foot to the hairline: in the 26th dynasty this grid was abruptly modified and the grid was extended to twenty-one squares.

It is thought that there were many different reasons for this change, but it is hard to believe artists had lost touch with tradition and then worked out a new frame of reference. In part it was a sort of adjustment of the system of measurement, from the small cubit to the royal cubit. In fact these two units differed in length, with the first measuring six palms, the second seven: the figure, in this way, was still inserted in a system with a height of three cubits, even though the royal cubit was nearly 3 in or about 7 cm longer. This unit of measurement was utilized almost exclusively in architecture and it is unlikely that it was just a simple conversion from one system of reference to another. It is probable that the adoption of the royal cubit should be interpreted in a theological sense, since the number seven has strong symbolic values, especially in the funerary and religious sphere with which the representations were connected.

19

20

19. Statue of Nekhthorheb, high dignitary of the pharaoh Psamtik II, about 590 BC. Paris, Musée du Louvre.

20. Basalt head representing a queen, about 664-525 BC. Glasgow, Burrell Collection.

21. Small bronze representing the sacred bull Apis, about 664-525 BC. Private collection.

ANIMALS IN ART

Ancient Egypt has left us splendid images of the animal world that often surprise us by their lack of conventionality. This was partly due to the careful observation of nature by artists, who found an inexhaustible source of inspiration in it, but above all it stemmed from the high symbolic value accorded to animals in Egyptian religion.

In pictures of animals realism and abstraction are fused in images that have the incisiveness of the detailed representation and the essentiality of the symbol. Hence those elements and those details that are considered necessary are depicted with extreme accuracy, while the less significant features, especially of the body, can sometimes be neglected or sketched in a few brushstrokes.

Animals are represented on the basis of their links with sovereignty or with particular deities, but also appear as ordinary animals, for example in the scenes of daily life painted on the walls of the tombs.

Contrary to what might be thought, it was not just animals regarded as "noble," like the lion and falcon, that were connected with the world of gods and kings: alongside the falcon of the god Horus, the lioness of the goddess Bastet or the ibis of the god Thoth, we find the simple goose, as symbol of the god Amon, the principal deity of the New Kingdom, and even the scarab or dung beetle, as emblem of the sun and of metamor-

I. Bas-relief with two
vultures. Cairo,
Egyptian Museum.

II. Scarab with heron,
from Tutankhamun's tomb,
about 1330 BC.
Private collection.

III.

III. Fresco depicting a
garden with a fishpond,
from Nebamun's tomb
at Thebes, about 1350 BC.
London, British Museum.

EGYPTIAN ART

IV

IV. Pectoral of Rameses II
with falcon's wings, ram's
head, uraeus and vulture,
about 1250 BC. Paris,
Musée du Louvre.

phosis. The scarab forms a ball of dung in which it lays its eggs. Thus new scarabs are born out of the dung: this ability to transform the humblest of materials into new forms of life became a symbol of metamorphosis and of the different manifestations of the reality.

Curiously, the horse, an animal fundamental to the development of the civilizations of the Near East, played no part in Egyptian religion. Not introduced until after the period of formation of the civilization in the 5th millennium, this animal did not assume a significant role in religious symbology. However, its image was closely linked to that of the warrior ruler of the New Kingdom, who is shown routing his enemies on his chariot drawn by a pair of rearing horses. In other contexts, such as the scenes of everyday life that adorn tombs, the animals depicted are simply companions of daily existence and sources of food. This is the case with cattle, associated with the goddess Hathor, but also with the geese of Amon, often represented bound by their wings while carried as an offering to the deceased.

We also find images of dangerous animals like the cobra, which is the symbol of kingship *par excellence*, and at the same time one of peril: Apopis, the enemy that threatened the nighttime journey of the sun god, was in fact represented as an enormous serpent, with huge coils.

V

V. Relief representing the offerings at the Opet festival, detail, about 14th-12th century BC. Luxor, Temple.

GUARDIAN LIONS
about 370 BC
Rome, Museo Gregoriano Egizio, Vatican

SUBJECT

The entrances of temples, palaces and avenues were regarded as places to be protected, in so far as they were passages from the dimension of ordinary life to the sacred premises of the residence of the pharaoh or the deity. Consequently a pair of guardian lions often placed in defense of gates and doors, with the aim of controlling access to the divine place. The splendid pair of crouching lions now in the Museo Gregoriano Egizio in Rome dates from the reign of Nectanebo I.

The bodies of the animals, perfectly modeled in the dark stone, are portrayed in a relaxed position, with no hint of aggressiveness or tension; the heads, on the other hand, give them an alert and watchful air.

The tails, which in this type of statue usually run along the animal's hind leg, are positioned in this case on the base, as a supplementary decoration to the hieroglyphs with the name of the pharaoh and a votive inscription.

COMPOSITION

In ancient Egypt the lion was a symbol of royalty and strongly connected with sun worship. The animal's strength determined its association with the figure of the king, and both defended the country from possible external attack. As the numerous statues of lions, commencing with the sphinx, bear witness, the Egyptian artist had a deep understanding of his subject.

In this work too we can see the masterly handling of the body, in the representation of both the muscles and the typical posture of a feline. Only the mane is deliberately simplified, to the point where it becomes a geometric disk surrounding the lion's muzzle; the locks are represented summarily by wavy lines and the mane as a whole has no volume, hanging softly like a piece of cloth.

STATUARY AND THE ECLECTIC REVIVAL OF TRADITION

In the last, long phase of the pharaonic age different traditions encountered and confronted one another, but with a common denominator: the rediscovery and recovery of identity. In the production of statues, without doubt remarkable, this had uneven results: the tradition seems to have been invigorated by new contributions, revitalized in its substance and made relevant to the present. But in some cases it appears that this was done only formally, as an end in itself, and the models of the past were reproduced faithfully, as if all that was sought in them was the nostalgic revival of a long-lost grandeur. Not a few works of art, for example, have been dated to the Middle Kingdom and then on careful examination

23

24

22. Facing page: Figure of a man called the Dattari Statue, 381-362 BC. New York, Brooklyn Museum of Art.

23. Statue of Amonirdis I, "divine worshiper" of Amon, from Karnak, about 700 BC. Cairo, Egyptian Museum.

24. Cube statue of the priest Ankhpakhered, from Karnak, about 680 BC. Cairo, Egyptian Museum.

turned out to have been created over 1000 years later. Even in this formal research, however, it is possible to discern something new, something all of its own: the search for perfection and the attention to plays of light hint at a different attitude toward the object and toward art. The first thing to note is that what had been the primary function of statues, the funerary one, has vanished: now it is the votive statue in a temple that provides a guarantee of protection and of the continuity of the rites. In addition, statues of rulers are rarer than in the past, and in any case no longer outsize. No one believes that the standing colossus re-erected in the first courtyard at Karnak is really an effigy of Pinudjem I, "High Priest of Amon" (21st dynasty): although it bears his name, the statue had probably been usurped and actually represents one of the usual suspects, Amenhotep III or Rameses II. At present finds from the period of the 21st to 24th dynasties are scarce, but a few surprising ones have come down to us from the 22nd dynasty, among other things displaying great skill in the working of metal. As well as images of deities that are small in size but genuine masterpieces, we have figures of female personages in which the surface of the bronze is meticulously decorated with gold, copper and silver damascening. Stone statues of female figures by themselves are rare, but one from the same period stands out for the way it combines a revival

25

26

**25-26. Statue
of Shebensopdet
and detail of the bust,
from Karnak,
about 850 BC. Cairo,
Egyptian Museum.**

EGYPTIAN ART

**27. Colossus with the
name of the high priest
Pinudjem I. Karnak,
First courtyard.**

28

28. Head of King Taharqa,
from Karnak, 690-664 BC.
Cairo, Egyptian Museum.

of the past with new "deviations": the niece of Osorkon II (22nd dynasty), Shebensopdet, was honored with a granite statue at Karnak by her husband. At first sight it seems to be a statue dating from many centuries earlier, even a goddess of the New Kingdom. But it is the style of the clothing that gives away its real age, along with the fact that her image has been covered with inscriptions, certainly to her benefit but distributed almost at random. The types of statue adopted were strictly limited by the fact they were almost exclusively located in temples: the dominant ones were the cube statue, the figure seated in what is called an asymmetric pose, with one knee raised and the other leg laid on the ground, and the pose of the scribe seated with crossed legs. There is no doubt that the Nubian kings, who came down into Egypt to restore order to a country they judged to be in the grip of chaos, gave a considerable boost to the search for canonical models. On the other hand, it seems to have been in this period that an interest emerged in

29

30

29. Cube statue of the scribe Hor, about 775 BC. Berlin, Staatliche Museen.

30. Statue of the vizier Hori, from Karnak, about 725 BC. Cairo, Egyptian Museum.

the unconventional "portrait," centered on the representation of individual characteristics, which sometimes seem to clash with the reproduction of attitudes of the old type. Some statues of Nubian rulers are also characterized by the novelty of their costume, which they clearly wanted to combine with the traditional Egyptian one: even the head of King Taharqa (25th dynasty) in the Cairo Museum is striking for its not purely Egyptian features, with a roundish face and elongated eyes, full lips and above all, despite being badly damaged, nose with a broad base, underlined by furrows at the sides, so typical they are known as "Kushite folds" (Kush was the Egyptian name for Nubia). These differences are made even more conspicuous by the fact that forehead and head are covered by an almost hemispherical skullcap, now of rough appearance but once clad with gold and surmounted by the true pharaonic crown resting on a more or less cylindrical element. The side view reveals the curly hair, next to the temples and behind the ears, on the round nape. The "realistic" tendency existed side by side with the "idealizing" one, which set out to revive fully styles of the past. There are different effigies of the same personage that can be assigned to one or the other tendency, as in the case of the statues of "divine

31. Statue of the superintendent Irigadanen, from Karnak, about 680 BC. Cairo, Egyptian Museum.

32. Statue of Harwa, administrator of the "divine worshipers," with two deities, about 700 BC. London, British Museum.

33   34

worshipers" and their administrators (e.g. Harwa and Montuemhat). We are instinctively more drawn to the images that combine a traditional attitude with an individualization of the features, capable of making us feel that the person has materialized in front of us. the full or exaggerated forms of Harwa and Irigadanen look very different from the ones, invisible to most people, that characterized the equally masterly statues of Khufu's architect Hemiunu or of Kaaper, from 18-19 centuries earlier. In the Saite age all the idiosyncratic elements introduced into artistic production by the Nubians were repudiated, while the tendency to archaism and

an idealized appearance was accentuated. These qualities were combined with a very accurate working and above all an extremely refined finish, which constitutes their dominant aspect.

The statue of Nespakashuty in the pose of a scribe relies unhesitatingly on the play of light, finding its very *raison d'être* in technical perfection, but for later masterpieces, as there were indeed to be, we have to wait for further developments in the tendency toward a greater "realism," even in attitudes, that can already be discerned in another statue of Nespakashuty, in an asymmetric pose.

33. Statue of the vizier Nespakashuty in the pose of a scribe, from Karnak, about 640 BC. Cairo, Egyptian Museum.

34. Statue of Nespakashuty seated in an asymmetric pose, about 640 BC. Cairo, Egyptian Museum.

STATUETTE OF KAROMAMA
about 860 BC
Paris, Musée du Louvre

SUBJECT

The statuette, probably from the Temple of Karnak, was acquired in Egypt in 1829 by Jean-François Champollion, the man who deciphered the hieroglyphic script, during a scientific mission that was given the name of the "Franco-Tuscan Literary Expedition" as it was Grand Duke Leopold II of Tuscany who funded the expedition led by the first Italian Egyptologist, Ippolito Rosellini.

It represents Princess Karomama, perhaps the granddaughter of King Osorkon I (22nd dynasty) and a "Divine Worshiper of Amon": the priestly title, reserved for daughters of royal blood, shows that she had been chosen for the role of "Bride of the God," consecrated solely to his worship. As such she lived in a residence with its own lands, run by administrators, and was accompanied by a group of women who, like her, could neither marry nor have children. These were the "divine worshipers" who adopted as "daughters" the girls destined to succeed them in their position, something that obviously lent itself to political jockeying.

COMPOSITION

Karomama is shown performing a ritual act, with her forearms raised to hold two objects that have been lost. The depiction of her sumptuous attire and the grace of her features and pose bear witness to the high level of technique and expressiveness attained in the Late Period.

The fine lineaments of the face are accentuated by the roundish wig, topped by a cylindrical element and the royal diadem, the uraeus, on her forehead.

The pleated dress with flared sleeves is densely decorated: the damascening of gold, silver and electrum renders the details with elaborate preciosity. A broad collar with many rows of floral and geometric motifs around the neck covers the shoulders.

A skirt adorned with plumed elements is tied under the breasts. Over it is laid a decoration formed of two large flaps that wrap around the hips, crossing on the pelvis.

STATUE OF MONTUEMHAT
about 670 BC
Cairo, Egyptian Museum

SUBJECT

The statue comes from the Temple of Karnak, where it was unearthed by the French archeologist Legrain in 1904 following the fortunate discovery of the "Cachette," a pit dug perhaps at the end of the Ptolemaic era to hold statues that were taking up too much room: 779 stone figures and about 17 000 smaller bronze ones were literally "fished" out of it. This statue represents perhaps the most powerful figure in Southern Egypt at a difficult time: Montuemhat was priest of Amon, "Mayor of Thebes" and "Governor of Upper Egypt" in the phase of transition between the Kushite 25th dynasty and the 26th; he lived through the sack of Thebes by the Assyrians and the reunification of the state by the princes of Sais. The size and the preciosity of decoration of his immense tomb, no. 34 in the Assasif necropolis, even though it has not yet been completely explored and studied, are sufficient by themselves to give a measure of the privileges he enjoyed.

COMPOSITION

The statue, just under life size, was displayed in the temple: for what we can now define as a "memorial," Montuemhat chose to hark back to a type of statue that had been traditional ever since the Old Kingdom: a standing male figure, with the left leg advanced and the arms hanging straight at the sides.

The figure is set on a base and supported by a dorsal pillar, both covered with inscriptions.

The breadth of the shoulders, the shape of the bust and the narrow hips correspond to the athletic ideal in vogue in the past, but the hips are girded with a plated *shendyt* kilt, like that of the king, and like the king Montuemhat's name is inscribed on the belt.

The face reflects both tradition and innovation: the full wig, inspired by 18th-dynasty models, creates an almost coloristic effect with its succession of waves over the curls at the sides of the neck. The strong features of the face combine the influence of the "style" of the Nubian kings with a more individual approach, as revealed by the narrow eyes and the shadows underneath.

THE VITALITY OF THE MINOR ARTS

The discovery of intact graves has shown that, even in such a troubled time, neither artistic creativity nor technical ability had been lost. Unfortunately we only possess works from the oldest phase of the period, but vestiges from later moments, some found by chance, provide evidence for a continuity.

Gold work in particular stuck to tradition, with a production of jewelry, furnishings and other objects intended for use as grave goods that are extremely refined from the viewpoint of their execution. The treasures of Tanis have not attracted as much attention as those of Tutankhamun, but they are certainly their equal on the level of craftsmanship. It is the royal tombs of the 21st and 22nd dynasty, in fact, that have yielded the works of the master goldsmiths of the Late Period: masters of a school that had maintained a high degree of technical ability and creativity. In fact the Assyrian king Esarhaddon wanted the craftsmen of this school deported to his own country to work for the court.

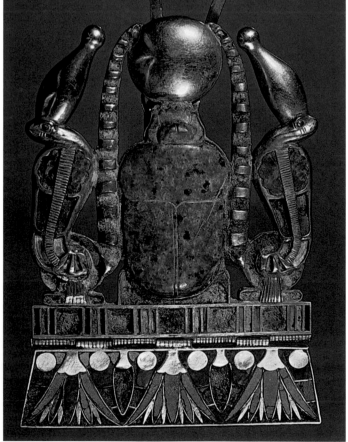

35

36

35. Gold pendant in the form of a shrine, containing a small lapis-lazuli statue of the god Ptah-Soker-Osiris, from the grave goods of Undjebauendjedet, at Tanis, about 1000 BC. Cairo, Egyptian Museum.

36. Inlaid gold pectoral with a lapis-lazuli scarab pushing the solar disk, from the grave goods of Sheshonk II, at Tanis, about 890 BC. Cairo, Egyptian Museum.

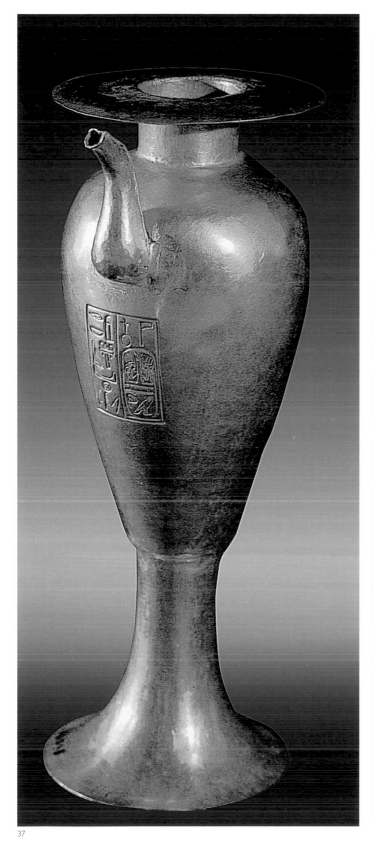

37. Gold vase for
libations, from the tomb
of Amenemope at Tanis,
about 990 BC. Cairo,
Egyptian Museum.

38. Sarcophagus of King
Psusennes I, detail of the
head, about 1000 BC.
Cairo, Egyptian Museum.

Bracelets, pectorals and collars are among the most significant pieces: semiprecious stones, especially lapis lazuli, were used extensively in their manufacture and were perfectly cut and set. Precious metals, gold as well as silver, were also used in large quantities: the gold collars of Psusennes, for example, weigh 18 lb or more than 8 kg.

The choice of themes also shows a continuity with respect to the production of the New Kingdom: the winged scarab, the vulture and the *udjat*, the eye of Horus, are some of the most frequent motifs, chosen for their symbolic value.

Among the innovations of the period are the rings that, for example, form the cascade of gold of the counterpoise of Psusennes' collar.

The use of silver for sarcophagi is another innovation of this time. The

39

39 and 41. Pendant with Osirian triad and, on following pages, detail, about 860 BC. Paris, Musée du Louvre.

**40. Collar of gold rings
of King Psusennes I,
about 1000 BC.**

anthropoid coffin of King Psusennes I is made of this material, with the details of the band on the forehead and the diadem-uraeus in gold, and so is that of Sheshonk II. Silver was not mined in Egypt but imported from the Near East, so it was very rare and thus considered extremely precious. In earlier times it was utilized in smaller quantities, but in the Late Period, perhaps as a result of the improvement in trade links with the countries to the northeast, it was more widely employed, in part for its symbolic value. Along with gold and silver less noble metals were worked, including bronze and wrought iron. Damascened bronze, made using the lost-wax technique, was an improvement on an older tech-

nique dating back to the New Kingdom and has left some stupendous examples. Hot-worked inlays in gold, silver and electrum were used to embellish bronze in a multiplicity of objects as diverse as statues and furnishings: celebrated are the ones made for the divine worshipers of Amon, of which the statuette of Karomama is the finest example. Joinery was also of the highest quality and included striking pieces like the coffins and furniture with incrustations of polychrome glass paste or ivory. Finally, furnishings have been found in the intact tombs which show that craftsmanship was far from in decline, but on the contrary capable of creating new models and taking in new ideas.

43

EGYPTIAN ART

42. Facing page: Bronze sculpture called the "Gayer-Anderson cat," about 600 BC. London, British Museum.

43. Pectoral of King Sheshonk I, detail with scarab between two female figures, about 920 BC.

Egyptian faïence, or glass frit, is a mixture of silica and copper salts that was fired at high temperatures. The copper in the mixture caused the faïence to take on shades of color ranging from bright blue to green, with a shiny surface resembling that of a crystalline glaze. The Egyptians used faïence as an inexpensive substitute for semiprecious stones, which were more difficult to obtain and therefore more costly, in the manufacture of objects for funerary and religious use. The most common types were amulets and votive statuettes. In addition, the blue and green colors of faïence had powerful symbolic associations: in fact blue recalled the element of water and was linked to concepts of fecundity and life, while green was the color of vegetation and thus of rebirth. Because of its color, therefore, faïence was used for various types of artifact whose symbolic value was connected with these concepts, such as votive statu-

I. Faïence bowl with papyrus plants, New Kingdom. London, British Museum.

II. Statuette of hippopotamus, Middle Kingdom. Paris, Musée du Louvre.

ettes that were included in grave goods with the aim of favoring the regeneration and rebirth of the deceased. The examples of a popular series of statuettes in the form of hippopotami also come from tombs. Motifs of papyrus or lotus plants are traced in black on the animal's body, to conjure up the aquatic element and the environment in which it lives. The scene of the pharaoh hunting and killing a hippopotamus on the banks of the Nile was a classic theme of royal iconography, as it represented the ruler's ability to overcome disorder and the aggressive forces that threatened the world. *Ushabti*, the figures of servants that were buried in graves in large numbers, were often made of faïence: this is another example of the use of frit for symbolic reasons linked to the desire for the rebirth and regeneration of the deceased. The manufacture of amulets was very widespread, again for religious motives. The most common were in the form of the *ankh*, the key of life. Other amulets frequently made out of faïence were the eye of Horus, the *udjat*, symbol of health and the wholeness of the body, and the scarab, whose base could also be used to inscribe short magic spells. These amulets were worn by people while alive, but they were also inserted between the linen bandages during mummification. Faïence was used for decorative purposes too: in the chambers of Djoser's step pyramid at Saqqarah, for instance, the walls were covered with panels of tiles made of this material, as its green shades recalled the color of the papyrus from which the mats that decorated homes and temples were made.

IV

III

III. *Udjat* amulet, Third Intermediate Period, 1069-664 BC. London, British Museum.

IV. *Ushabti* of Hekaemsaef, 26th dynasty, 664-525 BC.

EGYPTIAN ART

6. Ptolemaic Egypt

I n 332 BC Alexander the Great annexed Egypt, encountering hardly any resistance. With considerable political acumen, he immediately had himself recognized as the son of Amon at the Siwa Oasis and crowned pharaoh in the Egyptian manner, inaugurating the policy of respect for local traditions that would be followed by all his successors. Thus a small Greek and Macedonian minority became the ruling class: the official language of the state was now Greek, with demotic used for administration.

Two peoples, two languages and two cultures existed side by side, but it was the rulers who assimilated the local culture, identifying their own gods with the Egyptian ones and adopting their cults and traditions. After Alexander's death it was Ptolemy I who governed the satrap of Egypt. His dynasty, the 33rd according to Manetho's division, was to retain a firm hold for three centuries, keeping the traditions of pharaonic Egypt alive until the moment of its decline, with the arrival of a new power in the Mediterranean: Rome.

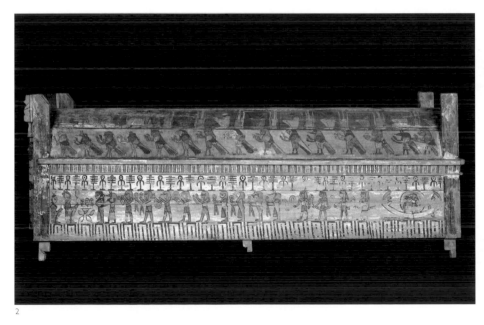

2

3

EGYPTIAN ART

1. Facing page: Statue of Cleopatra VII, detail, 51-30 BC. St Petersburg, State Hermitage Museum.

2. Sarcophagus of Cleopatra, from Sheikh Abd al-Qurnah, Thebes, 2nd century AD. London, British Museum.

3. Funerary mask of Hornedjitef, 220 BC. London, British Museum.

THE IMAGE OF KINGSHIP BETWEEN WEST AND EAST

The new pharaohs, rulers of two peoples and heirs to two artistic traditions, the Egyptian and the Greek, chose to preserve both, but without allowing them to contaminate one another. Royal statuary, destined for use within the court or at least to be seen by Greeks, remained closer to the Hellenistic tradition in its themes and its manner. The images of Alexander the Great and those of the Ptolemies, right up until the last ruler of the dynasty, Cleopatra, fit perfectly into the Hellenistic style and embody a heroic ideal of the conquering sovereign. They are images full of the dynamism and realism typical of the Greek art of the period. In sharp contrast to these works was the production of public statues, aimed at the people, a means of propaganda whose purpose was to prevent them from per-

ceiving their new rulers as a break with the past. The images carved on temples and votive statuary maintained a perfect continuity of style and theme with the pharaonic tradition. From the outset, Alexander the Great had realized that the best way to ensure the Greek minority retained its grip on the country was to link it to tradition, especially the religious one. Thus the Greek rulers were pharaohs through and through, and erected temples that adhered to the architectural rules of the New Kingdom. Even Manetho's history, commissioned by Ptolemy II, in which the Greek kings appear as the legitimate 33rd dynasty, was a way of connecting Greek rule with the past. So the artistic production of the Ptolemaic period drew on the same symbology and made use of the same techniques, proposing the immobility, hieratic character and even facial features that were characteristic of Egyptian statues. In the decorations of the great temple complexes the Ptolemies presented themselves in their ritual and military functions

4

5

4. Head of Ptolemy III Euergetes, about 246-222 BC.

5. Head of Cleopatra VII, about 51-30 BC. Berlin, Antikensammlung Altes Museum.

6. Facing page: Statues of Ptolemy II, Arsinoe II and a princess, about 280-250 BC. Rome, Museo Gregoriano Egizio, Vatican.

7

as enlightened sovereigns deified in their lifetimes, in accordance with the classical stereotypes. The two styles, Greek and Egyptian, never interpenetrated: neither Greek production nor still less the Egyptian one had any influence on one another. The sole exception was the occasional appearance of a number of attributes or objects. Typical of the Greek period was a change in the female figures, which grew increasingly sensual. Eroticism appeared in the representation of their bodies, perhaps due to the influence of the Asiatic rulers of the Late Period and Greek images of Venus.

The curves of hips and breasts were accentuated, as well as those of the belly, in which the navel became very pronounced. Queens and goddesses wear a long and closely fitting dress, and nothing but a faint line above the ankles shows that they are not nude. With the passing of the years, however, the schemes of the production in Egyptian style grew increasingly tired and stereotyped and lines became repetitive. Even in decorations the scenes looked clumsier in their modeling and composition and over time became more and more stiff and devoid of creative ideas.

**7 and 10. Bas-relief with
Ptolemy XII and Horus,
detail and whole,
about 80-60 BC.
Philae, Temple of Isis.**

THE GODS AND THEIR CULTS: CONTINUITY AND INNOVATION

The age-old Egyptian cults remained practically unchanged: preservation of the religion was a fundamental part of the policy of integration adopted by the Ptolemies. The majority of Egyptian deities were assimilated to the Hellenistic ones, and thus venerated by the Greeks themselves, as is shown by the numerous papyri containing prayers and oracles. At the same time, however, Ptolemy II introduced a new cult, that of Osorapis or Serapis, a divine figure born out of the fusion of Osiris, god of the underworld, with the sacred bull Apis. Some aspects of Hellenistic deities like Zeus and Dionysus also merged with Serapis. The cult was aimed almost exclusively at the Greek population, who found in it the hope of resurrection and an afterlife offered by the Osirian myth and absent from their own religion. Its iconography represents a rare example of the partial contamination referred to above:

the god was depicted in the Greek manner, with a thick beard and curly head of hair and dressed in rich drapery. As he was venerated along the lines of the Osirian cult, however, he was given attributes related to fertility and rebirth drawn from the myth of Osiris. This means that he was often portrayed with a measure for grain on his head, a symbol of fertility, since according to tradition Osiris was also the harvest god.

This measure or basket is adorned with leaves and vegetation because, as a god who dies and is reborn, Osiris is also connected with the cycle of plant growth. Serapis became extremely popular in the Hellenistic world and later in the Roman one: his cult spread throughout the Mediterranean. The largest temple dedicated to him was built at Alexandria, but there were others on Delos and at Tivoli. The cult of Isis, Serapis's wife, was equally popular: her image remained for the most part linked to Egyptian iconography, although some representations of her were influenced by the Greek style.

8

9

8. Bust of Serapis, about 2nd century AD. Cambridge, Fitzwilliam Museum, Cambridge University.

9. Statue of Isis, Ptolemaic period. Rome, Museo Gregoriano Egizio, Vatican.

THE GREAT TEMPLES: GOD'S CREATION

The sanctuaries that were constructed by the Ptolemies derived from the Theban temples of the New Kingdom. Their plan was based on that of the Temple of Amon at Karnak and represented a natural development of it, since it retained the salient elements while harmonizing the irregularities. The great temple complexes of the Ptolemaic dynasty were all conceived with a well-defined plan, and even if they were built under the reign of several kings have a single and homogeneous layout, not the fruit of successive additions like the complex at Karnak. The sense of unity is also suggested by the high walls that enclose them and keep them within a compact structure. The temple of the Ptolemaic period evokes the creation on earth: it is the myth of the primordial hill transposed into stone. The ceiling covered with stars is the sky, while the slight raising of the thresholds toward the shrine reproduces the first mound of sand that emerged from the waters at the moment of creation. According to the myth in fact, the "first time," the beginning of everything, was when a heap of sand rose from the chaos of the primeval waters, the first piece of land on which the creator god appeared at the dawn of time. The temples are a translation of that event into stone, and the *sancta sanctorum* represents the top of the primordial hill, the only place worthy of housing the deity. Thus the structure proceeds from the most sacred to the less sacred as one moves from the seat of the god toward the boundary wall; by analogy creation is an emanation that moves outward from the unmovable statue of the deity set at the heart of the temple. The process of creation by divine emanation is also suggested by the illumination of the spaces: from the total darkness of the sanctum, a darkness that enfolded the god, one proceeded through the semidarkness of the intermediate rooms toward the brilliance of the light outside.

11

11. Temple of Horus, hypostyle hall, about 3rd-1st century BC. Edfu.

12. Temple of Hathor, relief on the ceiling with the rising sun, first half of 1st century AD. Dandarah.

THE TEMPLE AT EDFU

One of the masterpieces of the Ptolemaic era is the temple dedicated to the falcon god Horus at Edfu, in Upper Egypt, still in excellent condition today. The structure was conceived in a unitary manner and is practically the typical one of the Ptolemaic period, with a naos, called the venerable seat, isolated by a corridor that runs around it and preceded by another room, called the Hall of the Ennead, dedicated to the nine deities who made up the god's court. Onto the corridor surrounding the sanctum opened nine chambers, used for activities of worship.

During the annual festivities the statue of the god was brought out of its venerable seat to see the light of the sun again: it was an opportunity for the people to admire the sacred image, otherwise inaccessible. Proceeding toward the outside, the statue passed through a pillared hall, called the Hall of Appearance as the statue of the god appeared there, glittering, to receive offerings and gifts. These rooms were lit by small windows set in the ceiling, in such a way as to enhance the polychromy

of the painted capitals and bas-reliefs, today completely lost and very hard to imagine.

The next space is the canonical and indispensable element of the Egyptian temple from Karnak onward: the hypostyle hall, so called because it was filled with columns that were taller than in the rest of the temple. It was the most brightly lit part of the building, thanks to the openings in the wall that separated the hypostyle hall from the large external courtyard. In reality this hall was considered a separate element from the core of the god's house, as is shown by the fact that it hooked onto the main wall of the temple in a pincer-like manner. The hypostyle hall at Edfu still has its original ceiling and allows us to appreciate, emerging from the gloom, the sensation of being immersed in the light and warmth of the sun's rays that flood the courtyard. Here the divine statue appeared to the people, who were able to participate in the festival of the god and his regeneration through contact with the sun. Thus the courtyard was the temple's public space, enclosed by the boundary wall and the monumental entrance formed by the pylon. This, again perfectly preserved,

13

14

13. Temple of Horus, east colonnade of the courtyard, about 3rd-1st century BC. Edfu.

14. Temple of Horus, detail of the front of the pronaos, about 3rd-1st century BC. Edfu.

15

rises to a great height to represent the hieroglyph of the horizon. Stairs with landings had been constructed inside it to provide access to the top, and let people reach the point closest to the sun god.

Striking statues of Horus in the form of a falcon can still be seen in front of the entrance: they take the place of the statues that, in the New Kingdom, usually represented the pharaoh and were set one on each side to defend the entrance of the temple. Even the solar bark in the sanctum has survived: in reality it is a wooden litter made in the shape of a boat on which stood a shrine, used to carry the statue of the god in processions.

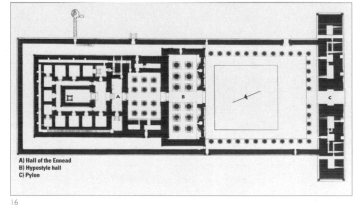

A) Hall of the Ennead
B) Hypostyle hall
C) Pylon

16

15. Temple of Horus,
detail of the colonnade
and the statue of Horus,
about 3rd-1st century BC.
Edfu.

16. Plan of the Temple
of Horus at Edfu
(from C. Aldred, F. Daumas,
C. Desroches-Noblecourt,
J. Leclant, *Egitto, il crepuscolo
del mondo egizio*, Milan 2005,
p. 325, fig. 237).

THE TEMPLE AT ESNA

The temple at Esna was dedicated to the god of fertility Khnum and his female counterpart, the goddess Neith. In no other temple was as much emphasis placed on the god's role as creator. Khnum in fact is the potter who, according to myth, made the image of man in clay on his wheel and then brought it to life with his divine power.

In the shrine of the birth in the temple at Deir el-Bahri, where the myth of the divine conception of Queen Hatshepsut is related, Khnum is also represented modeling the image of the little princess.

But it is at Esna that this deity fully assumes the role of demiurge, of creator of the world. The temple is a paean to his work, i.e. to creation and to nature. The capitals of the hypostyle hall are phytomorphic, with papyrus and lotus plants whose colors, now faded, ranged from red to blue to white to green in order to enliven the scene and vary the repetition of the same scheme. In their observation of nature, artists had noticed that it remained fundamentally the same while changing in the details: thus the architectural model of the temple, which was intended to be a "reproduction of the creation in stone," repeats the same plan, making only slight modifications.

Alongside the venerable seat are set rooms that were used for the purposes of worship, housing materials used for rituals and the care of the statue, which was washed, dressed and fed by the priests three times a day.

17

17. Temple of Khnum, façade of the hypostyle hall. Esna.

18. Facing page: Capital with lotus leaves, second half of 3rd century BC. Temple of Khnum, Esna.

THE TEMPLE AT DANDARAH

The temple of the goddess Hathor at Dandarah, planned and begun in the Late Period but constructed for the most part during the Roman era, represents the last stage in the evolution of temple structures.

The plan, conceived in a unitary fashion, is the most complete and functional of all those designed up to this moment. The only element missing is the pylon, which was never constructed. The boundary wall that encloses the temple and the annexed buildings, such as the *mammisi* (the place where the union of the goddess with her husband and the birth of their divine son was celebrated) of Nectanebo and the one from the Roman period, surrounds the entire complex, just as at Karnak. The management of the spaces, designed to meet liturgical needs, has been studied with particular care, and is perhaps the most functional of any temple. To the east of the sanctum a chapel called the *uabet*, the "pure chapel," was used for rituals of purification and

regeneration of the divine image. It was preceded by a small courtyard open to the sky where the statue could be exposed to the sun without being taken out of the building. One basic need, in fact, was to bring the statue, usually kept in total darkness inside the naos, into contact with the rays of the sun, god of light and life, to re-forge the link between deity and statue.

Immersed in darkness, the naos contained an enormous, unmovable shrine, carved from a monolithic block, and the solar bark used to carry the statue in processions. From the sanctum the deity had to renew creation every day, and the priests who took care of its image had to make sure that the necessary conditions were maintained for it not to leave: the statue, in fact, like the temple, had to be made in accordance with divine laws and with strictly harmonious proportions in order for it to be animated by the deity. Hathor, goddess of joy, music and women, was venerated by herself in this temple, whereas a structure of such dimensions was usually dedicated to a male deity and his

19

**19. Temple of Hathor,
main north front with six
Hathor-headed columns
above low walls, about
early 1st century AD.
Dandarah.**

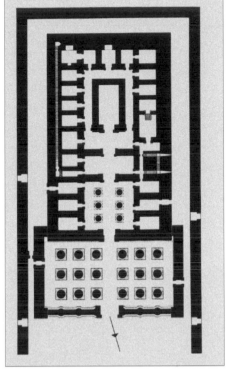

21

22

20

female counterpart. In this case, however, the sacred image of Horus's bride emerged from the temple once a year to go on a pilgrimage to Edfu, sailing along the Nile to her husband's temple.

Although constructed at the end of the era of Egypt's independence, the Temple of Hathor has a freshness and a perfection of composition worthy of earlier periods, from the viewpoint of both its architecture and its decoration. The columns of the large hypostyle hall, for example, have fine Hathor-headed capitals with the face of the goddess looking in all four directions, at the whole of creation. Each decoration in the temple is an invitation for the faithful and for the priests themselves to share in the goddess's joy, a necessary condition for them to celebrate her cult in a fitting manner.

Finally, the sacred lake constructed inside the precinct in keeping with the tradition of the complexes at Karnak has been perfectly preserved, with its four gateways providing access to four flights of steps leading down to the pool.

20. Temple of Hathor, roof terrace with a kiosk supported by Hathor-headed columns (Chapel of the New Year) in the southwest corner, about mid-1st century BC. Dandarah.

21. Plan of the Temple of Hathor at Dandarah (from C. Aldred, F. Daumas, C. Desroches-Noblecourt, J. Leclant, *Egitto, il crepuscolo del mondo egizio*, Milan 2005, p. 323, fig. 230).

22. Temple of Hathor, Hathor-headed capital supporting the entablature, about early 1st century BC. Dandarah.

THE BAS-RELIEFS OF THE TEMPLES: MYTH CARVED IN STONE

The temples of the Ptolemaic era are covered in their entirety with bas-reliefs and hieroglyphs, decorating the pylons, walls and columns. These carvings were made by artists still in the grip of the *horror vacui* that had characterized the decorations of previous periods.

The temple at Edfu, for example, is lavishly decorated with bas-reliefs relating the myth of the falcon god Horus and depicting the Ptolemaic rulers making offerings. The themes and symbology of these bas-reliefs are in keeping with Egyptian tradition. Only the line has changed slightly: in the best examples we note the introduction of a sense of move-

ment, represented with flexibility and naturalness, even though most of the human figures are rigid, portrayed in canonical poses. While in the classical age the immobility of the model and the rigor of the canon did not compromise the harmony of the composition, in the reliefs of this phase the movements look stiff and the style lacks the grace of that period. In the bas-relief, as in contemporary statuary, there is an accentuation of the sensuality of female bodies, with a greater emphasis of the breasts and the belly and the navel clearly visible.

Here too, as elsewhere and at Philae in particular, the bas-reliefs have not escaped the religious superstitions of those, in all probability the early Christians, who believed that the figures of the gods could be rendered "innocuous" by chiseling away their faces and extremities.

23

23. Relief with Ptolemy IV receiving the document confirming his legitimate succession to the throne from the god Horus, about 210 BC. Edfu, Temple of Horus.

24

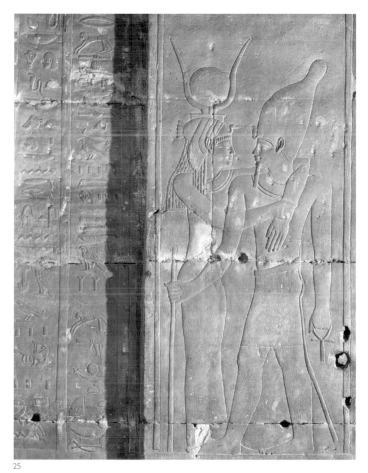

25

26

24. Relief representing the myth of Horus, mid-2nd century BC. Edfu, boundary wall, Temple of Horus.

25. Relief depicting the goddess Hathor embracing Ptolemy IV, about 210 BC. Edfu, Chamber of the Throne, Temple of Horus.

26. Relief with Ptolemy VIII Euergetes II appointed king by Nekhbet and Wadjet, goddesses of Upper and Lower Egypt, about 164-116 BC. Edfu, Temple of Horus.

SYRIANS, LIBYANS AND NUBIANS: EGYPT'S ENEMIES

The Egyptians held their civilization in very high regard, considering themselves to be a superior people. They made no attempt to disguise this opinion, not even in their international relations with the great empires of Mesopotamia. "The Two Lands," as Egypt was known in antiquity, since the country was made up of the regions of the Delta and the Valley, were seen as the permanent seat of a universal order established by the gods at the dawn of time. From this perspective, the neighboring peoples, considered inferior and consequently looked down on, represented a danger and a threat to the order and unity of Egypt. As the fundamental duty of the sovereign was to guarantee the security of the Two Lands by crushing their enemies through his

strength and with the guidance of the gods, he was often portrayed in public images in the act of trampling nine bows under his feet. In Egyptian iconography, in fact, all possible enemies were represented by the "Nine Bows": the bow symbolized military aggression from the outside, while nine indicated all: since the number three was used to indicate "plural," nine, as the result of the multiplication of three by itself, represented the "plural of plurals" and therefore all. There were three peoples who had always been enemies of Egypt, Libyans, Syrians and Nubians, depicted according to fixed canons that identified them by their features and clothing. They were the three peoples who lived in areas bordering on the country and thus represented the main

I. Relief with prisoners, from the tomb of Horemheb at Saqqarah, about 1310 BC. Bologna, Museo Civico.

threat. The Nubians and African peoples in general were portrayed with dark skin and Negroid features, such as fleshy lips and curly hair; they often wore conspicuous earrings and short, brightly colored garments. The Syrians had their own iconography: the skin is pale, the eyes narrow and they have beards and mustaches, while the hair is long at the back and gathered in a band on the forehead. Their clothes, unlike those of the Nubians, always reach down to their feet. The Libyans, finally, are characterized by an olive complexion and a braided lock of hair. They wear short garments and a long cloak tied over one shoulder. The iconography of the enemies was fixed so that their identification would be unambiguous, and the representation of one

alluded to them all. Thus a scene very frequently used to decorate the pylons of temples shows the king holding a Syrian, a Libyan and a Nubian by the hair: in this way it was asserted, partly for magical reasons, that the pharaoh held all the country's enemies in his power. The latter are often depicted on a smaller scale to underline their weakness with respect to pharaoh, and they are always bound, terrified or in the act of fleeing, and thus rendered inoffensive. We should not forget, in fact, the magical value of images, which were believed to make what they depicted come true: thus the enemy was rendered impotent, because the negative forces he embodied could in no way act through the material support provided to them by the representation.

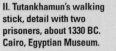

II. Tutankhamun's walking stick, detail with two prisoners, about 1330 BC. Cairo, Egyptian Museum.

III. Bas-relief with prisoners bound by their hair, about 1295-1186 BC. Cairo, Egyptian Museum.

IV. Tile with African prisoner, from the palace of Rameses III at Medinet Habu, about 1160 BC. Cairo, Egyptian Museum.

V. Tile with Semitic prisoner, from the palace of Rameses III at Medinet Habu, about 1160 BC. Cairo, Egyptian Museum.

EGYPTIAN ART

345

THE SARCOPHAGI OF THE ALEXANDRINE NECROPOLISES

After the country came under foreign domination funerary cults also underwent changes, especially those of the Greeks. In fact the rulers found a prospect of eternal life and resurrection in Egyptian culture that did not exist in their own, and were quick to appropriate it. But the funerary cult of their subjects continued to be what Egyptian culture had developed over the centuries, with the same symbols linked to rebirth, like the winged scarab or the *djed* pillar, commonly used in tombs and on sarcophagi, and with the same rituals.

Beautiful sarcophagi have been found in the necropolises of the Alexandrine period. Made of stone or more frequently painted wood, they are derived from those of the Late Period: they are anthropomorphic and characterized by a marked expressiveness of the face, often painted in gold or covered with gold leaf, a symbol of purity. A new technique was also developed to reduce the cost of making the sarcophagi and render burial according to the Egyptian rite accessible to a larger number of people. Called cartonnage by the archeologists, this entailed constructing the sarcophagus, as well as the funerary mask, out of several layers of wet papyrus strips that were then covered with plaster and painted. Papyrus scrolls containing written texts, considered no longer useful, were often used in cartonnage. Sometimes archeologists have chosen to destroy ancient sarcophagi forever in order to recover literary works of inestimable value that would not otherwise have come down to us. The funerary mask also evolved in the direction of portraiture, acquiring greater expressiveness through large painted eyes that attract the attention of the observer. But there was no realism in the colors, since the choice of gold for the masks and the sarcophagi was made for symbolic reasons, and was linked to the concepts of purity and rebirth associated with this material. It quickly became the practice in the Greco-Roman era to place a very large number of amulets in sarcophagi, with the aim of ensuring undisturbed sleep for the deceased and protecting the parts of the body considered weakest. The net of beads and stones decorated with symbols of rebirth like the winged scarab, already in use in the New Kingdom, was intended to serve this fundamental purpose.

27

28

29

27. Sarcophagus of the priest Hornedjitef, from Assasif (Thebes), about 220 BC. London, British Museum.

28. Wooden sarcophagus, Ptolemaic period.

29. Funerary mask, Ptolemaic period. Rome, Museo Gregoriano Egizio, Vatican.

30. Facing page: Cartonnage mask of mummy, Ptolemaic period. Private collection.

THE EL-FAIYUM PORTRAITS

The last stage in the evolution of the sarcophagus and the funerary mask is represented by the pictures painted on wood in the imperial era and known as El-Faiyum portraits, since the majority of them have been found in the oasis of that name in Lower Egypt. Executed using a highly sophisticated encaustic technique, the face of the deceased was reproduced on wooden panels that were then placed on top of the head in the sarcophagus, instead of the funerary mask. These faces remain emblematic for their realism and for the expressiveness and incisiveness of their gaze, into which the artist has instilled all the hope of rebirth and survival after death, as well as immortalizing the character of the deceased. The El-Faiyum portraits provide an extremely useful means of reconstructing techniques of painting in the Alexandrine and Roman periods, as contemporary paintings in Greece and Rome have been almost completely lost. Above all they offer us an insight into the customs, usages and fashions of the last "pagans" in Egypt, followers of age-old funerary cults and the ancient religious practices of this country. The arrival of Christianity put an end to the Egyptian religion and the whole culture of which it was the fruit.

31

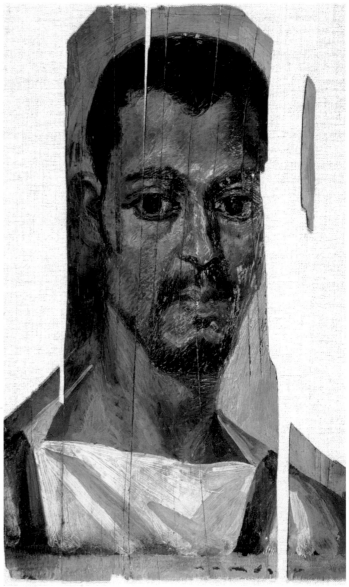

32

31. Portrait of a young woman, from El-Faiyum, 2nd century AD. London, British Museum.

32. Portrait of a man, from El-Faiyum, 2nd-3rd century AD. Paris, Musée du Louvre.

33. Facing page: Portrait of a young woman, from El-Faiyum, AD 120-130. Paris, Musée du Louvre.

PORTRAIT OF A YOUNG WOMAN
2nd century AD
Florence, Museo Archeologico

SUBJECT

In the sarcophagi of the age of imperial Rome, found mostly at the oasis of El-Faiyum, it was the custom to cover the head with a wooden panel painted with the face of the deceased. This portrait, like the other examples, has been executed with the encaustic technique, i.e. by mixing the pigment with hot wax before applying it to the panel.

The face of the young woman shares with other portraits the intensity of the enigmatic gaze with which she seems to meet our eyes.

The features of the face are delicate and accurately represented; the thick head of hair gathered in an elaborate bun on top of the head suggests that she was well-off, as does the jewelry she is wearing.

The encaustic technique helps to give the face, and the gaze in particular, a brilliance that makes the portrait a vivid presence. The eyes express the desire for life and the hope for resurrection of those who venture into the unknown. In this portrait the artist has succeeded in capturing the feelings of doubt in the face of death, the disappearance of that blind faith in the afterlife which had been typical of the past. The features are those of a young woman, and no longer an idealized representation as was the custom in the previous period. The technique of chiaroscuro has been perfectly mastered by the artist, who uses several different shades of pink and white for the flesh tones and to emphasize the area of the eyes in order to render the gaze more expressive.

GLOSSARY

A

AMON-RE or AMON-RA: the origins of Amon, the god almost always represented in human form, wearing two tall plumes on his head, are not easy to trace, but during the Middle Kingdom his importance increased in step with the rise of the royal houses from Thebes. He rapidly assumed the characteristics of a national and universal deity, assimilated to the principal god of Egypt, the Sun, in the form of Amon-Re.

ANUBIS: god of the dead, represented in the form of a black jackal. His main place of worship was Asyut, in Middle Egypt. He presided over the rites of embalming.

APIS: a sacred bull, originally a symbol of fertility, he was the object of a cult at Memphis as a "manifestation" of the god Ptah. He went on to acquire characteristics of a funerary deity, associated with Osiris. Like the god, the bull was mummified when he died and buried in gigantic catacombs. The priests sought his successor by looking carefully for patches or "cowlicks" on the coats of bullocks.

ATON: the term used for the visible aspect of the Sun, and thus translated as "solar disk." For a short time in the 18th dynasty Aton was also the only god, in the religious reform which the pharaoh Akhenaton tried to impose on his subjects.

B

BAST or BASTET: cat goddess, linked to her main place of worship, the city of Bubastis in the Delta (now Tell Basta, near Zagazig); originally a lioness, she then became the peaceful aspect of the dangerous Sekhmet and the Greeks identified her with Aphrodite.

BOOK OF THE DEAD: name commonly used for "The Chapters of Coming-Forth-by-Day," the title given by the Egyptians to a collection of magical spells placed in tombs and the most widely used from the New Kingdom until the Ptolemaic period, especially among private individuals. The texts are based on legends and myths and intended to ensure the rebirth of the soul by providing it with the means to overcome all the adversities it might encounter in the afterlife. Usually written on papyrus, it is accompanied by illustrations that are often of very high quality.

C

CANOPIC JARS: name mistakenly given to the vessels used to hold the viscera extracted from the body during the mummification process. There were four of the jars, placed the protection of the gods called the Sons of Horus. Canopus is the name of a city in the Delta where the god Osiris was worshiped in the Greco-Roman period in the form of a human-headed vessel.

CORBELED VAULT: a way of roofing a space by means of successive courses of stones each of which projects beyond the next, creating the effect of an arched vault.

D

DAMASCENING: named after the city of Damascus, which was famous for its wares produced by this technique in the Middle Ages, it indicates the inlaying of wires of precious metal or metal of a different color in narrow undercuts made in the surface of the metal from which the object is made.

F

FAÏENCE: derived from the name of the Italian city famous for the production of tin-glazed earthenware or majolica, Faenza, the term is also improperly used for a frit, i.e. the calcined or partly fused materials of which glass is made, with a shiny blue-green or turquoise surface deriving from the presence of copper salts.

FALSA DOOR: structure imitating the jams and lintels of a door and marking, in the tombs of the Old Kingdom and every subsequent period, when it was reproduced in paint alone, the point where it was imagined that communication took place between the dead and the living. In the Old Kingdom, offerings of provisions were deposited at its base.

H

HATHOR: highly complex female deity, goddess of the sky who brought life. She was represented in the form of a cow, or with a cow's ears and horns. She was also linked to the "lioness" deities and was a truly "universal" goddess, assimilated to Nut and Isis.

HORUS: ancient sun god, represented in the form of a falcon, with whom the reigning pharaoh was identified. Inserted into the myth of Osiris, he was the latter's son who avenged his killing by Seth and inherited his kingdom on earth.

HYPOSTYLE HALL: the term, derived from the Greek, is used for a hall filled with pillars or columns supporting the roof.

I

ISIS: the goddess was the sister and wife of Osiris, who discovered and reunited the pieces of her husband's body after he was killed by his brother Seth, and the mother of his posthumous son, Horus, heir to his royal throne. As a mother, she was linked to other fundamental female deities, like Hathor and Nut.

J

JUBILEE: the term, which in the Old Testament and in the tradition of the Catholic Church indicates a year declared to be holy, is also used for the festivities and ceremonies held to renew the sovereignty of the pharaoh in Egypt, called the Sed Festival. Of very ancient origin, from at least the Middle Kingdom onward it was held in the thirtieth year of reign and then every three years after that.

K

KA: incorporeal element of the human personality, almost a personification of its vital force; it survives in the tomb after death, and the offerings of food are intended for it.

KHENTI-IMENTIU: literally "Foremost of the Westerners," i.e. the dead, was the god venerated at Abydos, represented in the form of jackal. He was soon assimilated by Osiris, the principal god of the dead, and the god's name became one of his epithets.

KHNUM: god originally venerated on the island of Elephantine, he was represented in the form of a ram, and as such as a creator; in particular, he was the god who turned newborn children on his potter's wheel.

M

MAAT: "Truth" or "Justice," the name of the goddess represents the concept of universal order established by the gods. This is written in hieroglyphics with the symbol of the ostrich plume, pronounced *maat*, and so the image of the goddess bears a plume as an emblem on her head.

MASTABA: the Arabic word for a stone bench constructed outside a house, it is also applied, because of the similarity in appearance, to the typical private tomb of the Old Kingdom, an oblong structure that tapers slightly toward the top. Royal tombs prior to the pyramids were also of this type, and private individuals continued to use them throughout the Middle Kingdom.

MONTU or MONT: deity originally worshiped at Hermonthis, he became the "Lord of Thebes" and was represented with a falcon's head and wearing two tall plumes. He was a warrior god, characterized by his virility, but was later surpassed in importance by Amon. However, he still had a sanctuary to the north of the great precinct of Karnak, and the cities of El-Tod, El-Madamud and Hermonthis, close to Thebes, were always devoted to him. His sacred bull, called Buchis, was buried at Hermonthis, now Armant.

MUT: companion of Amon and assimilated to lioness goddesses like Sekhmet and Tefnut in the complicated myths that refer to the Eye of the Sun, protector of kingship.

N

NAOS: the Greek term for the part of a temple (as distinct from the portico) in which the image of the deity is housed.

NEITH: goddess of the city of Sais in the western Delta, perhaps originally a goddess of the hunt carrying a bow; although of very ancient origin, she did not become important until the 26th dynasty, which had Sais as its capital, and was then considered a creator goddess like the male deities.

NEMES: Egyptian name for the royal headdress that, presumably made of cloth, swept back from the forehead to cover all the hair and ended in two broad bands on the breast, often with horizontal stripes, while the strip at the back was twisted and tied under the nape.

NOME: administrative division of ancient Egypt, usually translated as province.

O

OBELISK: derived from the word for a "spit," it was the name that the Greeks gave to the monuments typical of the solar cult in Egypt. A tall monolithic pillar on a square base with a tip in the form of a pyramid, it was considered to be a "petrified" ray of sunlight and alluded, especially in that pyramidal top, to the primordial mound that emerged from the waters and allowed the Sun to rise on the first day of the universe's existence.

OPET: name of one of the principal religious festivals at Thebes, which could last for almost a month. On that occasion the statue of the god Amon was carried on a processional bark from the sanctuary at Karnak, by land or river, to the Temple of Luxor, called the *ipet resyt* or "southern place of seclusion"; it was accompanied by statues of the other members of the Theban triad, Mut and Khonsu, each on its own boat. The king also took part, and probably repeated the ceremonies of his coronation at Luxor.

OSIRIS: according to the cosmogony of Heliopolis, he was the son of Geb and Nut (Earth and Sky respectively) and the husband of his sister Isis. Protagonist of one of the most widespread of Egyptian myths, but one of which no complete version has survived, he was the god who, like others in the Mediterranean, died and was then reborn. In the Egyptian myth, it was his brother Seth who killed him in order to take his place as king, and in some versions tore his body into pieces and scattered it. His sisters Isis (who was also his wife) and Nephthys were able to gather the members and put them back together to make the first mummy. In addition, Isis conceived from her husband their son Horus, who would avenge his father. Osiris was made king of the underworld by the tribunal of gods, while his son was declared legitimate heir to the kingdom of the earth, which was that of every ruler of Egypt.

■ P

PAPYRUS COLUMN: an architectural element used for support or decoration, the column in Egypt was inspired by the plant world. The most common type was the papyrus column, which reproduced a bundle of papyrus stalks in more or less stylized form. The capital usually represented its closed foliage, but could also be open, in the shape of an "umbrella" or bell.

PHARAOH: title of the king of Egypt, mentioned in the Bible but not found in Egyptians texts before the New Kingdom. It derives from the Egyptian *per 'aa*, "great house," i.e. the palace, and thus describes the ruler in terms of the place in which he resides.

PROCESSIONAL (or SACRED) BARK (or BOAT): a boat or model of a boat used to transport the image of the god, hidden by curtains, during festivities. It was carried on shafts by the priests along special routes used for processions.

PROCESSIONAL WAY: route created for processions of priests carrying sacred images.

PRONAOS: Greek term for the portico on the front of a temple.

PTAH: originally the local deity of Memphis, he was creator god and patron of craftsmen and artists, always represented in human form and with a royal beard.

PYLON: from the Greek, it indicates the monumental gateway which in the pharaonic period consisted of two towers flanking an entrance, and was perhaps intended to reproduce the sign for "horizon" in the hieroglyphic script.

PYRAMID: the term, now in universal use, even for the geometric solid, was introduced by the Greeks, like other names for Egyptian monuments, almost as if they were trying to reduce their grandeur or extraordinary character to a more "human" dimension. Although its etymology is controversial, it may derive from *pyramis*, the Greek word for a wheaten cake, and be based on a vague resemblance in shape. The royal sepulchral monument in vogue from the Old to the Middle Kingdom and shortly afterward, it was called *mer* in the Egyptian texts and alluded to the primordial hill of creation, which at Heliopolis, the center of sun worship, was identified with the *benben* stone, perhaps a meteorite of conical form.

■ R

RA-HARAKHTY: sun god, represented with a falcon's head, who combined the aspects of the principal solar deity, Re, and the god Horus, qualified as "Horus of the horizon," i.e. the rising sun.

RENENUTET: goddess of the harvest, particularly venerated in one part of El-Faiyum and represented in the form of a cobra.

■ S

SACRED BARK (or BOAT): see Processional bark.

SARCOPHAGUS: from the Greek *sarkophagos*, "flesh eater," it is the term used for the coffin made from stone for the preservation of mummified bodies. While the word sarcophagus usually refers to the outer casket made of stone and the word coffin is used for the inner casket or caskets made of wood, the terms are sometimes interchangeable, especially when the casket is anthropoid, or in the shape of a human being.

SED FESTIVAL: see Jubilee.

SERDAB: "cellar, storeroom" in Arabic. It is the name given to the small chamber used to house the statues of the owner inside a mastaba, or to one of the chambers inside the royal pyramid of the Old Kingdom.

SETH: a deity that seems to personify the concept of disorder; a member of the group of Nine Gods of Heliopolis, he was Osiris's brother and, according to the myth, his murderer. In the New Kingdom he assumed the characteristics of several gods of the Near East, and like them became the lord of storms.

SPHINX: Greek term, perhaps a back-formation from sphingein, "to squeeze, bind," or derived from the Egyptian *shesep-ankh*, "living image," used for symbolic representations of the king with the body of a lion and a human head. The definition is extended to sculptures of a lion with the head of a ram or falcon, found in a number of Egyptian temples.

SHENDYT: name of the kilt typically worn by the king, with two strips of cloth wrapped around the waist and crossed at the front, on top of a third and narrower strip.

SOKER or SEKER: god of the region of Memphis. Originally, like Ptah, connected with craftsmen, he then became a god of the dead like Osiris. He was represented as a mummified falcon.

STELE or STELA (plural STELAE): standing monument (from the Greek *stellein*, "to set up"), usually a stone slab or pillar used for commemorative purposes, bearing the name of the person commemorated alone or alongside those of members of the family or colleagues involved in the funerary or memorial function of the stele.

■ T

TALATAT: an expression of uncertain origin, perhaps formed from the Arabic word for three, used for blocks of sandstone (at Karnak) or limestone (at Tell el-Amarna) of a standard size introduced during the reign of Amenhotep IV-Akhenaton. Their small size (about 21 × 10 in or 53 × 25 cm) made them easy to transport and speeded up the construction process.

THOTH: main deity of Hermopolis, "the city of Hermes," the god whom the Greeks considered most similar to the Egyptian one. Represented with the head of an ibis or in the form of a baboon, he was the scribe of the gods, lord of learning, numbers and measurements, and measurer of time, as he was also associated with the moon.

■ U

URAEUS: name of the diadem in the form of an asp or cobra worn by the ruler of Egypt; it was identified with the cobra goddess Wadjet or Buto of Lower Egypt. The name, in the Greek form, derives from one of the many epithets given to the royal emblem, perhaps *iâret*, "the (serpent) that rises."

■ V

VESTIBULE: antechamber, providing access to a room or serving as an entrance.

CHRONOLOGY

■ 4TH MILLENNIUM BC

4000-3200 BC: of Naqadah I (or Amratian) culture, in Upper Egypt, and Naqadah II (or Gerzean) culture, in Upper and Lower Egypt, with influences from the Near East.

3200-3000 BC: Naqadah III, last phase of the Predynastic period.

DYNASTY 0 (3100-3000 BC): First documented kings.

· "Scorpion," Narmer, at Abydos and Hierakonpolis.

· Narmer Palette.

1ST-2ND DYNASTY (3000-2686 BC): Protodynastic period: royal necropolis at Abydos, mastabas at Saqqarah.

· The use of stone for monuments commences.

· Royal funerary stelae.

■ OLD KINGDOM (2686-2160 BC)

3RD DYNASTY: Djoser.

· First sepulchral monument built entirely of stone and first pyramid at Saqqarah.

· Statue of Djoser from the *serdab*.

4TH DYNASTY: Snefru, Khufu, Djedefra, Khafre, Menkaure.

· Age of the pyramids, rise of sun worship.

· Royal statuary; Sphinx of Giza.

· Private statues from the mastabas, Rahotep and Nofret, Hemiunu, Ankhhaf, Kaaper.

· "Spare" heads.

· Grave goods of Hetepheres.

· Ceremonial boat of Khufu.

5TH DYNASTY: Userkaf, Sahure, Neuserre, Unas.

· Pyramids and solar temples.

· Private mastabas.

6TH DYNASTY: Teti, Pepi I, Pepi II.

· Decline of the power of the monarchy, emergence of regional independence.

■ FIRST INTERMEDIATE PERIOD (2160-2055 BC)

7TH-11TH DYNASTY: Age of autonomous regions.

· Provincial necropolises, rock-cut tombs.

■ MIDDLE KINGDOM (2055-1650 BC)

11TH DYNASTY: capital at Thebes.

· Sepulchral monument of Mentuhotep II at Deir el-Bahri; his statue in Jubilee dress.

12TH DYNASTY: Amenemhet I, Sesostris I, Amenemhet II, Sesostris II and III, Amenemhet III and IV, Sebeknefru.

· Capital transferred to El-Lisht.

· Pyramids at El-Lisht, Dahshur, El-Lahun, Hawara.

· Statues of Sesostris I from El-Lisht.

· Temples at Heliopolis, El-Faiyum (Qasr es-Sagha, Medinet Madi, Biahmu), at Thebes (Karnak; White Chapel of Sesostris I) and at Abydos (Cenotaph of Sesostris III).

· Statues of Sesostris III and Amenemhet III from El-

Faiyum and Thebes, and, usurped, from Tanis.

· Rock-cut tombs of princes (Beni Hasan, El-Bersha, Meir, Qaw el-Kebir).

12TH-13TH DYNASTY: Private statuary from tombs and from Abydos (creation of the cube statue).

· Wooden coffins and Canopic jars; jewelry from tombs at Dahshur and El-Lahun.

■ SECOND INTERMEDIATE PERIOD (1650-1550 BC)

14TH-17TH DYNASTY: Occupation of Northern Egypt by the Hyksos, with capital at Avaris; Thebes remains independent.

■ NEW KINGDOM (1550-1069 BC)

18TH DYNASTY: Ahmose, Amenhotep I, Thutmosis I and II, Hatshepsut, Thutmosis III, Amenhotep II, Thutmosis IV, Amenhotep III, Amenhotep IV-Akhenaton, Tutankhamun, Ay, Horemheb.

19TH DYNASTY: Rameses I, Seti I, Rameses II, Merneptah.

20TH DYNASTY: Rameses III, Rameses IV-XI.

· Thebes capital of the 18th dynasty, then the Ramessides prefer Pi-Ramesse in the eastern Delta.

· Development of the national sanctuary of Karnak and the temple of Luxor.

· Royal tombs in the Valley of the Kings, mortuary temples on the fringes of the desert: Hatshepsut at Deir el-Bahri, Amenhotep III with the Colossi of Memnon, Ramesseum and Medinet Habu.

· Development of the Theban private necropolises and of painted decoration.

· Statues of private individuals in the temples.

■ THIRD INTERMEDIATE PERIOD (1069-664 BC)

21ST-25TH DYNASTY: Thebes remains the main religious center, Tanis is the official capital of the 21st dynasty, but other cities in the Delta are dynastic seats: Bubastis, Leontopolis, Sais.

· The 25th dynasty is formed by rulers from Nubia (Kush, with its capital at Napata), then defeated by invaders from Assyria.

· Royal burials inside the temple precincts; pyramids in Nubia.

· Royal grave goods from Tanis. Palace tombs of the administrators of the divine worshipers at Thebes.

· Enlargement of Karnak. Bronze and stone statuary, with archaizing tendencies.

· "Realistic" style in the statuary of the Nubian period (Taharqa).

■ LATE PERIOD (664-332 BC)

26TH DYNASTY (664-525 BC): Psamtik I, Apries, Amasis.

· Capital at Sais.

· Period of artistic "revival," with recovery of models of the past.

· Serapeum of Memphis.

27TH-28TH DYNASTY (525-399 BC): The Persian king Cambyses II conquers Egypt and founds the 27th dynasty.

· Temple of Amon in the oasis of Kharga.

29TH-30TH DYNASTY (399-343 BC): Constructions at Karnak, Saqqarah and the temple of Isis on Philae.

· Second Persian conquest.

· Alexander the Great conquers Egypt.

■ PTOLEMAIC ERA (332-30 BC)

332-305: Macedonian dynasty: Alexander the Great, Philip Arrideus, Alexander IV.

305: Ptolemaic dynasty: Ptolemy I Soter officially ascends the throne as legitimate pharaoh.

· Alexandria, a new city founded by Alexander the Great, becomes capital and the center of Greek bureaucracy and culture.

· Construction of the great Ptolemaic temples: Edfu, Esna, Dandarah.

48: Julius Caesar lands in Egypt to defend Cleopatra VII.

30: Cleopatra VII kills herself after the defeat of Mark Antony at the battle of Actium. End of Egypt's independence.

INDEX OF NAMES

The names of people mentioned in the volume are listed in alphabetic order. Numbers in plain type refer to citations in the text, numbers in italics to the caption of an illustration, numbers in bold type to the sections on masterpieces.